T0057427

HOW TO BE AN ASTROLOGER

*Everything You Need to
Interpret Anyone's Birth Chart
for a Complete, Accurate,
and Revealing Astrological Reading*

CONSTANCE STELLAS

Adams Media

New York   London   Toronto   Sydney   New Delhi

◢adamsmedia

Adams Media
An Imprint of Simon & Schuster, Inc.
100 Technology Center Drive
Stoughton, MA 02072

Copyright © 2020
by Simon & Schuster, Inc.

All rights reserved, including the right to
reproduce this book or portions thereof
in any form whatsoever. For information
address Adams Media Subsidiary Rights
Department, 1230 Avenue of the
Americas, New York, NY 10020.

First Adams Media hardcover edition
April 2020

ADAMS MEDIA and colophon are
trademarks of Simon & Schuster.

For information about special discounts
for bulk purchases, please contact
Simon & Schuster Special Sales
at 1-866-506-1949 or
business@simonandschuster.com.

The Simon & Schuster Speakers Bureau
can bring authors to your live event. For
more information or to book an event
contact the Simon & Schuster Speakers
Bureau at 1-866-248-3049 or visit our
website at www.simonspeakers.com.

Interior design by Julia Jacintho

Manufactured in the
United States of America

2 2022

Library of Congress Cataloging-in-
Publication Data has been applied for.

ISBN 978-1-5072-1301-8
ISBN 978-1-5072-1302-5 (ebook)

Many of the designations used by
manufacturers and sellers to distinguish
their products are claimed as trademarks.
Where those designations appear in
this book and Simon & Schuster, Inc.,
was aware of a trademark claim, the
designations have been printed with
initial capital letters.

Blank chart on page 250 is reprinted by
permission from *Celestial Guide 2004*.
© 2004 Jim Maynard,
www.quicksilverproductions.com.

Charts and tables on pages 251–261 reprinted
with permission from Matrix Software,
6212 NW 43rd Street B, Gainesville, FL
32653, www.astrologysoftware.com.

Charts, tables, and all other material
taken from Ivy Goldstein-Jacobson's
books reprinted with permission.

Contains material adapted from the
following title published by Adams Media,
an Imprint of Simon & Schuster, Inc.:
Advanced Astrology for Life by Constance
Stellas, copyright © 2005,
ISBN 978-1-59337-197-5.

TO MY TEACHERS, BETTY THOMPSON,
CARL STOUGH, LEOR WARNER, RAFAEL LUGAY,
AND VIVIAN EVERETT, FOR THEIR WISDOM
AND HELP IN KEEPING ME ON THE GROUND
WHILE I LEARNED ABOUT THE STARS.

FOREWORD BY
ARIN MURPHY-HISCOCK

Astrology is the art of studying the position and movement of the planetary bodies in the sky and determining a connection between those movements and the events in our lives on Earth. Astrologers of the past held prestigious positions in temples and courts and were consulted by kings and emperors. Although now a less honored and certainly less visible practice in official life, consulting an astrologer is still undertaken today by many members of governments, both in North America and worldwide.

While modern scientific theories contradict those arguments stating that natural events may be a reflection of the motions in the heavens, the ancients did develop sophisticated civilizations based on the study and interpretation of the stars. Our secular calendar is still based on astrological observation. The days of the week are named after ancient gods and goddesses of cultures such as Norse, Greek, and Roman; they also lend their names to the planets of our solar system. Astrology is not an outdated or primitive practice. You can search for deeper meaning and explore the knowledge available to you by engaging in the art and science of astrology today.

Modern astrology goes much deeper than the necessarily superficial horoscopes seen on websites and in newspapers. With a little time and thought, you can acquire the basic knowledge necessary to interpret the position of the planets and apply that interpretation to your life, the lives of others, and even upcoming events. The snapshot of the heavens at the moment of birth offers a unique method of interpreting an individual's personality and life path. Known as a natal, or birth, chart, this simple map becomes a key to understanding deep unconscious motivations and influences and can help you plan for upcoming events in your life.

The world of astrology is a distinct blend of mathematics and intuition; as such, it can often be overwhelming for a student seeking to know more. With Constance Stellas as your guide, you can be confident and at ease. She clearly sets out the information necessary for someone ready to learn about more than just their Sun sign. Terms such as *ascendant* and *midheaven* are clearly defined; concepts such as *synastry* and *electional astrology* are explained in a fashion easily understood by the new astrologer. *How to Be an Astrologer* also explores creative uses of astrology and introduces you to applications of astrological interpretation such as medical and mundane astrology.

With astrology, you can take the reins of your life firmly in your hands. By arming yourself with astrological knowledge and interpretation, you will no longer have to ride out desperate storms wondering when the seas will calm. The astrological interpretation of planetary positions can benefit those seeking counsel regarding any life event, big or small, including areas such as investment, career, relationships, and travel. With the knowledge contained within *How to Be an Astrologer*, you can become your own astrologer. Studying the stars is a rewarding way for you to examine the connections between Earth and sky—humanity and the cosmos—allowing you to dance with the stars to the music of the spheres.

ACKNOWLEDGMENTS

Writing a book is a solitary occupation, but putting it together requires expert and wonderful help. I would like to acknowledge my clients who helped me to learn astrology. I would like to thank Karen Cooper and everyone at Adams Media who helped with this book. To Brendan O'Neill, Katie Corcoran Lytle, and everyone else who worked on the manuscripts. To Frank Rivera and Julia Jacintho for their work on the book's cover and interior design. I appreciated your team spirit and eagerness to dive into the riches of astrology.

CONTENTS

INTRODUCTION

Welcome! *How to Be an Astrologer* invites you to join a four-thousand-year-old tradition that has fascinated and guided people throughout time, helping them to understand themselves better, answer questions about their life, and find love and happiness. Studying the divine art of astrology is a rich and mystical pursuit that combines logic and intuition. The left brain calculates and traces the physical motion of the planets and the patterns that influence a birth chart, while the right brain, the seat of intuition, tunes in to the rich metaphors and energies of a person's chart.

A birth chart is a mathematical fact: It states where the planets were on the date, time, and place of a person's birth. You can also calculate a chart for other events, like a beloved pet's birth date or the "birth" of an airline flight, and this book will teach you how to read your chart or someone else's chart. However, that's only part of the astrological puzzle. You have probably seen email newsletters, *Instagram* accounts, and *Twitter* feeds that offer astrological forecasts. Though they may be fun to read, these interpretations are generic and computer-generated. With the wisdom in this book, you'll discover how to understand events and trends in your own life so you get a deeper and more personalized sense of what's to come.

In ancient times, astrology was frequently used to protect leaders from ill-advised wars or subversive elements. Few of you will encounter dire situations such as those, but you can still use the astrological predictive techniques in this book to determine the best time to schedule a wedding, make financial investments, or consider a career change. *How to Be an Astrologer* offers guidance both for making decisions about your own life and for helping someone else with their choices.

Predictive astrology is fascinating but can be tricky. For example, you might want to use your astrological knowledge to determine whether or not you will get a job for which you've applied. Astrology can help you predict the likelihood of getting the job—but whether you enjoy the job, whether it will pay well, or whether it will be permanent are other matters. A more fruitful approach to predictive astrology is to learn to read the astrological currents. You can then understand the overall energy of a particular time without setting firm expectations.

Knowing more about astrology can also improve your relationships. *How to Be an Astrologer* will teach you techniques for quickly assessing the compatibility and pitfalls of any romance, friendship, or working relationship. Once you have learned these techniques, the later chapters of *How to Be an Astrologer* will introduce you to specialized interpretations for astrology, such as understanding karmic influences, critical degrees, and fixed and benevolent stars.

The planets and stars do not determine events; they simply offer you likely outcomes. However, you have free will and the power to change. Discerning which events or courses of action are meant to be—and which can be changed—takes wisdom, experience, and knowledge. The more you learn about astrology, the better equipped you will be to figure out whether fate is pointing a finger in a helpful direction or whether there are actions that you should be avoiding. After reading this book, you will have begun a lifelong dialogue between yourself and the planets that can clarify and grace your life.

HOW TO USE THIS BOOK

Throughout *How to Be an Astrologer*, I will assume that you have access to your chart, and an astrology software program for more advanced techniques. I have given simple instructions for all the techniques I describe. I recommend using Win*Star 6.0 or Kepler 8.0 (available from www.astrologysoftware.com) or Solar Fire V9 (from www.alabe.com) as good software choices. You can also use a free astrological website, such as *Astrodienst*, to calculate your basic natal chart and do chart comparisons. You can access this site by going to www.astro.com. It can do basic chart calculations and store your results.

You'll find a blank chart at the back of this book you can use as a template. You'll also find sample charts in the back of the book that are referred to in the text. Although these example charts are from people born years ago, this in no way means that the astrological analysis is outdated in any way. Astrology is all about cycles and how the planets move throughout time. We have to consider the society in which a person is born, but the analysis and chart comparison outlines principles of how the planets work together. Studying charts from all eras is fascinating and will enrich your astrological knowledge.

More experienced astrologers will notice that I place more emphasis on aspect patterns instead of strictly observing the common rules for orbs. This is a result of my years of astrological practice and personal experience. I feel that it is important to understand that the rules give us a place from which to start—but should not be rigidly adhered to. After all, astrology is an art of interpretation as well as calculation. I do not believe in strict mathematical precision for all parts of astrology. Creative thinking is an essential part of the process of learning and practicing astrology. It is more important to me to communicate a way of looking at the astrological world that takes into account fluidity, subtlety, feelings, and interpretive skill rather than simply accumulating mathematical facts. The Internet offers accurate calculations, but does not give a seeker the feeling or intuition to integrate all of the rich possibilities that astrology has offered people for more than four thousand years.

Astrology can inform you about planetary cycles that define major life changes. If you think about the planets as circles within circles, you can see that daily life concerns a small circle of planetary motion through the signs. For this information, we examine the small circle containing the Sun, the Moon, Mercury, Venus, and Mars. The second, larger circle encompasses Jupiter and Saturn. These two planets tell us about the principles of expansion and contraction in our lives. The outer planets—or Uranus, Neptune, and Pluto—form the largest circle, and their motion through an individual's chart describes and informs generational concerns as well as major transformative periods of life.

Astrology also provides a cosmic blueprint of your past lives, as we have lived many times before. Sometimes there is no explanation for an event, an illness, an attraction to a person, or extraordinary luck when you look at the transits or major planetary life cycles. You should then examine your chart to see if there is a past-life influence that is dominating the chart. You will learn to look for clues to interpret how past-life influences help or hinder the current lifetime.

These tools and techniques will empower you to learn more about yourself than you thought possible. Enjoy!

CHAPTER ONE

COSMIC INGREDIENTS

An astrological chart is a map of exactly where the planets were at the specific date, time, and place a person was born. These positions are objective and mathematical, so anyone who is calculating an individual's chart would arrive at the same information. This book assumes that you know the basics of obtaining astrological information and the meaning of the astrological symbols, signs, and planets. It also assumes you are using an astrological software program to make charts (although keep in mind that, even if today's students may not know how to hand-calculate a chart, it's still a great skill to have to understand spatially how the planets move).

A chart is essentially a cosmic recipe that outlines the ingredients that go into making each individual or moment in time. In a chart, you can see how all those ingredients are working or not working together and what to do when they are not. No matter what kind of chart you are calculating, the basic components remain the same: the planets, signs, houses, and elements. In this chapter, we'll review the basic ingredients and then move on to more advanced and sophisticated techniques.

THE PLANETS

In ancient times, there were five planets that astrologers could identify and observe in addition to the "lights," that is, the Sun and Moon. The farthest known planet was Saturn, or Chronos in Greek.

In ancient times, the planets were characterized by different attributes that delineated their natures and aided astrologers in interpreting what the planets' positions in a chart meant. Certain planets were considered benefic and others malefic. Most basically, the benefic planets were fortunate and denoted ease, and the malefic planets were unfortunate and indicated struggle. Venus is called the *lesser benefic* and Jupiter the *greater benefic*. Mars and Saturn are the lesser and greater malefics, respectively. Since astrology was used in ancient times almost exclusively as a predictive art, it was prone to more black-and-white interpretations than we use today. The terms *benefic* and *malefic* are still used, but it is more helpful to read the planets in terms of the energies they represent.

Saturn and Mars are malefic, but that does not begin to describe the quality of experience that either of these planets brings. Look further and see how this energy is operating. Jupiter, our jovial benefic, can signify extravagance and waste as well as generosity, while Saturn, the greater malefic, can encourage brilliant planning and structure. Saturn also can mean delay, frustration, and lack of fruition. Astrology is a subtle art, and thinking only in terms of good and bad will limit your understanding of the riches that astrology has to offer. The ancient astrologers also characterized the planets as dry or moist and cold, hot, or warm. This characterization delineated individual temperament as well as weather conditions.

Planets are also considered masculine or feminine. As those words are undergoing dramatic changes in contemporary society, I believe the Chinese words *yin* and *yang* are more appropriate. The yin (feminine) signs are receptive, yielding, and introverted; the yang (masculine) signs are assertive, active, and extroverted. In keeping with the yang or yin nature of the signs, in this book I refer to yang signs as *he* and yin signs as *she*.

MERCURY ☿

Mercury, or Hermes in Greek mythology, was the messenger god. The planet Mercury is the closest to the Sun, moves swiftly, and completes a tour of all the zodiacal signs in one year. Mercury is both dry and moist, and it was sometimes considered an androgynous planet. Mercury is neither benefic nor malefic; he is the intermediary who brings and takes messages. If you have seen the statue of Hermes with his winged feet, you will understand the meaning of this planet. Mercury tells us how a person communicates.

VENUS ♀

Venus, or Aphrodite in Greek mythology, was the goddess of love. Her planet, Venus, is warm, moist, and decidedly yin. Venus is called the *lesser benefic* as she denotes pleasure, good times, and affection. Her orbit through the zodiac takes 255 days, and she spends about four weeks in each sign. Venus, as the morning and evening star, is visible to the naked eye. Venus in a chart shows where and how a person experiences pleasure.

MARS ♂

Mars, which has been called the "red planet" since ancient times, is hot and fiery. In ancient Greece, the god and planet were named Ares; and in both Greek and Roman mythology, he was the god of war. Mars is called the *lesser malefic*; his influence is challenging, but he also brings great energy and passion. The energy is yang. Mars takes 687 days to travel through the zodiac and stays in each sign for six to eight weeks. Mars symbolizes passion, sexual energy, and assertiveness. These planetary principles have nothing to do with sexual preference. Rather, they connote the way a person expresses his or her yang and yin energy.

JUPITER ♃

Jupiter is the largest planet in the solar system. The planet is yang, warm, and moist. Jupiter, also known as Jove in Roman mythology or Zeus in Greek mythology, represents the principle of expansion and generosity. Jupiter stays in a zodiacal sign for about one year and takes about twelve years to pass through all the zodiacal signs. Jupiter is called the *greater benefic* as he denotes luck, fruition, and justice. Since Jupiter moves more slowly than the luminaries and personal planets, his character influences a wider group of people. Therefore, Jupiter pertains to the interrelationship between an individual and society. Together with Saturn, Jupiter is called a *transpersonal* (or *impersonal* or *nonpersonal)* planet. On the Internet you may see other descriptions for Jupiter and Saturn, but classically they have been designated as the transpersonal planets.

SATURN ♄

Saturn was the farthest planet known to the naked eye until advances in the telescope led to the discovery of Uranus in 1781. Saturn, or Chronos in Greek mythology, has many images, such as the ancient image of Father Time with his scythe.

Saturn is yang, cold, and dry. Saturn is called the *greater malefic*, and many students of astrology shudder when Saturn forms difficult aspects in their charts. Saturn is larger than Mars (the lesser malefic) and is a slower-moving planet and therefore influences a chart for a longer period of time. Saturn is also called the greater malefic because the planet's effects on a chart are usually deeper and more serious than those of Mars. Although Saturn's influence may not always be cheery, it is always necessary to bring about personal growth. Saturn stays in a zodiacal sign for approximately two and a half years. When you study transits and larger planetary cycles, you will see that it is Saturn's motion that describes some of the major turning points of life. Saturn provides structure and limitation but also shows how you can create your life within these parameters.

URANUS ♅

Uranus, the planet of rebellion, was predicted many years before its discovery in 1781. It is the first of the outer planets. Uranus stays in a sign for seven years. Because Uranus stays in each sign for such a long period of time, it identifies people born within a seven-year period and gives a particular character to this group of people. The planet is cold, moist, and yang. Uranus's very nature is exciting and disruptive; older texts refer to the planet as "the awakener." It is the "out of the blue" planet. Although Uranus is a malefic planet, it makes more sense to interpret the planet's effect as surprising and uncontrollable. Sometimes the surprises are positive, such as an unexpected love affair; other times they can be challenging, such as an accident. In any case, in a chart, Uranus shows where to expect the unexpected.

NEPTUNE ♆

Neptune is the planet of spiritual love, ideals, and the imagination. The planet is also associated with illusion, foggy impressions, and subtle energies. Neptune, or Poseidon in Greek mythology, ruled the seas and all sailors prayed to Poseidon that they would reach land safely. When a person feels "lost at sea" with confusion and too many feelings, Neptune may be strong in the chart. Discovered in 1846, Neptune was thought to be the last planet in the solar system. It is yin, warm, and considered moist by some, dry by others. Neptune stays in a zodiacal sign for fourteen years, so the planet characterizes a generation of people. Neptune's zodiacal position can define the highest ideals of a generation and the illusions that sometimes prevent their realization.

PLUTO ♀

Pluto, discovered in 1930, is the last known planet of our solar system. Due to the effects of Pluto's eccentric orbit (it orbits at an elongated ellipse and on a more inclined plane than the other planets), astronomers posited that there must be another planet after Neptune, but there was no proof until Clyde Tombaugh, following research and a prediction by Percival Lowell, discovered Pluto and announced his findings on March 13, 1930. The name Pluto came from Roman mythology as the name of the Lord of the Underworld. Although it's now considered a dwarf planet, there is nothing small about Pluto's power in a chart.

Data is still being collected to see how Pluto influences life. Due to the irregularity of Pluto's orbit, he spends varying amounts of time in each sign. For example, Pluto was in Leo for eighteen years (from June 1939 to August 1957), then in Virgo for fourteen years, and in Libra for twelve years. In addition to his significance in personal charts, Pluto is the major defining planet of each generation. Pluto rules the masses, and since he can remain in one sign for a longer period of time than Uranus or Neptune, his influence is more extensive. By the very energies that Pluto represents, he signifies what the collective values are.

Pluto pertains to the use and abuse of power. In a personal chart, Pluto shows where deep transformation and psychological growth occur.

The planets tell us *what* energies or principles are active in a chart. The Sun, Moon, and signs, which we will consider next, tell us *how* these energies manifest in a chart.

THE SUN ☉

The Sun and the Moon are not considered planets and are usually referred to as "the lights" or luminaries. In occult philosophy, the Sun and the Moon indicate the beginning of spiritual consciousness. The Sun is the male representation of the conscious ego.

The Sun's movement through the zodiacal signs is connected to the seasons of the year and gives the major astrological tone to each month. We begin the astrological year at the spring equinox, when the Sun is at 00 degrees of Aries. In Greek mythology, the Sun god Apollo drove his fiery chariot through the heavens to provide light and warmth to humanity. The Sun is yang energy; it was termed hot and dry by ancient astrologers. It is considered a benefic planet, representing men in general as well as the father role. The passage of the Sun through the zodiac takes 365¼ days and forms our present-day calendar. The Sun in a natal chart shows how a person's personality shines.

THE MOON ☽

The Moon is a feminine, or yin, light. She is the female representation of reflected feeling and emotional nurturing. She is cold and moist. Her cycle takes approximately twenty-nine days, and all liquids on Earth are influenced by the Moon's motion. The Moon remains in a zodiac sign for approximately two and a half days. She is the swiftest moving light. The Moon is considered neither benefic nor malefic, because she reflects feelings from moment to moment. The Moon also represents women in general as well as the mothering role. The phases of the Moon govern the ebb and flow of not only the tides but the currents of emotion affecting everyone. The Moon shows how a person reacts and feels.

THE SIGNS AND THEIR ELEMENTS

There are twelve zodiacal signs. The astrological year begins with Aries, the Ram, and concludes with Pisces, the Fish. Each sign, in addition to having its own nature, is ruled by a planet, an element, the triplicities, and the quadruplicities:

- The four elements are fire, earth, air, and water.
- The triplicities are composed of three signs in each element:
  - Aries, Leo, and Sagittarius form the fire triplicity.
  - Taurus, Virgo, and Capricorn form the earth triplicity.
  - Gemini, Libra, and Aquarius form the air triplicity.
  - Cancer, Scorpio, and Pisces form the water triplicity.
- The quadruplicities consist of four signs in three descriptive modes: cardinal, fixed, and mutable.
  - The start of spring, summer, fall, and winter describes the cardinal nature of the signs of Aries, Cancer, Libra, and Capricorn.
  - The months when each season is well established characterize the fixed signs: Taurus, Leo, Scorpio, and Aquarius.
  - The months in which the seasons change characterize the mutable signs: Gemini, Virgo, Sagittarius, and Pisces.

When considering the zodiacal signs, the elements will tell you immediately what "language" each sign speaks:

- The fire signs are energetic and inspirational.
- The earth signs are practical and concrete.
- The air signs are communicative and intellectual.
- The water signs are emotional and sensitive.

The quadruplicities tell you how the signs express their basic natures:

- The cardinal signs initiate activity. They are, after all, the first signs of each season.
- The fixed signs establish and maintain activity; each season is well established when the fixed signs dominate.

- The mutable signs change according to what is needed in any endeavor. Mutability and flexibility are their major characteristics. In each season, the mutable signs are the harbinger of what is to come.

With these characteristics in mind, let's take a brief look at each of the twelve signs.

ARIES ♈ (MARCH 21–APRIL 19)

Aries is a cardinal fire sign. This is a yang sign, ruled by Mars. The part of the body ruled by Aries is the face and head. Frequently, Aries have very pronounced brows that resemble their symbol, the Ram. Aries love to butt heads with life, assert their individuality, and campaign for justice and social causes.

The Aries personality can provide the spark for launching any project into activity. He has energy to burn and frequently is a leader. It is usually a good idea for Aries to engage in a dynamic sport or physical activity as a way to channel his energy. In his zeal for activity, Aries can launch too many projects and fail to complete them. When his energy is harnessed, he can be a pioneer and inspirational leader.

TAURUS ♉ (APRIL 20–MAY 20)

The second sign of the zodiac is a fixed earth sign. The sign is yin and ruled by Venus. In the body, Taurus rules the throat, neck, and ears. Taurus's symbol is the Bull. Taureans are usually placid and content, but when they are provoked, their tempers can blow the roof off. An outburst may not happen often, but when it does, it is a doozy. Taurus is practical and concerned with security and accumulating possessions. Building projects concretely is Taurus's greatest talent.

Taurus is a sensual sign and has exquisite senses of touch and smell. Taureans can become set in their ways and bogged down with security needs. Keeping the body flexible is one way for Taurus to avoid mental and physical rigidity.

GEMINI ♊ (MAY 21–JUNE 20)

Gemini is the third sign of the zodiac. It is mutable, air, and yang in nature, although some would describe Gemini as androgynous. Ruled by Mercury, his symbol is the Twins (Castor and Pollux).

The hallmarks of the Gemini personality are mental agility and the ability to communicate. Geminis can investigate and research a variety of subjects at once. "Do two" is their motto, and they are not happy with any kind of routine in work, love, or play. The lungs, respiratory system, and hands are the body parts ruled by Gemini. Versatile Gemini's greatest challenge is to focus and concentrate the mind so he does not get lost in a mental whirl, which leaves him exhausted. The best practice for Gemini is deep rhythmic breathing. This will help calm and focus the mind.

CANCER ♋ (JUNE 21–JULY 22)

Cancer is a cardinal water sign, and the fourth sign of the zodiac. A yin sign, Cancer is ruled by the Moon. Her personality and feelings shift with the Moon's motion through the signs. Cancer is thin-skinned and feels everything keenly. There is no such thing as an impersonal remark or relationship. Cancerians' feelings can be overwhelming, and they must cultivate objectivity.

Cancer's symbol is the Crab, who carries her protective shell or home on her back. A crab also walks backward and forward, testing the waters toward its goal; this tentative movement also gives Cancer the security to feel confident enough to proceed. The breasts and stomach are the areas of the body ruled by Cancer. Both male and female Cancerians are nurturing and maternal. Cancerians can ferociously defend home and country, and love to be surrounded by family.

LEO ♌ (JULY 23–AUGUST 22)

Leo is a fixed fire sign and the fifth sign of the zodiac. He is ruled by the Sun and is yang. The heart and spine are the parts of the body ruled by Leo. Leo's symbol is the Lion, king of the jungle. When Leo feels he has enough attention, there is no sign more generous. Leo always commands attention and has abundant energy. He is the most vital sign of the zodiac.

Where Cancer represents the maternal instinct, Leo represents the traditional paternal instinct. He is the leader of the household, spreading joy and protection to those under his care. His courage in defense of his kingdom is formidable. When Leo feels as though he's not the center of attention, his hidden side appears as insecurity. If his immature ego drives his personality, there are difficulties. But when Leo can cooperate and share his enthusiasm and fire with others, he shines.

VIRGO ♍ (AUGUST 23–SEPTEMBER 22)

Virgo is a mutable earth sign. She is yin and the sixth sign of the zodiac. Virgo is the second sign ruled by Mercury. Gemini, an air sign, represents Mercury's rapid ability to accumulate knowledge; Virgo, as an earth sign, represents the earthy dimension of Mercury's ability to analyze and categorize knowledge. In the body, Virgo represents the intestines and all assimilative processes. Virgo usually has a very sensitive physical system, and if Virgo becomes ill, it is sometimes from nervous tension.

Virgo's symbol is the Maiden gathering the harvest. She is pure, and Virgo quests for perfection throughout life. The important word here is *quest*. If Virgo reaches perfection, there is nothing left to do! The quest keeps Virgo occupied and relieved of the burden of self-criticism. Virgos also like to serve and be helpful. They enjoy working and making life, projects, or their minds tidy. There are some disorganized Virgos, but they almost always have an innate sense of order, even if it is indiscernible to others. Virgo's greatest challenge is to allow creativity and happiness to flow without constant comment and negative criticism.

LIBRA ♎ (SEPTEMBER 23–OCTOBER 22)

Libra is a cardinal air sign. The seventh sign of the zodiac, he is yang. Libra is the second sign to be ruled by Venus. Venus as Taurus's ruler describes and emphasizes the earthy, sensual side of pleasure and aesthetics. In Libra, Venus emphasizes pleasure in relationships and communication. Venus as Libra's ruler denotes love, romance, and marriage. In the body, Libra rules the kidneys and adrenal glands.

The first six signs of the zodiac represent the development of a personality. When we reach Libra, the sign of relationships, we are at the pivotal point between the individual and the individual in relationship with others. It is interesting that Libra's symbol, the Scales, is the only inanimate symbol of the zodiac. There is an abstract quality to many Libras, as they constantly weigh the justice or rightness of their thoughts, feelings, and actions. This constant need to balance life frequently means that Libra goes from one extreme to the other, but it is all in search of harmony and balance. Libra seeks to please others and instinctively knows what is required in any social situation. It is more difficult for Libra to locate his own feelings and responses. The famous Libran indecision is merely an attempt to look at all sides of the question and balance the equation. Libra, as the sign of partnership and marriage, constantly seeks harmony between himself and others. Though it may be a daunting task for him at times, Libra must first understand his own feelings.

SCORPIO ♏ (OCTOBER 23–NOVEMBER 21)

Scorpio is a fixed water sign. The sign is yin and the eighth sign of the zodiac. Until the discovery of Pluto in 1930, Mars was the sole ruler of Scorpio. Since then, Pluto has joined Mars in ruling Scorpio. In the body, Scorpio rules the sexual organs and all eliminative functions.

Scorpio is the strongest sign of the zodiac because of the amount of power she can harness and creatively express through creation. The choice to use creativity for good or ill is a challenge for most Scorpios. The sign has three symbols, which describe Scorpios at different levels of development: the Scorpion, the Eagle, and the Phoenix. The Scorpion would rather sting itself to death than forgo the pleasure of the sting. This represents the unevolved Scorpio who can be stuck in a cycle of self-destructiveness. The Eagle represents the soaring spirit who travels close to the Sun and is a fierce hunter. These Scorpios are learning to use their power creatively without controlling people. Lastly, the Phoenix re-creates itself from its own ashes. The Phoenix characterizes Scorpio's interest in life-transforming experiences that move the soul forward. Scorpios have the ability to transform the darkness in their own souls into light and to help others do the same. The sign loves hidden matters and may be very quiet, but you will always feel Scorpio's presence.

SAGITTARIUS ♐ (NOVEMBER 22–DECEMBER 21)

Sagittarius is a mutable fire sign. Sagittarius is the ninth sign of the zodiac, yang, and a sign ruled by Jupiter. The areas of the body ruled by Sagittarius are the hips and thighs. His symbol is the Centaur, the half human and half horse who, with his bow, aims his arrows high into the world of ideas.

There are two types of Sagittarian personalities:

1. The first is the extroverted, happy-go-lucky gambler who can be superficial but charmingly cheerful and engaging. These people need space to roam and cannot be fenced in.
2. The second type begins to emerge in midlife. At this time, many Sagittarians begin to be interested in philosophy and to consider the big questions of life. Sagittarians rarely brood; they enjoy inquiring about the roots of spiritual development.

As the last sign in the fire triplicity, Sagittarius has the characteristic energy and enthusiasm of all the fire signs. Here, the energy is concentrated and geared toward understanding, wisdom, and personal values. The greatest challenge for Sagittarius is to moderate his bluntness and take others' feelings into consideration.

CAPRICORN ♑ (DECEMBER 22–JANUARY 19)

Capricorn is a cardinal earth sign, ruled by the planet Saturn. She is yin and the tenth sign of the zodiac. The knees and entire skeletal structure are under Capricorn's dominion. In Roman mythology, Saturn—or the Greek god Chronos—fled Mount Olympus and went to Italy where his rule initiated a golden age, a time when people lived in perfect harmony. At the Roman feast of Saturnalia held every winter, no war could be declared; slaves and masters ate at the same table and people gave each other gifts.

A goat traveling sure-footedly up a mountain is an appropriate symbol for Capricorn. The way may be rocky and hard, but Capricorn will get to where she is going. The astrological glyph that denotes Capricorn is actually a mythical creature called the Sea Goat (encompassing the earthy goat who climbs and a sea creature that lives in the fluid realms of spirituality). Capricorn enjoys the maturity and knowledge that comes with age and development. Capricorns always set goals and, as earth signs, are concerned with creating concrete structure in the world. As the final earth sign in the earth triplicity, Capricorn's aspirations also can be spiritual in nature. Capricorn's greatest challenge is to flow with life rather than worry obsessively.

AQUARIUS ♒ (JANUARY 20–FEBRUARY 18)

Aquarius is a fixed air sign. He is the eleventh sign of the zodiac and yang in nature. In the body, Aquarius rules the ankles, circulation, and the nervous system. The sign has two rulers. In ancient times, his ruler was Saturn; however, since the discovery of Uranus, many Aquarians exhibit traits more consistent with the unexpected energy of Uranus. If you examine the chart, you will see whether the individual leans toward a more conservative status-quo personality characterized by Saturn, or the surprising, unpredictable personality of Uranus.

Aquarius's symbol is a youth pouring water from a large vase (the Water Bearer). This is frequently confusing, because some students think Aquarius's element is water. Remember, Aquarius is an air sign: a sign of mental pioneering, not of emotions, because the water the youth pours represents knowledge for humanity. Aquarius, the sign of rugged individualism and even eccentricity, uses his knowledge to benefit society at large. He is the inventor who serves the collective. Lest you conclude that Aquarius is self-sacrificing, remember that, as a fixed sign, Aquarius is interested in power. Aquarians are mindful of actions that are for the good of humanity, but are also very interested in exercising their own personal power and will. Aquarius's challenge is to recognize that many people operate emotionally rather than reasonably.

PISCES ♓ (FEBRUARY 19–MARCH 20)

Pisces is a mutable water sign. She is yin, and the twelfth and final sign of the zodiac. Aries represents the spark that launches a soul into matter; Pisces represents the completion of the journey. Pisces—symbolized by the Fish—describes the return of the personality to the waters of the unconsciousness. The two fish are tied together; one is above the water, participating in life, and the other is hidden under the sea.

The Piscean personality may be unfathomable to others, or even to themselves, but such are the depths of their imagination, creativity, and dreams. Feeling the pain of the world can lead to a tendency toward escapism, and all Pisceans need to spend time in retreat to regenerate themselves. Before the discovery of Neptune, Jupiter ruled Pisces. Now we associate Pisces with Neptune, and the gaseous swirl of Neptune fits the sensitive, sometimes dreamy nature of Pisces. Pisces rules the feet; she must keep her feet on the ground if she is to make her dreams come true. Physically sensitive, Pisceans are usually musical and have compassion for all creatures. A relaxing bath, a trip to a hot tub, or a mental health day spent in bed are the best ways for Pisces to maintain her vitality.

THE TWELVE HOUSES

Now that we have looked briefly at all the signs and planets, we have learned *what* is operating in the chart (the planets) and *how* they are operating (the signs). Next, we look at *where* these energies are happening. For this information, we turn to the twelve houses in the chart. The houses delineate areas of life that tell us how to apply the meanings of the planets and signs.

The best way to learn what each house signifies is to consider the Aries, or natural, wheel. The natural wheel follows the season order of the zodiac: It begins with Aries and finishes with Pisces. An Aries wheel places the Sun's position at the vernal equinox, which is 00 degrees Aries, in the ascendant position, which is the First House cusp. The *ascendant* is the position of the chart that orders the house cusps around the chart. All the signs follow around the wheel in their natural order. This format establishes Aries as the ruler of the First House; Taurus, the Second; Gemini, the Third; Cancer, the Fourth; Leo, the Fifth; Virgo, the Sixth; Libra, the Seventh; Scorpio, the Eighth; Sagittarius, the Ninth; Capricorn, the Tenth; Aquarius, the Eleventh; and Pisces, the Twelfth. When you cast an individual natal chart, the sign on the ascendant will vary. For the purposes of reviewing the meaning of each house, keep the natural sign in mind, because it will inform you of the matters that each house concerns. The ruler of a house is both the sign and planet indicated on that house cusp (a house cusp is the degree that shows where the house starts). In the Aries wheel, the sign ruling the First House is Aries, and the ruling planet is Mars.

The areas of life governed by each house may at times seem confusing. Why should friendship be linked with goals and wishes in the Eleventh House, for example? If you look at the meaning of the natural signs ruling each house, you will find that each one is like a poem describing specific qualities of that house. Astrology is not a mathematical science; it is an interpretive art. As you familiarize yourself with the houses, you will get a feeling for all the areas of life relevant to that house. Keeping this in mind, it is time to look at the twelve houses.

THE FIRST HOUSE

Aries is the sign of the first spark of life and begins the natural wheel. The First House's element is fire, and Mars is the ruling planet. This house describes the way a person appears and is perceived by others. The First House is an angular house, meaning it is a place of action and strength. It is the strongest of the four angular houses. When a planet falls in the First House, it will have a very strong influence on a person's life. All the angular houses (1, 4, 7, and 10) in the natural Aries wheel correspond to the cardinal signs. When you want to know where the action is in a chart, look to the houses ruled by these signs.

THE SECOND HOUSE

Taurus is the natural ruler of the Second House. It is an earth house ruled by Venus. This house rules money, a person's movable possessions, and all matters of economy or spending. The Second House shows a person's strongest desires in determining his or her lifestyle. This house's location is called *succedent*; it is not as strong as the angular houses. The succedent houses (2, 5, 8, and 11) are all ruled by the fixed signs.

THE THIRD HOUSE

Gemini is the natural ruler of the Third House. It is an air house ruled by Mercury. The Third House tells us about the mind's power to communicate and synthesize knowledge. It also governs siblings and near-blood relations other than parents. Short journeys, one's neighborhood, neighbors, and acquaintances also fall under the domain of the Third House. It is known as a *cadent house*. The cadent houses (3, 6, 9, and 12) are ruled by the mutable signs. While they are the most flexible and service-oriented houses, they remain the least dominant houses in a chart.

THE FOURTH HOUSE

Cancer is the natural ruler of the Fourth House. It is an angular water house ruled by the Moon. The Fourth House rules the home, one's roots and foundation, and all domestic matters. This house also concerns real estate and land as opposed to movable possessions symbolized by the Second House. The Fourth House also rules one of the parents. There is controversy over whether it rules the mother or the father. The rulership of Cancer leads us to believe that it would be the mother and that the father would be shown by the opposite Tenth House, ruled by Capricorn. Capricorn can describe a conservative personality and teacher in the ways of the world, which corresponds to the traditional image of a father. However, many people have very maternal, nurturing fathers and/or career-driven mothers, so traditional definitions are not applicable. This is where the interpretive art of astrology comes into play. The best rule is to try and assess which parent had the dominant influence and to consider the signs ruling the Fourth and Tenth houses in a natal chart to give you information about the childhood home. The Fourth House is also called the nadir of the chart, and it represents where we find ourselves at the end of life.

THE FIFTH HOUSE

The Fifth House is ruled by Leo. It is a succedent fire house ruled by the Sun. The Fifth House rules creative and procreative urges. It is the house of pleasure, romantic love, speculative income, gambling, and children. All manners of artistic endeavors fall under the Fifth House. Love affairs, not marriage, are Fifth House subjects. The sign of Leo rules the heart, and the Fifth House concerns all matters of the creative heart. It might seem a little peculiar to lump together stock speculation and children, but both of these activities are slightly uncontrollable and arise from a creative, pleasurable impulse. The Fifth House also rules drama and the desire to express one's feelings.

THE SIXTH HOUSE

The Sixth House is ruled by Virgo. It is a cadent earth house ruled by Mercury. It is the house of health, work, and service. The Sixth House rules work and labor, but not career or professional standing. This house also gives us information on daily health habits and a person's physical sensitivities. Employees and pets also fall under its domain. Food, cooking, sewing, crafts, and domestic maintenance activities come under the auspices of the Sixth House. The Sixth House is not a strong placement for any of the personal planets.

THE SEVENTH HOUSE

Libra rules the Seventh House. It is an angular air house ruled by Venus. With Libra as the sign of partnership, the Seventh House rules partnerships and marriages, including spouses or significant others, business partners, and professionals with whom one does business, such as doctors, attorneys, or contractors. The Seventh House rules open enemies and therefore is the house to examine for any dispute adjudicated in a court of law. The Seventh House is the house of public interaction between the self and others. Marriage, governed by the Seventh House, does not have to be a legalized relationship. Any partnership that is mutually beneficial to two people, endures over time, and is entered into with mutual feelings falls under the auspices of the Seventh House. Common-law relationships and long-standing cohabitating couples come under the domain of the Seventh House.

The Seventh House is opposite the First House, and the sign on its cusp is called the *descendant*. The First House represents the self outside of relationships; the Seventh House represents the self in its relationship to others. The First through the Sixth houses inform the development of the individual soul. The Seventh House begins the soul's journey in relationship to others. The Seventh House is the third-strongest angular house.

THE EIGHTH HOUSE

The Eighth House is ruled by Scorpio. It is a succedent water house ruled by Pluto and Mars. Dubbed the house of sex, death, and taxes, the Eighth House is basically the house of transformation. Consistent with the powerful sign of Scorpio, the Eighth House shows us where the person undergoes experiences that force him or her to evolve psychologically and spiritually. The transformation can come in many forms. Sex is a transformative experience, death is the ultimate transformation, and taxes transform the taxpayers' money into, we hope, the public good.

The Eighth House is opposite the Second House; it represents a partner's money, inherited wealth, and all dynamics concerning other people's money. It governs loans, insurance policies, wills, and all aspects of a deceased person's goods.

THE NINTH HOUSE

The Ninth House is ruled by Sagittarius. It is a cadent fire house ruled by Jupiter. As with all the cadent houses, it is not considered to be in a strong position. The Ninth House rules publishing, universities, the legal profession, philosophy, and the higher mind. It is also concerned with long journeys, grandparents, and in-laws. As the house opposite the Third House, the Ninth House represents the superconscious, abstract mind that seeks a guiding philosophy. The Third House represents the concrete, everyday mind. The Ninth House governs nighttime dreams and religious and spiritual yearnings. It is concerned with organized religion as well as individual spiritual pursuits. A person's values and sense of justice are also matters for Ninth House consideration.

THE TENTH HOUSE

Capricorn is the natural ruler of the Tenth House. It is an earth house ruled by Saturn and the strongest angular house after the First House. The Tenth House represents the career, a person's standing in the world, one of the parents, and all manners of exposure, successful or not, before the public. The Tenth House also governs relationships with all those who have authority over a person. The sign on the Tenth House cusp is called the *midheaven* or *medium coeli*. Next to the ascendant, it is the most important position in the chart for determining the path of success in life. The midheaven and transits affecting it are always involved with major events that concern the career and good standing in the world.

THE ELEVENTH HOUSE

The Eleventh House is ruled by Aquarius. It is a succedent air house ruled by Uranus and Saturn. The house governs friendship, goals, and wishes. Adoptive children and all work with the nonprofit sector fall under the Eleventh House's domain. As the opposite house to the Fifth, the Eleventh House rules pleasurable situations for the individual in society. The Eleventh House gives us information about a person's wishes for life and whether he or she will be able to attain them. Consistent with the Aquarian rulership, the Eleventh House also indicates higher levels of consciousness and humanitarian instincts.

THE TWELFTH HOUSE

Pisces is the ruler of the Twelfth House. It is a cadent water house and represents the final destination of the soul as it travels on the astrological wheel. Jupiter and Neptune rule this house. Psychologically, the Twelfth House represents the unconscious and the energy that may never be brought into the light of day. It is the house of institutions of retreat and reflection, such as monasteries, prisons, and hospitals. In keeping with the mystical associations of the Piscean sign, many of the associations with the Twelfth House are unfathomable. Here we have hidden desires and feelings. For example, the Twelfth House governs *hidden* love affairs or unrequited love. The Twelfth House has been called the "house of self-undoing" and can indicate self-destructive tendencies. It is also the house of limitless spiritual growth and compassion. Many great mystics and holy people have had very strong Twelfth Houses.

SYNTHESIZING ALL THE INGREDIENTS

When you analyze a chart, it is sometimes helpful to group all the houses in categories according to their elements:

- The fire houses (1, 5, 9) are called the Trinity of Life.
- The earth houses (2, 6, 10) are called the Trinity of Wealth.
- The air houses (3, 7, 11) are called the Trinity of Relationships.
- The water houses (4, 8, 12) are called the Trinity of Psychism.

Working with a variety of charts is the best way to observe how planets in the different houses operate. In the natural Aries wheel and in a solar wheel, all the house cusps equal 30 degrees. When you calculate a chart with an exact birth time, the ascendant marks the beginning point of that natal chart. Therefore, the house cusps will reflect different degrees. Some houses are intercepted. This means that one and perhaps two entire signs are included in that house, and the house is prominent because it covers a lot of territory. An example of this is if the sign on the Seventh House cusp, or the descendant, were 20 degrees Cancer and the Eighth House cusp were 15 degrees Virgo, it would mean that all 30 degrees of Leo are included within the domain of the Seventh House. If you were born with Pluto at 19 degrees of Leo, then Pluto would be intercepted in the Seventh House. When a planet is located close to a house cusp, you must consider its influence on the house it has just left or the one where it will shortly arrive.

The ascendant, or rising sign, can only be calculated with an exact birth time. It is the sign and degree that was rising on the eastern horizon of the zodiac at that particular time. If you are casting a chart for a person, it is the time of a child's first breath, as this is the moment that the child exists independently. If you are casting a chart for a business, the ascendant would be either the time when the entity first opened for business or the time that the contracts that formed the corporation were signed. The ascendant for an airplane flight is calculated from the departure time. You can calculate a chart for an event, the birth of a child, or your pets. Whatever the reason for calculating the chart, the ascendant gives an immediate character to the entire chart.

For people, the ascendant or rising sign is the face they wear to the outside world. It may be in great contrast to their Sun sign or their Moon sign. The ascendant will also give information about the physical stature of a person, their hair and eye color, and whether he or she tends to be robust physically. When you begin to interpret charts, you will learn quickly about people if you concentrate on the ascendant, the Sun, and the Moon. These are the three signposts of anyone's character. Consider the elements: Is someone an earth ascendant with an airy Sun and Moon? Or perhaps a person has a lot of fire in their chart but is a water ascendant? Clearly, the water ascendant will dampen their fiery exuberant energy, and this person will have to work to express their fire nature.

If you learn the basic meanings of the signs and get a feel for them, you will be able to interpret what each ascendant means and integrate its meaning with the rest of the chart.

THE PERSONAL PLANETS

In everyday life, we are not usually concerned with large philosophical, spiritual, or karmic questions. Something may happen that causes you to question what you are doing with your life, or it causes great pain, but all in all, these moments are few. Even in the midst of great turmoil your daily activities keep you busy, and you often move on without much contemplation. Personal planets indicate how a person deals with everyday life. The personal planets in a chart are Mercury, Venus, Mars, and the two lights, the Sun and the Moon. For larger issues and life changes, you need to examine the transpersonal planets, Jupiter and Saturn, and the outer planets, Uranus, Neptune, and Pluto. As you examine your chart and the charts of others, you can quickly see what ingredients make up one's character:

- The Sun tells you information about the personality.
- The Moon helps you understand a person's emotions and habitual responses.

- Mercury informs you about a person's mode of communication.
- Venus tells you how a person shows affection, where they like luxury, and how they spend money.
- Mars tells you about someone's temper, whether they are accident-prone, what their passions are, how they feel about sex, and how they handle conflict.

PLANETARY POWERS

Certain planetary positions are considered strong, while others are considered difficult for the expression of the planet's native energy. The Table of Planetary Powers illustrates the ruler, detriment, exaltation, and fall of each planet. I recommend that you memorize this table.

TABLE OF PLANETARY POWERS				
PLANET	RULER OF	DETRIMENT	EXALTATION	FALL
Sun	Leo	Aquarius	Aries	Libra
Moon	Cancer	Capricorn	Taurus	Scorpio
Mercury	Gemini	Sagittarius	Aquarius	Leo
	Virgo	Pisces		
Venus	Taurus	Scorpio	Pisces	Virgo
	Libra	Aries		
Mars	Aries	Libra	Capricorn	Cancer
	Scorpio	Taurus		
Jupiter	Sagittarius	Gemini	Cancer	Capricorn
	Pisces	Virgo		
Saturn	Capricorn	Cancer	Libra	Aries
	Aquarius	Leo		
Uranus	Aquarius	Leo	Scorpio	Taurus
Neptune	Pisces	Virgo	Cancer	Capricorn
Pluto	Scorpio	Taurus		

When a planet is in the sign it rules, it is at home and powerful. When a planet is in its opposite sign, we say the planet is in its *detriment*. The power is lessened because it is not at home in that sign. Capricorn is ruled by Saturn. Saturn, as stated earlier, is the ruler of time and limitations; it rules structure. Saturn in Capricorn feels at home. The planet and the sign have affinity. However, Saturn in watery, maternal, free-flowing, and emotional Cancer is not an easy fit. Therefore, the planetary placement can be described as in detriment. The person with Saturn in Cancer is going to have a more difficult time with rules, obligations, deadlines, and structure because his or her nature wants to flow and feel things out.

Each planet also has a sign apart from the one it rules that enhances the energy of the planet and allows easy access and expression to its energy. This is called the *exaltation* of a planet. It is a powerful and favorable placement. The exaltation of a planet is always in a similar element to the sign the planet rules.

The Sun's exaltation is Aries. The Sun in Aries is comfortable. Aries supports the bright fire of the Sun. The sign opposite a planet's exaltation is considered its *fall*. When a planet is in its fall, its power is weakened; it does not deny success, but it means that the planet cannot easily express the energy of the sign. For example, the opposite sign of Aries is Libra. The Sun flourishes in Aries but has trouble burning brightly in cool, airy Libra. Libra is a mental, abstract sign and challenges the Sun's energy.

You have now reviewed what is operating in a chart (the planets), how they are operating (the signs), and where they are operating (the houses). We have also learned the importance and meaning of the ascendant and the Table of Planetary Powers. All of your future work in astrology will utilize these basic cosmic ingredients.

HOW TO ORGANIZE THIS INFORMATION

To organize all of this knowledge, get a piece of paper to write down key points. First look at the elements that are present in the chart being analyzed. Using a point system, make a list of each element: fire, earth, air, and water. Assign 1 point for each sign and give 2 points to the signs that the Sun and Moon are in. This is because these two luminaries are so important to our basic natures. Also, give 1 point for the ascendant and the midheaven. Example charts are located at the back of the book. For Chart 1, your tally would look like this: fire 2 points, earth 5 points, air 1 point, and water 6 points. Or, for Chart 2, your tally would be fire 3 points, earth 7 points, air 2 points, and water 2 points.

The total number of points cannot exceed 14 points unless you consider asteroids and the part of fortune. I do not recommend that you include these positions in a basic chart analysis. When you are analyzing a chart, you want to go to the heart of the matter, and the planets, Sun, Moon, ascendant, and midheaven describe that perfectly. If you notice an absence of one element, then that is crucial information for a person. No fire means low enthusiasm and limited good spirits. No earth means a person does not think and plan practically. No air means a person may have trouble communicating. And no water means that a person's emotions are not readily available. You can easily see how to evaluate this score sheet for the elements.

You can also evaluate which signs dominate in the quadruplicities. Using the point system again, give 1 point for each cardinal, fixed, or mutable sign, and tally them. For the quadruplicities, do not use the ascendant and midheaven, because you want to see how the chart describes the way the planets act. I also do not give 2 points to the Sun and Moon in determining the strength of the quadruplicities. In Chart 1, note that you have no cardinal signs (0 points), three fixed signs (3 points), and seven mutable signs (7 points). In Chart 2, there are four cardinal signs (4 points), five fixed signs (5 points), and no mutable signs (0 points). Next, quickly count up the number of yang signs and the number of yin signs and write them down. Some men are predominantly yin. Some women are predominantly yang. Some people are balanced between the two or have a 60/40 split. This information will tell you about a person's quality of energy.

Lastly, note whether or not any of the planets are in the sign they rule, their exaltation, their detriment, or their fall.

At this juncture, it is important to learn a new definition: *mutual reception*. In Chart 4, the Sun is in Cancer and the Moon is in Leo. Cancer is ruled by the Moon and Leo is ruled by the Sun, but in this chart the planets are in the sign of each other's rulers. The Sun and Moon are linked together by mutual reception and each partakes of the strength of the other planet. In Chart 3, we see that the Sun is in Aquarius and Uranus is in Leo. The Sun rules Leo, and Aquarius is ruled by Uranus; therefore, you would describe the Sun and Uranus as being in mutual reception; these two planets are linked together.

Finally, list all the planets that are noteworthy for the strength of their position. Using these techniques, you can develop a thumbnail sketch of any person's character.

CHAPTER TWO

HOW YOUR PLANETS WORK TOGETHER

This chapter will teach you about the aspects, or relationships, between planets. An aspect is a specific measurement between two planetary positions. Isabel M. Hickey defines aspects in her excellent book *Astrology: A Cosmic Science* as "lines of force between centers of energy (planets) in the magnetic field of the individual." The major aspects are the conjunction, opposition, square, trine, and sextile. In this chapter you will also learn about the semisquare, the semisextile, the quincunx or inconjunct, and the quintile. The Aspects Table outlines all these aspects.

Astrology is based upon mathematics, and aspects are a refinement of these mathematics. Once you understand the simple arithmetic needed to identify certain astrological patterns, it becomes easier to blend the intuitive right-brain mode used for interpretation with the analytical left-brain mode. With this in mind, let's look at aspects.

If you visualize each sign as a slice of pie, imagine that each slice, or sign, takes up 30 degrees of space or arc. There are 60 minutes in each degree. When you look at your chart, you will see that the Sun is located not only in a sign but also in measured degrees of that sign. For example, the Sun might be at 10 degrees 56 minutes of Libra or 10♎56 in a person's chart. Without using astrological symbolism, you write this as 10Libra56.

ASPECTS TABLE		
ASPECT	ORB OF MEASUREMENT	SYMBOL
Conjunction	0–10 degrees apart	☌
Opposition	180 degrees apart	☍
Square	90 degrees apart	□
Trine	120 degrees apart	△
Sextile	60 degrees apart	✶
Quincunx (inconjunct)	150 degrees apart	⚻
Semisquare	45 degrees	∠
Semisextile	30 degrees	⚺
Quintile	72 degrees	Q

Learning to recognize aspects in a chart requires that you note the elements of each sign as well as the degrees of the sign. In addition to the orb of measurement for aspects, the orb tells you the distance allowed for an aspect to be considered significant; an orb is the measurement that describes the space within which an aspect is effective. It is helpful to look first at the sign's elements and then examine the degrees. The elements of the sign will tell you whether the signs are square, opposite, or trine, but if the degrees of the signs are too far away from each other, or out of orb, the planets do not form an aspect. A basic orb of 10 degrees is reasonable for the conjunction, square, trine, and opposition. The sextile, semisextile, quincunx, and semisquare use orbs of between 6 and 8 degrees. (Remember, it is more important to get a feeling for the orbs than measure exactly. That being said, more than 10 degrees is too far apart.) The quintile must have an orb of 1 degree or less. When the number of degrees is the same in an aspect, the aspect is called *exact*. An exact aspect is particularly significant because it indicates the strongest energy link possible between those two planets. For example, in Chart 4, not only are the degrees square when the Sun is at 21♋09 and Neptune is at 21♎08, but the aspect is also within 1 minute of being exact. This creates a very tight square, and this aspect is a focal point of the chart.

Aspects are either applying to, or separating from, each other. If a faster-moving planet is applying, it is moving toward an exact aspect; the energy is approaching, and its energy is strong. When the planet has passed the aspect, it is leaving, or separating, and the intensity is lessened. For instance, in Chart 2, Mars at 6♏ is applying to an opposition with Venus at 11♉, but it is separating from an opposition with Jupiter at 3♉. The terms *applying* and *separating* are used for all the aspects. Aspects are referred to only when they are between a faster-moving planet and a slower-moving one. In the case of conjunctions, consider the number of degrees to identify which planet is applying and which is separating. Venus can apply to an aspect with Saturn, but Saturn cannot apply to an aspect with Venus. This is why it is helpful to memorize the order of the planets.

THE MAJOR ASPECTS

Detailed descriptions of the major aspects follow.

THE CONJUNCTION ♂

The conjunction is the most powerful aspect in any chart. In the conjunction, the energies of the planets involved are blended and act as a single source of power. When the conjunction is with planets that are at home with each other, the result is beneficial; when the conjunction is with planets that are antagonistic, then the effects can be difficult. For example, a conjunction between Jupiter and Venus doubles the luck and benefic nature of each planet. If Jupiter and Venus are also in strong signs, then the planets' energies are further enhanced. A conjunction between Mars and Uranus can bring a great deal of energy, even genius, but it gives an explosive temper and a tendency toward self-defeating actions. When more than two planets are conjunct in the same sign, it is called a *stellium*. Chart 7 has a major stellium in Scorpio. Chart 1 has two stelliums, one in Virgo and one in Pisces. In Chart 4, there is a very fortunate conjunction of Venus and Jupiter in Gemini, and a strong challenging conjunction between Uranus, Mars, and the Sun in Cancer. This person has a combination of good luck, many talents, and a great deal of self-defeating behavior. In other words, all the planets in a stellium should be considered as a cluster of energy and one of the most important parts of the chart.

Please note that it is possible for two planets to be conjunct in different signs. If a planet is at the end of the sign's arc, for example, at 25 degrees of one sign, and there is another planet at 2 degrees of the next sign, these planets are conjunct. For example, 25Leo42 is conjunct 2Virgo15. This is called an *out-of-sign conjunction*; there is a blending of Leo and Virgo energy for these planets. This particular combination can inspire a person to accomplish a good deal of work but can also lead to fussiness and self-criticism. In Chart 2, Jupiter at 3 Taurus is conjunct Mercury at 28 Aries. This person has considerable mental ability, but a very sharp, blunt way of communicating that can be hurtful.

THE TRINE △

To recognize the other aspects, you need to turn your attention to the elements, degrees, and quadruplicities. Signs in the same elements are trine relationships. Leo is trine Aries, and Sagittarius is trine both Leo and Aries. The same is true for the earth, air, and water signs. Another way to recognize a trine aspect is to count the degrees between the signs. Since each sign has 30 degrees of arc and there are four full signs before we reach the next fire sign, the trine measures 120 degrees (four signs × 30 degrees equals 120 degrees). The mathematical relationship of the trine is the same for the earth, air, and water signs. The trine is the most flowing, harmonious aspect; all the signs like each other and their energies move easily. The trine brings ease to a chart and to relationships. But too many trines can lead a person to be lazy and complacent. When life comes too easily, one becomes spoiled and may not be able to cope with misfortune. A few trines to ease the way are helpful, but too many, and a person can become self-indulgent.

THE SQUARE □

The cardinal, fixed, and mutable signs in incompatible elements are all square each other. This aspect is challenging and inharmonious. For example, the fire sign of Aries is square the water sign of Cancer. They are both active cardinal signs, but the elements are incompatible. They speak a different language. Fire puts out water; the relationship is uncomfortable, but it has power. Fire produces steam, and energy is released. The square always shows where the action is in a chart. In the fixed signs, Aquarius is square Scorpio and Leo is square Taurus. With the mutable signs, a couple of examples are: Gemini is square Virgo and Pisces is square Sagittarius. The square aspect measures 90 degrees. To count the aspect, begin with one sign and count three full signs until you reach the next sign of the same quadruplicity; this will measure 90 degrees. For example, Aries, Taurus, Gemini equals three signs. Three signs × 30 degrees equals 90 degrees. In Chart 2, there is a square between the Sun and Pluto. It is a square in fixed elements and holds great energy but offers challenges regarding use and abuse of power. Many squares in any of the elements means challenges and difficulties. However, these challenges frequently give people the drive to accomplish a great deal in their lives. Sometimes people with squares say their chart is doomed because it is difficult. There is no such thing as a doomed chart.

THE OPPOSITION ☍

The other aspect between signs in a quadruplicity is the opposition. You can either memorize which signs are opposite, or recall the natural, or Aries, wheel and notice the oppositions as they occur on the wheel. Aries is opposite Libra. Taurus is opposite Scorpio. Opposites attract. Their elements are complementary because they provide the balance the signs lack on their own. Cancer is opposite Capricorn; her watery nature complements Capricorn's pragmatic earthiness. Gemini is opposite Sagittarius. His airy nature fans the flames of Sagittarius's fire. The opposites are like a seesaw. These are just a few examples. Sometimes one planet and sign dominate and sometimes the other one takes over, but they are tied together. Please note it is the planets in the signs that are opposite. Mars in Gemini is opposite Saturn in Sagittarius. The only time it would be necessary to count degrees for an opposition is when the aspect is out of sign. For example, 25 degrees of Libra is opposite 2 degrees of Taurus because 2 degrees of Taurus is just 3 degrees away from the end of Aries at 29 degrees Aries. The aspect between the two planets in these signs, in this case, would be an opposition. If you measure the arc count from Aries and six full signs ahead, six signs × 30 degrees equals 180 degrees. The best way to recognize out-of-sign aspects is to pay attention to all degrees at the end and beginning of signs. In Chart 1, notice that the stellium of the Sun, Mercury, and Saturn in Pisces are all opposite Uranus and Pluto in Virgo. The stellium would not be opposite Mars, although he is also in Virgo, because he is out of orb.

THE SEXTILE ⚹

The sextile aspect measures 60 degrees and is formed between planets two signs apart in compatible elements. Gemini (air) is sextile to Leo (fire). Scorpio (water) is sextile to Capricorn (earth). The degrees of each planet that are sextile are important, but because a sextile is a milder aspect, 8 degrees is the maximum orb between signs. For example: 8 degrees of Scorpio would be sextile 12 degrees of Capricorn, but 8 degrees of Scorpio would not be sextile 20 degrees of Capricorn. You can calculate this by subtracting 8 from 20. The remainder is 12 degrees, and that is larger than the 8 degrees of orb that is usually allowed. The term *allowed* is a convenient one; the prescribed orbs are not meant to be dogmatic. Judgment of an aspect's significance comes from accumulated wisdom from past astrologers and your own experience. Astrology is an interpretive art, and noticing how a sextile operates in a variety of charts is more important than strictly following a rule.

The meaning of a sextile in a chart is opportunity. The planets are in a harmonious relationship and move well together. This brings a positive flow, which encourages opportunities. Whether or not a person activates the opportunities that are available is their choice. In Chart 4, there is a sextile between Venus and Mercury within 2 degrees of orb. A nearly exact sextile between the Moon/Pluto conjunction in Leo and the Saturn/Neptune conjunction in Libra shows this person to be a writer and very good communicator. These aspects give opportunities for expression, in turn tempering more difficult aspects.

THE QUINCUNX OR INCONJUNCT ⚻

The quincunx is an aspect that measures 150 degrees. It is also called the *inconjunct*. This aspect was not one of the major aspects that Ptolemy, the premier ancient astrologer, considered important. Ptolemy believed that only aspects based on the numbers 3 and 4 and their multiples constituted sufficiently strong lines of force for an aspect to be important. The quincunx is based on the number 5, with five signs × 30 degrees equaling 150 degrees. Astrologers today are using the quincunx more frequently because it has proved to be valuable in ascertaining matters of a fateful quality, especially in terms of health and accidents. When a chart has many quincunx aspects, events occur that a person has little control over. The aspect is particularly useful in examining flight charts and charts for operations. The two signs involved in an inconjunct are neither friendly nor hostile; they just rub each other the wrong way. The most common word used to describe this aspect is *irritating*.

Recognizing the inconjunct is sometimes tricky. The aspects are five signs away and an inconjunct is between planets of dissimilar elements and quadruplicities. The easiest way to recognize the quincunx is to see if there are any signs that are one sign less, or more, than an opposition's sign. For example, Aries is inconjunct Virgo. Virgo is one sign before Libra, the opposite sign to Aries. Aries is also inconjunct Scorpio because Scorpio is one sign after Libra.

The orb allowed for a quincunx (inconjunct) is 5 degrees. Therefore, 5 degrees Aries is quincunx 10 degrees Virgo, but 19 degrees Virgo is out of orb. You can also have an out-of-sign quincunx, which is hard to recognize but is nonetheless important to know. If a planet is located at 27 degrees Aries, it is inconjunct a planet at 2 degrees Libra. If you do not pay attention to the degrees, you would say that Aries is opposite Libra, but the degrees tell us that the relationship is, in fact, inconjunct.

Here's how the math works: We begin with 27 degrees of Aries, then count a whole 30 degrees sign, to 27 degrees of Taurus, then 27 Gemini, followed by 27 degrees of Cancer, Leo, and Virgo. That is 5 signs of 30 degrees, which total 150 degrees. But our aspect has 3 degrees left in Aries and 2 degrees of Libra. We have to add these 5 degrees to 150, for a total aspect of 155 degrees. This is within the 5-degree orb allowed for the quincunx, or inconjunct, aspect. As mentioned before, it is important to pay special attention to planets at the end and beginning of a sign. For instance, in Chart 2, Venus is inconjunct Saturn. The aspect between these two planets would lead you to suspect that a romantic life has been difficult and that there are problems with sweets and diet. Both areas of life have been frustrating to this person.

THE UNCOMMON ASPECTS

Detailed descriptions of the uncommon aspects follow.

THE QUINTILE Q

The quintile is an uncommon aspect, and many charts will not have any planets that are quintile each other. The standard aspects used in astrology come from Ptolemy, but the quintile was introduced by Johannes Kepler in the seventeenth century. The aspect measures 72 degrees, and occult authors claim it is the hallmark of spiritual initiation. This information has been handed down to present-day astrologers and needs further research. In my own experience, the quintile aspect does indicate a special and focused creative gift. When a person has a quintile aspect, there are typically only one or two in a chart. As with all other configurations in astrology, we must activate an aspect to gain the greatest benefit.

The only way to recognize the quintile is to count degrees. If you look at Chart 1, you'll see that the Sun is located at 6♓24 and Jupiter is located at 19♉28. If we count from 6 degrees of Pisces to 6 degrees of Taurus, we have a 60-degree aspect, but we must account for the remaining degrees of Taurus, which is 13 degrees 28 minutes. Adding this to 60 degrees gives us the aspect between the Sun and Jupiter of 73 degrees 28 minutes, which is a quintile.

This person's goal in life was to achieve spiritual growth and enlightenment. Other clients have mentioned their spiritual development as one aspect of their lives, but for this client it was the most important pursuit.

It is interesting to note that the quintile connotes spiritual aspirations and is not easy to recognize. Frequently, soul growth is neither flashy nor heralded. Look at the planets that are involved with the quintile and you will be able to tell where a person can grow artistically and spiritually.

THE SEMISQUARE ∠

The semisquare is an aspect that measures 45 degrees. I jokingly call it "square-lite" because it measures half of the 90 degrees of a square, and it is a nudgey, irritating aspect, but it does not have the energy potential of the square. Planets forming a semisquare to each other are like a bothersome habit. It does not define an individual's character; it influences it. If you examine planets semisquaring each other, you will see where a person can learn patience and tolerance. In Chart 4, there is a semisquare between Venus and Mars. This person has great personal charm but a knack for getting on people's bad sides, especially in romantic relationships. This can hamper some of the more flowing aspects in the chart.

THE SEMISEXTILE ⊻

The semisextile measures 30 degrees and is half a sextile both in degrees and importance. It is a benevolent aspect. The semisextile connotes everyday harmony between the two planets under consideration. Because the signs are next-door neighbors, there is a cordial relationship, not one of intense involvement. In Chart 3, there are three semisextiles. The Sun is semisextile Saturn, Jupiter is semisextile Saturn, and the Moon is semisextile Uranus. This individual is a good friend and easily maintains relationships with people very different from her.

ASPECT FORMATIONS

Once we have analyzed the individual aspects in a chart, there are sometimes major combinations of aspects that create a special pattern called an *aspect formation*. These patterns work together defining and influencing a chart. All charts have aspects, but not all charts have specific aspect patterns. In ancient times, astrology was sometimes called a science of celestial geometry. The aspect patterns build on the aspects already discussed and create a larger pattern that is significant for refining interpretation. The orbs between aspects in an aspect pattern are frequently wider than between planets not in a specific pattern. The important interpretive information is that in a pattern, a group dynamic operates that is more significant than specific orbs. The closer the degrees are to the prescribed orbs, the more powerful the aspect pattern will be. When considering aspect patterns, pay special attention to the elements of the signs. The elements will help you quickly identify the entire aspect pattern, and concentrating on the elements of the signs involved will give you an immediate feel for the type of energy involved in any aspect pattern.

THE T-SQUARE

The T-square is formed when two planets oppose each other and a third planet squares the opposing planets. If you look at Chart 1, you will see that the planets involved in the T-square are Neptune, Jupiter, and Venus. Neptune and Jupiter are opposite each other, and both square Venus: ♆☍♃□♀. This T-square is also in the fixed signs and is therefore called a *fixed T-square*. It is not an uncommon aspect and is prominent in charts of many people who have made an impact on the world. This is not to say that you cannot be successful if you don't have a T-square. The aspect is energizing and dynamic, helping to motivate a person to overcome obstacles. The planet carrying the square aspects is the focal point of the opposition, and a person must work to integrate that planet into his or her life.

A T-square can be compared to a seesaw on top of a powder keg. The square is the powder keg, and unleashing that energy in life can cause a person to go up and down like a seesaw. Equilibrium is achieved when the force of the powder keg is just enough to balance the seesaw without toppling it. When you study transits, you will see that with a T-square, the entire pattern is affected by a transit and potentially stirs up a great deal of activity.

THE GRAND TRINE

A grand trine occurs when three planets are trine each other and form a large triangle in the chart. The trines will usually all be in one of the four elements, but can contain out-of-sign planets. All grand trines have great internal flow because the planets are moving in sync with each other. The challenge for anyone with a grand trine is to express energy outwardly. The fire grand trine can be a one-man band and must take others into consideration. The earth grand trine can plow through the most difficult situations, but tends to bulldoze other team members. The air grand trine can entertain themselves with constant mental activity, but needs to communicate their thoughts. Lastly, the water grand trine is awash with feeling, but needs to open the gates to share with others. Chart 5 contains water grand trines involving the Moon, Uranus conjunction, trine Venus, trine Pluto: ☽ ☌ ♅ △ ♀ △ ♀. There is another grand trine between Jupiter, the Moon/Uranus conjunction, and Pluto. Because of the strength of this watery grand trine for interpretative value, all these planets in water work together to describe a major dynamic in this person's life. This person had a great deal of feeling, but could not express it and therefore came across as very cold.

THE GRAND CROSS

This aspect pattern is also called a grand square and a cosmic cross. The pattern is formed when two oppositions square each other. The pattern is strengthened when all planets are in the same quality, that is, cardinal, fixed, or mutable. Look at Charts 2 and 3. In Chart 2, note the grand cross in cardinal signs. This is a difficult aspect pattern. The Moon is opposite Uranus, square Neptune, and square Mercury: ☽ ☍ ♅ □ ♆ □ ☿. You've already learned about chart patterns and, with that, know that some of the orbs in this particular grand square (Chart 2) are wider than usual; nonetheless, the pattern is a powerful one and definitely part of this person's character. The grand cross contains a great deal of creative potential but usually brings frustrating conditions that require enormous self-discipline to overcome and unleash the grand cross's potential. Handling a grand cross requires that people address their inner dilemmas before life can flow. If you pay attention to the quadruplicity of the grand cross, you will have an immediate summary of the kind of energy the person is dealing with. Can you spot the fixed grand cross in Chart 3? The fixed grand cross is perhaps the most difficult quality as it implies energy and rigidity. The mutable grand cross has scattered and restless energy that requires discipline to focus.

THE MYSTIC RECTANGLE

This is an interesting configuration that was first brought to astrologers' attention by Dane Rudhyar, one of the great influences on modern astrological thought. The Mystic Rectangle involves two sets of oppositions whose ends trine and sextile each other. If you look at Chart 2, you will see that the Moon is sextile Mars, and Venus and Jupiter are sextile Uranus. Also, Mars is trine Uranus and Venus/Jupiter are trine the Moon. The two oppositions are Moon opposite Uranus and Mars opposite Venus and Jupiter. Rudhyar called the Mystic Rectangle representative of practical mysticism. People with this pattern have a great yearning for mystical and spiritual experiences, and they have the challenge of implementing that desire while juggling the demands of the everyday world. The oppositions bring stress and discord, and the trine and sextile planets allow the person to retreat into a comfortable personal vision of the way life should be. Part of their life will be about balancing these incompatible desires.

THE YOD

The Yod has also been called "the finger of fate." It is formed when two planets are sextile, both forming an inconjunct to a third planet. The configuration looks like a large Y. Usually, if there is a Yod in a chart, there are at least two inconjunct aspects. These aspects are involved with health concerns, accidents, and seemingly fateful events.

When I calculate charts for airplane flights, I pay special attention to the Yod aspect. If some other aspects, which I will discuss later, join it, I advise clients not to fly.

In a personal chart, a Yod tells us which planets would be involved with events that come out of the blue. The Yod has a Uranian feel to it. In Chart 6, note the sextile between Jupiter and Neptune. Both planets are inconjunct Uranus, which is located in the Sixth House of health. This person had a great and fortuitous career but was taken ill in his forties and died suddenly. Not every chart with a Yod will mean that a person has such a fate, but, in combination with other factors in this particular chart, the Yod described the surprising and fateful quality of this particular event.

The aspect patterns are descriptions of the way a person's energy will most likely manifest. When energy has a difficult time expressing itself creatively, a person can become mired in self-destructive patterns that do not serve him or her. You do bring over challenges from other lifetimes to work on in the present life. If you are studying your chart or helping another person to understand theirs, you must accept that the chart gives you the problem *and* the solution. There is no point in rolling your eyes and wincing when you see a tough aspect pattern. Astrologers can be as guilty of whining as much as anyone else. But mental conversations such as "My life would be perfect if it weren't for my Neptune aspects" are not productive. You must use the planets, signs, aspects, and aspect patterns you were born with. The advantage with astrology is that you have before you the best guide possible for understanding who you are, what your assets and liabilities are, and how to emphasize the best parts of your chart.

HOW TO SYNTHESIZE
AND ORGANIZE THIS INFORMATION

In a computer-generated chart, the aspects are usually found in the inner circle of the wheel with many lines drawn to show the connection between planets as well as the symbol for the particular aspect located on the line. Most computer charts indicate the conjunction, trine, square, opposition, and sextile. The chart patterns are usually delineated separately. This basic blueprint is the best place to begin looking at a chart. But to really understand a chart, you can draw an aspectarian. This is a grid that looks like a series of steps where you can note the aspects between planets. It helps you to think about the Sun's relationship to the Moon, decipher if they aspect each other, and see the relationships between the other planets. There is a blank aspectarian at the back of the book, or if you like, you can draw your own. Once the aspectarian is drawn, fill in the aspects between all the planets. Note in the corner of each box whether the aspect is applying or separating. After all this information is filled in, count the number of applying and separating aspects and see where the majority are. Put that information on the aspectarian sheet, as well. If there are any major aspect patterns, put them on top of the sheet. Once you have finished with this exercise, you should have a good feel for how all these planets interact.

Lastly, note the aspects between the planets, ascendant, and midheaven. Does the individual have a face toward the outside world that easily allows his or her emotions to flow? To answer that question, you would look at the relationship between the Moon and the ascendant. What is the aspect between Saturn and the midheaven? This will tell us what kind of effort a person is willing to make for career and public standing. Create a tally sheet of how many squares, trines, sextiles, oppositions, and conjunctions the chart shows. If there are a number of squares, the person has a challenging chart. If trines predominate, expect ease and not too much angst. With practice, you will get a general impression of the entire chart, but it is always a good idea to individually study the aspects between the planets. This is the only way you will find the quintile, the semisquare, and the quincunx if those aspects aren't included in your astrology software program. Learning to recognize aspects is one of the major building blocks of chart interpretation. When you look at the transits of the planets, as you will in the next chapter, you will examine the aspects that the transiting planets make to a chart.

One of the greatest uses of astrology to a cosmic planner is to identify when the time is right for particular activities. If you have mastered all the information in the first two chapters, you are ready to start applying it to the daily motion of the personal planets.

CHAPTER THREE

YOUR PERSONAL PLANETS AND THEIR DAILY MOTIONS

A natal chart captures a specific, unchangeable event, but influences from the transiting planets to your natal chart occur throughout life. A planet's transit means the passage of any planet as it moves through a designated sign. The effect of specific transits that a planet makes to a native's personal planets or progressed chart—or even a planet's passage through a particular house—is defined by the aspects the transiting planet forms to a person's personal planets, progressed chart, house cusps, and other important points in the chart. In the same way that you feel differently when spending time with different people, planetary motion affects you in varied ways. Studying the planetary movements and their effects upon your chart is perhaps the most fascinating part of astrology. Have you noticed that certain times of the year are productive and buoyant for you and other times are difficult? If you look at the positions of the personal planets during these times, you might begin to see a pattern. You will know which activities are the most beneficial during these times. If it is a low period for you, this is not the time to launch a job search, build a new house, or plan a vacation.

Although the Internet can be a good source for daily astrological transits, it may be more convenient to have an ephemeris or astrological calendar. An ephemeris is a book that tells you the position of all the planets on a daily basis. As we are now in the twenty-first century, you'll need two books: an ephemeris for the twentieth century, which covers the years 1900–2000, and an ephemeris for the twenty-first century, for 2000–2050. You will find some good suggestions for ephemerides in the resources section at the back of the book.

Another tool that is crucial for looking at daily planetary motions is a calendar that tracks the monthly lunar cycle. This can be found in the ephemeris, but, because ephemerides are calculated for Greenwich Mean Time (GMT) and the Moon moves rapidly, you would be a step behind if you took the Moon's position without calculating the difference between GMT and your time zone. A simpler solution is to purchase an astrological calendar for your time zone. For instance, the *Daily Planetary Guide* (published annually by Llewellyn Publications) clearly shows the daily lunar aspects as well as the Moon void periods. (You can also find this information on the web at https://lunarium.co.) Both an ephemeris and an astrological calendar keep daily track of the Moon's motion as well as the major aspects between all the planets. With these tools, you can follow the daily motions of the personal planets and determine their effects on you. In this chapter, you are going to learn how the planets' motion and aspects affect a personal chart and how planetary motion affects everyone. All people are governed by the planetary transits. When there is an eclipse, for example, everyone will feel the event even if they are not conscious of it. However, an eclipse will be more powerful for some people if it falls on a planet or position in an individual's chart that corresponds to the degree and sign of the eclipse. Always keep in mind that in astrology, you are examining the small world of a personal chart, or a nation's chart, with the larger world of cosmic planetary motion. As the ancient seer Hermes Trismegistus said, "As above, so below."

THE SUN ☉

You have already learned the twelve Sun signs, their elements, and their basic meanings. When you consider the Sun's motion, you are intimately connected with the seasons. If you note which seasons are your favorites, they are usually synchronized with harmonious aspects between your natal Sun and the transiting Sun. The simplest way to consider how the Sun affects your daily life is to look at which house the transiting Sun falls in and focus on the areas of that house. When the Sun is in the Eleventh House, it is a good time to make new friends or get in touch with friends you may have forgotten for a while. When the Sun is in the Twelfth House, pay attention to your unconscious currents, meditate, or turn your attention toward any kind of service with less fortunate people. When the Sun crosses your ascendant and moves into the First House, you may find you are physically energized and able to project your wants and needs more clearly. When you plan for the upcoming year, see if you can maximize your efforts by paying attention to the house through which the Sun is traveling. This can be particularly useful in family situations. For example, let's say the Sun is passing through your Sixth House and you are busy with work, but that month is also the time when the Sun is passing through your partner's Seventh House, and they want your time and attention. Knowing about the different transits of the Sun offers the opportunity to work out a compromise between your needs and their needs. If you consider that the planets motivate both people's expectations, you can eliminate personal blame and avoid countless arguments. The Sun is simply shining in different areas.

Next come the aspects between the transiting Sun and your natal personal planets. This will tell you how easily you will be able to express that particular solar energy or sign. The trines bring ease, the squares bring challenge, the sextiles bring opportunities, and the conjunctions bring intensity. If you have a chart that has planets concentrated in only a few signs, such as Chart 7, then you will find that from the time the Sun is in Scorpio until it enters Sagittarius, life will be particularly intense. The area of focus will be work and health because the concentration of planets in Scorpio in the Sixth House is so extreme.

THE MOON ☽

The Moon spends approximately two and a half days in each zodiacal sign and takes approximately twenty-nine days to complete her journey through the zodiac. When considering the effects of the Moon, you'll first want to know the aspect between the Moon's sign in the heavens and your natal Moon. If you keep track of this motion, you will see that when the Moon is square or opposite your natal Moon, you feel more energized, but with the square, you are more easily frustrated when things do not go your way. When the Moon is trine or sextile your natal position, you may feel more at ease and harmonious. The conjunction is also an energetic aspect and magnifies the feelings of your natal lunar placement.

When you look at the sign the Moon is in and the aspects she is forming with the other planets, you can tell the emotional tenor of any day. For example, as I am writing this section, there was a total lunar eclipse at 16 degrees of Taurus. The night was clear and cold and the view of the Moon was spectacular. The entire day had a luminous, bouncy feeling. You can draw up a chart for the moment of the eclipse and see that the Moon was trine Jupiter at 13 degrees of Virgo, sextile Saturn at 13 degrees of Cancer, and forming a separating square from Neptune at 16 degrees of Aquarius. That makes two harmonious aspects and one challenging. All in all, it felt like a benign eclipse. Jupiter in Virgo helps to make plans concrete, Saturn in Cancer indicates structured nurturing, and Neptune in Aquarius urges idealism and peace for all people. Because the Moon in Taurus was square Neptune you could conclude that, on a larger scale, hopes for peace would be challenged. Can you see how you can blend the meanings of the signs, planets, and aspects to get the feel for any astrological event?

You can also outline the aspects of the Moon with the planets on an ordinary day. There may be many different aspects or only a few. Sometimes your brain can get too busy looking at all the planetary motions. To simplify the use of the Moon for planning, just note the sign the Moon is in, and concentrate on activities that are harmonious to the meaning of the sign. Plan a party when the Moon is in Libra. Consider volunteer work or dealing with your pets when the Moon is in Virgo or Pisces. The Moon in Taurus is a good time to look for a house, buy furniture, or cook a good meal.

THE MOON'S PHASES

In addition to the sign the Moon is in, it is very important to look at the Moon's phases. The lunar cycle begins with the waxing phase; that is the time from the new moon until the full moon. The waning phase commences after the full moon and is called the third quarter moon, and concludes with the dark of the moon.

The New Moon

Noted on most calendars, the new moon is the time when energy is increasing, making it the time to initiate new projects. Each month's new moon is in the same sign as that month's Sun sign, and the full moon is in the opposite sign. There is a feeling of renewal with each new moon. This is the time to start looking for a new job, begin a new health or eating plan, start or continue exercising, or plan a trip. When you plan around the lunar phases, you are synchronized with your feelings and the flow of energy. If you begin a project during the new moon, work on it until the full moon. This is approximately two weeks. This is the sowing phase, and you are planting seeds for the future.

The Full Moon

Astrologers are not the only people who note the full moon. Some people say hospital emergency rooms, police stations, and bars are more active at the full moon than at other times. Everyone feels intense energy at this time. Cancerians, in particular, may need to let off some steam and howl a bit. No matter where your Sun or Moon may be, you may feel more vibrant than usual, very moody, or excited. Contact with water is restorative during the full moon. It is also a good time to consider your feelings rather than your mind. Meditation groups sometimes meet at the full moon because it adds luminosity to their prayers and meditations. Some seeds that we have sown at the new moon may reach fulfillment at the full moon.

The Waning Moon

Right after the full moon, you may notice that things become a little slower and you feel as if nothing is happening. This is a time to keep up your actions and finish up the projects begun at the previous new moon. Some projects, of course, take a good deal longer than a single lunar cycle. When the Moon is waning, give yourself some downtime and don't go full tilt. A little relaxation and fun is the best medicine during the waning moon.

The Dark of the Moon

The last three days of the lunar cycle can feel dull and you may be more tired than usual. This is a time to rest. I don't necessarily mean stay in bed, but relax, and if you do need sleep, try to get as much as you can. Pay attention to your dreams and be as inwardly oriented as your nature allows. After all, what you are doing is preparing for the next new moon, which comes soon enough.

The Void-of-Course Moon

Another term that is important to learn when considering the Moon's motion is *void-of-course*. This is also written as the *v/c* or VoC Moon. The term *void-of-course* relates to a period of time when the Moon is changing from one sign to the next, and is not connected in a major applying aspect to any other planet. It is important to note the times when the Moon is void-of-course, because it usually has an influence on everyday events and affairs. If you recall that the Moon outlines or pertains to our feelings and moods, then it is not an imaginative leap to see that when the Moon is unconnected to other planets, a person can feel unmoored or confused.

The v/c Moon period is a time to take a break and connect with your center. This is a time to postpone decisions and wait until the Moon connects to the other planets again before you sign contracts or enter into a serious commitment of any kind. Marriages finalized in a void-of-course Moon usually do not last. There are other reasons a marriage may break up, but I have never seen a marriage of long-lasting significance that began during a void-of-course Moon. Businesses that open during a void-of-course Moon usually struggle to find their niche and do not easily prosper.

The void-of-course Moon can bring unexpected results. Usually I counsel clients to avoid making purchases during a v/c Moon. The Moon doesn't make something defective—usually it's your judgment that might be off, so please do not conclude that a v/c Moon means a negative time. Keeping track of the Moon's motion is an opportunity to keep in contact with feelings, and you know that sometimes you might not feel in touch with your own feelings. When you want unity between your feelings and whatever activity you are pursuing, you should pay attention to the v/c Moon.

The major *don'ts* for a v/c Moon include elective surgery (except in case of an emergency), beginning a plane flight or a long journey, entering marriage, buying stock, signing a rental lease, closing on a home, or signing any other contract. Don't make important appointments while the Moon is void-of-course, as you probably will find that they are canceled, you are unable to make the deadlines, or you are unable to complete the appropriate work or business. Meetings or court cases held during a v/c Moon have unpredictable outcomes that frequently change at a later date. If a project has already begun, the phase of the Moon is not as significant. The v/c Moon pertains more to the beginning of an event or project.

The major *dos* for the void period are scaling down your activities, relaxing, reviewing your plans for the immediate future, and keeping steady in your pace. If you don't feel comfortable doing something when the Moon is v/c, do it later. Sometimes you might not have the luxury of doing what you feel like doing, but knowing that you may be swimming upstream helps you have patience with yourself and fosters a certain benign detachment from the multitude of events and influences swirling around you.

THE MOON'S MOTION THROUGH THE HOUSES

The last feature of the Moon worth noting is the passage of the Moon through the houses. When the Moon is in a particular house, you will feel keenly about the matters governed by that house. If you keep a copy of your chart handy, you can see which house the Moon is in and plan your activities accordingly. This does not mean that if you need or feel like doing something, and the Moon is passing through a house that has nothing to do with the activity, you will have difficulties. As events occur, it is always interesting to note if the Moon reflects the meaning of the event. Now that you understand the two luminaries, the Sun and the Moon, as they move through your chart, let's look at the planet of communication: Mercury.

MERCURY ☿

Mercury is the planet closest to the Sun and the smallest in the solar system. Mercury can never be farther than 28 degrees before or after the Sun. Therefore, the only possible aspects with the Sun are the conjunction or semisextile. When you interpret Mercury in a chart, look to see whether it is in the same sign as the Sun or in a different sign. When there is a conjunction between the Sun and Mercury, the person lacks objectivity in his or her thinking. The personality, signified by the Sun, and the thought processes, signified by Mercury, are so closely connected that it is difficult for people with this conjunction to entertain other people's viewpoints. When you examine the signs that Mercury and the Sun are in, regardless of the aspect, you will also have a good idea of the way a person thinks.

The other significant position of Mercury to consider is whether he is rising before or after the Sun; this simply means whether he is positioned before or after the Sun. If Mercury is located before the Sun, a person is cautious and thinks before they act. Such people also tend to be self-taught. If Mercury is located after the Sun, a person can feel "in the dark" about their thoughts and communications and be correspondingly pessimistic.

Lastly, consider whether Mercury was direct or retrograde when a person was born. If you see ℞ next to any planet in a natal chart, except for the Sun or Moon, it means that planet was retrograde when that person was born. If this does not show up, the planet was moving in direct motion.

People born with a retrograde Mercury have a unique thought pattern and way of communicating. Since Mercury retrogrades three times a year, the pattern is not uncommon. A person with a retrograde Mercury is a close observer of the facts, but they can become overly fussy with details. In Chapter 6: Assessing Compatibility Between Charts, you will learn how to communicate with a retrograde Mercury person. Mercury direct people are sure of their thinking and move directly toward their goals. Mercury direct allows the person to isolate the important points in an argument without getting bogged down in details. They may, however, be easily persuaded and lack mental discernment.

MERCURY TRANSITS

Noting which house Mercury is transiting through in a chart can give you some good information about where your thoughts and communication energy is focused. For example, when Mercury transits the Second House, you may be particularly involved with organizing finances and dealing with money matters. As you learned about the Sun and Moon, you can now examine the sign that transiting Mercury is in, noting where he is located in charts, and gear mental, communicative, and writing activities according to the meaning of the sign and house. You might pay more attention to your dreams when Mercury is in Pisces or communicate more directly when Mercury is in Aries. If a person is a writer, he or she will find writing easier when transiting Mercury is in a harmonious aspect to natal Mercury. Most people, however, are not that aware of Mercury's passage through their charts because thoughts move so quickly. You become aware of Mercury only because of the famous—or infamous—Mercury retrograde.

RETROGRADE MERCURY ☿℞

Mercury spends about fifteen days to two months in each sign and takes a year to go through all the signs of the zodiac. When Mercury spends two months in a sign, it is because Mercury is in retrograde motion. A retrograde planet does not physically move backward through the zodiac. When the motion of Mercury is retrograde, it is because Mercury slows in its orbit. The Earth maintains its speed and seems to be overtaking the slower-moving planet. Most planets have longer orbits than Mercury, and you will not notice their motions as often. Mercury, however, retrogrades three times a year, and you can be aware of this transit because it causes so much confusion.

This is the time when people roll their eyes because they get error messages on their computer that don't make sense and apps that worked just yesterday seem to have developed strange glitches. People sign contracts and then realize that the small print has some information or clause that is the opposite to what they expected. Appointments seem haphazard; people have a tendency to be late. In general, communications, thoughts, and electronics go askew. There is a reason for this planetary event, and, of course, there is a way to handle it. The message of Mercury retrograde is to practice your nonlinear, intuitive radar rather than logical, linear thought processes. Mercury retrograde is the time to suspend thoughts and, instead, operate on your feelings and hunches. Get the feel of the day's rhythm and stay centered as those around you fume and fret; you might be amazed at how many touchy situations you can glide through.

Specifically, you can expect to redo, rearrange, recommit to, rework, and review plans and activities during this retrograde time. You may go back to a project that you had abandoned. You may want to review plans. One client had *definitely* decided to leave her husband. She had her boxes packed and had purchased the plane tickets to Florida to stay with a friend. She had been married a long time and even knew that Mercury retrograde tends to confuse thoughts, but she was angry and planned to go anyway. Right before Mercury straightened out, she got intestinal flu and had to cancel her plans. In between trips to the bathroom, she had plenty of time to pay attention to her feelings. She recovered from the flu, Mercury went direct, and she and her husband came to a new understanding. No one knows what would have happened if she had gone to Florida, but certainly the hurt feelings on both sides would have added more stress to their relationship.

Mercury retrograde is a time to expect delays in traveling. Practical precautions include labeling luggage so it does not go astray, or packing lightly and keeping your bags with you. Don't schedule a meeting immediately after you arrive; leave a margin of time for any retrograde shenanigans such as a massive traffic jam or a computer foul-up with your reservations. Do not buy smartphones, cars, or major electronic equipment. Expect delays with construction and wait until Mercury is moving forward to begin construction projects.

The two signs most personally affected by a retrograde Mercury are Gemini and Virgo, because Mercury is their ruling planet. During the retrograde periods, these signs may feel more discombobulated than other signs. These retrograde periods offer other pathways for these signs to think and express themselves, which will help them in every area of their lives. Gemini and Virgo have such active minds that it may be all they can do to keep their thoughts from overwhelming them. For Gemini, this is the time to experiment with playing with one thought; for Virgo, it is the time to allow free association rather than the need to put things in order. Virgos might imagine that three times a year, they will be entertained by the unpredictability of their thoughts and communications. This will help them breeze through the retrograde Mercury periods.

Geminis may find the retrograde period a time during which they can focus their minds more easily, because trying to be clear and organized takes more effort than their usual scattered mental energies. You certainly don't have to sit and twiddle your thumbs while Mercury is retrograde. The best approach is to use these periods to explore a fluid, intuitive approach to communication and scheduling. So take a mental holiday three times a year.

By using the planet's motions, you will be able to allow yourself to work with the planets rather than against them. Some people hate the feeling of not being in control, but knowing the rhythms of life and the planets actually gives you more control because you can be more attuned to these rhythms.

VENUS ♀

Venus is the next personal planet that we consider when planning daily life and gathering information about our pleasures and enjoyment. Venus takes 255 days to orbit the Sun and spends approximately one month in each sign. Venus retrogrades every eighteen months, and there are special considerations to make when she is moving backward. Venus is visible twinkling on the horizon as the evening star in much of the Northern Hemisphere, and she was worshiped in ancient cultures even before the advent of astrology. The Mayan culture used Venus's orbits and retrogrades for agricultural planning. Venus is always considered a fortuitous, lucky planet.

When interpreting Venus, you first must look at the sign and house she occupies in a natal chart. The element that Venus is in will give you good information about what kinds of social and pleasurable activities that person enjoys. Then, as you have done with the Moon and Mercury, note the sign that Venus is in at the present time or for the time period you are interested in examining. What are the aspects between

Venus and your other personal planets? Venus aspects enhance life. They are not usually connected with major events, and watching Venus in your chart will clue you in to different ways of enjoying yourself. Venus is also the key planet to consider when buying gifts for someone or for yourself. If you know what sign a person's Venus is in, you will immediately have an idea of what sort of gift to buy them. For more details on this, take a look at my book *The Astrology Gift Guide*, which includes lists of gift suggestions for each sign.

VENUS TRANSITS

Venus transits will show you where to plan social activities and will give you some good insight into what kinds of pleasurable pursuits would be particularly inviting. If transiting Venus is squaring your personal Venus, don't expect a social whirl. The oppositions can bring short-lived romance or a fad that you enjoy for a while. In general, Venus transits do not bring about major events.

Venus can also indicate personal luck in all matters of gambling. When she is passing through the Fifth House and in good aspects to your Sun and Moon, then you might have luck with the lottery or games of chance. Venus and Uranus are both involved in extraordinary luck, but as far as I know, no one has ever become a winner solely through astrology. Venus rules speculative sports as well as pleasure sports, and there are some indications that Venus aspects help in breeding racehorses and winning races, although this is a specialized area.

The house that Venus is transiting, regardless of the aspects she makes to your chart, will tell you what pleasurable activities would be most successful. When she is in the First House, spend time and money on your physical being. This is a good month to get a massage or begin a new exercise program. When she is in the Second House, you will feel like spending a lot of money. If you have it, indulge; if you don't, watch out because Venus can beguile you into spending more than you have. The Fifth House would be the time to look around for a new romantic interest or flirt with the one you have. As you acquire a good working knowledge of all the houses, you can apply that knowledge to Venus transits. One particular note regarding Venus and sweets: They tend to go together, and if you have Venus in Taurus or Libra, you may be prone to having a sweet tooth. Other Venus placements, especially in the water signs of Cancer, Scorpio, and Pisces, may also have this problem. If you have this inclination and notice too many harmonious aspects coming up where you can easily polish off an extra glass of wine or devour a few too many chocolates, try to be moderate. Alas, Venus does not care for moderation and you may not be able to pay heed to this suggestion, but at least you will know what is prompting you. If you wait until Venus is in a less indulgent sign, you can undo the damage.

When purchasing furniture, art, jewelry, or expensive clothing, look at the sign occupied by Venus. If she is compatible with your natal Venus when you're shopping, then your taste will be on the mark and you will feel comfortable with your purchase. When you are considering buying something that is very expensive, you need some backup planetary assistance. Venus will help you choose and ensure good taste in your choice, but for reinforcement, remember to make sure the Moon is in a sign that harmonizes with Venus.

RETROGRADE VENUS ♀℞

The retrograde for Venus comes every year and a half and lasts approximately six weeks. The two major areas affected by a retrograde Venus are romantic relationships and shopping. It is never harmful, but it can lead you into some peculiar desires that usually do not work out.

During a retrograde Venus, don't spend large sums of money on any luxury products. You will find after Venus turns direct that you do not like what you purchased. This sometimes takes a little discipline, but it's worth the effort.

Venus retrograde is the time to frequent flea markets and garage sales for real finds. You will be pleased with your purchases; because most other shoppers don't know about the retrograde, they will be busy spending a lot of money and leaving the good deals for you.

The other traditional *don't* with Venus retrograde is planning a wedding and marrying while Venus is retrograde. There are other factors to consider when marrying, which will be discussed later, but it is easy to see whether Venus is direct or not as soon as you set a date for marriage. Love affairs begun under a retrograde Venus may be very bumpy. It doesn't necessarily indicate the end of a relationship, but you will notice that things change when Venus turns direct. For long-standing relationships, Venus retrograde can indicate a reevaluation of the romance and partnership. Romance is usually dampened and intimate relationships do not feel cordial. In and of itself, though, Venus retrograde does not indicate separation or divorce.

MARS ♂

Mars is the last of the personal planets and perhaps the most influential and challenging. Mars stands for passion, energy, assertiveness, and anger. Learning the difference between assertiveness and anger is a challenge for everyone, and Mars's position tells us exactly how to attempt this. Mars also tells a lot about sexual relations and feelings. When you look at compatibility charts, the position of Mars between two people describes how they relate as sexual partners. Since antiquity, Mars has been called the "red planet" and is visible to the naked eye. It stays in a sign for six to eight weeks and retrogrades approximately every two and a half years.

Before we consider Mars transiting through the chart houses, there are a few Mars aspects you should examine. If you have Mars in a challenging aspect to Saturn or Uranus in your natal chart, your difficulty with anger and passion is particularly acute. The aspect is a karmic indicator and will be a focal point for life. Specifically, Mars square Saturn and Mars conjunct Uranus are difficult. With Mars conjunct Uranus there is tremendous energy present, but it may take a person awhile to stabilize his or her erratic energies and master the tendency to explode.

When a person has Mars and Uranus conjunctions, they explode as a matter of course, and frequently spend a good deal of their life picking up the resulting debris and trying to stabilize themselves. Mars conjunct Saturn is a different kind of challenge. Saturn limits and binds Martian energy and it puts too many strictures on him. It can depress the spirit until the person learns that Mars needs due attention. Rules, regulations, and caution only serve life in certain areas, while at other times we need a bit of recklessness. What is Mars good for? Mars can be a planet of thrills and joy. It is a masculine exuberant energy, and when you are using this planet well, you will feel challenged and alive. Look at the sign Mars occupies in your chart and note the aspects he forms with transiting Mars in the sky. When Mars is trine and sextile, expect an even flow of energy. The conjunction will bring you face-to-face with your potential for joy and assertiveness or, if you are feeling pent up, for anger. If you feel self-possessed during the conjunction, this is the time to ask for a raise. If you are spilling over with Martian resentment, wait until a trine or sextile comes up. The opposition is usually a good time for sports and physical activity. Bedroom activity can be particularly satisfying during a Mars opposition. The square aspect, as you might guess, is a time to tread carefully. Because the challenge of handling a Mars square means compression of energy, this is a time to avoid any kind of reckless behavior, particularly concerning cars and thrill-seeking sports. If you have a motorcycle, be extra careful when Mars is squaring your natal Mars.

Mars also rules surgery because he rules metal, knives, and scalpels. Pay attention to Mars aspects when planning an elective surgery. In your chart, if the aspects are challenging, ask your doctor if you can wait until Mars moves into an easier relationship. It is best to consult a professional astrologer when planning any nonemergency surgery. There are a few basic rules, but serious surgery needs a lot of experience to maximize success and a good recovery.

MARS TRANSITS

As we have done with the other personal planets, examine the house that Mars is passing through in your chart. This is where you can concentrate your yang energy for the time that Mars is a tenant in that house. Also look at the house opposite to your Martian placement; this is where you may feel frustration. If Mars is passing through your Second House and you are working overtime trying to make money, while your partner (represented by the Eighth House) is totally unconcerned with any moneymaking efforts, Mars's energy will make you feel frustrated and angry. It could be challenging to resolve this situation. It is worth your while to examine Mars transits through your chart in terms of how you are relating to the people around you. If you feel angry with your friends, see if Mars is passing through your Eleventh House; if you are having a difficult time when you are around your children, Mars might be passing through your Fifth House. Mars, as the last of the personal planets, stays in a sign longer than Mercury, Venus, and the Sun do. You can concentrate on his effect on the chart for a longer period of time.

Mars transits are great times to get a lot of physical work done. Exercising regularly is always a good idea, but when Mars is directly affecting your chart, you are supercharged and need to work off energy in more ways than your usual stint at the gym. If you are moving furniture, clearing out brush from your backyard, or toting things from one place to another, Mars is your friend. He will give you stamina, and the physical exercise will be enjoyable. Because Mars does have destructive potential, it is worthwhile to regularly examine the aspects between Mars and other planets in the current sky. Most astrology software programs have a helpful feature called an astrology clock. This is a chart wheel giving you the positions of all the planets and how they move. The clock can register changes every 10 seconds. You can look up the position of the planets daily on www.astro.com to see if Mars is aspecting any of your personal planets.

On the clock, you can watch the Moon change signs and see the house cusps adjust accordingly. When outer planets move from one sign to another, the astro clock tells you exactly when a new planetary phase begins. Of course, you can also find this information in your ephemeris. When you notice that transiting Mars is conjunct, square, or opposite Uranus, you can expect strained nerves on a global scale. Mars in a hard aspect to Pluto magnifies anger. In both cases, accidents can occur and conflicts will increase. Tracking astrological transits for nations and global events is a specialized branch of astrology that will be discussed in Chapter 8. The value of noting the relationship between Mars and the outer planets is that it will tell you when you will want to exercise caution. Examine your astro clock and see if the planetary picture indicates dicey Mars, Saturn, and Uranus aspects. It is not superstitious to take the planets' positions into consideration when planning activities; it is wise. Mars, in particular, gives you a good indication of the temper and violence quotient that is present in the atmosphere. If Mars is conjunct Uranus, I would suggest staying off the road or, at least, driving very carefully. It is a very meditative activity to look at the astro clock first thing in the morning and connect with the heavens. It can give you patience and compassion for the day ahead.

RETROGRADE MARS ♂ ℞

Mars retrogrades approximately every two and a half years, which means that whatever sign Mars occupies when the retrograde occurs, he will remain in that sign for almost four months. A retrograde motion of a planet causes the planet's energy to be internalized. In the case of Mars, this usually means that people's egos are bursting with desire to assert themselves, but there is a great tendency to do so without restraint. People get angry at the drop of a hat, engage in power struggles with those in authority, or step up warlike activity quickly. When Mars goes retrograde, it is as if the balance tips in favor of aggression and angry expression. I have also noticed that every time Mars retrogrades in New York City, the street in front of my apartment goes under repair with an annoyingly loud jackhammer that seems to last exactly until Mars straightens out.

Those people who are restraining their tempers will definitely feel a buildup of energy, which must be expressed in some way. You might consider two activities during a Mars retrograde, when your energy or frustration level builds up. The first would be to visit a boxing gym and take out your frustrations on a punching bag. The second involves trees, which are your friends during a Mars retrograde. Go and shout your frustration to them, or wrap your arms around a particularly sturdy oak and express your feelings. There is no use denying that everyone has these feelings. The key is to find ways to express your emotions without setting up a chain of additional problems.

If you do have to communicate sternly and assertively with anyone during a retrograde Mars, try as much as possible to give the other person his or her space. If you engage in "I am right" and "You are wrong" positions, the argument will escalate quickly. Retrograde Mars is a perfect opportunity to agree with the other person's feelings, no matter how outrageous they are, *and* assert what you have to say. During these times, Mars may give you courage. Let it be effective courage. A more practical consideration for the retrograde Mars period is postponing any kind of surgical or dental procedures. Emergencies cannot be helped, but do not schedule anything that can wait. Court cases or issues involving fractious parties would also best be postponed. Be conservative with your driving because dealings with law enforcement officers will not be pleasant during this time. A retrograde Mars makes those who are involved in Martian activities, such as the police and the military, especially keen on doing their job well.

In conclusion, the major "dos" during a retrograde Mars are to find physical outlets for your energy that do not involve arguing with others; keep breathing; start an exercise program; and watch people's ego demands. The major things to avoid are scheduling elective surgery, carelessly handling sharp instruments or knives, driving recklessly, and provoking conflict and unnecessary confrontation. This can be a challenging time, and luckily occurs only about every two years.

HOW TO USE AND ORGANIZE THIS INFORMATION

When looking at the daily transits of the Sun, Moon, Mercury, Venus, and Mars, you should be able to mentally calculate the aspects between these planets and your chart. If this is too abstract for you at first, then practice by keeping a copy of your chart handy and plotting each planet on the outside of the wheel with a pencil. Then, when the Moon changes, or Venus moves into a different house, you can erase the planet and place it in the current house. This exercise will also give you a good feel for the way the planets move.

Note the aspects each planet is making to your chart. You can use your aspectarian until you can identify all the aspects easily. Also consider which house each transiting planet is in. By minding the house position without even dealing with particular aspects, you can zero in on the areas of life that need your attention. With practice you will be able to think like this: The Sun is in Scorpio, Scorpio rules my midheaven (the Tenth House cusp), so now is the time to pay particular attention to all career matters and work with the public. Or perhaps I need to pay attention to one of my parents (also indicated by the Tenth House cusp)? Life will let you know which interpretation of the houses to use. When you note the aspects between all your personal planets and the transiting planets, you can see if you will have an easy or a challenging time. Your aspects with Mercury will tell you how you are communicating. Aspects with Venus will tell you about your social life and pleasure, and aspects with Mars will tell you about your physical energy, temper, passion, and assertiveness. The quickly changing aspects with the Moon will tell you how you feel about everything day by day. When the aspects are challenging, for relief look to other parts of your chart where the aspects are easier. Concentrate your energy on the free-flowing department and you will skate through any sticky wickets in other departments. There is always some positive planetary aspect occurring in a chart.

CHAPTER FOUR

THE BIG PICTURE

As we have discussed already, the daily motions of the personal planets, the Sun, and the Moon can help us with everyday life. Contemplating life's big questions—such as how to apply your talents, how to figure out your life's purpose, and what is meaningful to you—requires looking at the transpersonal planets, Jupiter and Saturn, as well as the outer planets, Uranus, Neptune, and Pluto. All these planets stay in one sign from one to twenty years, depending on the planet; their effects are longer lasting than the hurried transits of Mercury, Venus, and Mars. Jupiter and Saturn help us set down roots and direct attention to where we can grow and develop. Uranus shakes us up and surprises us. Neptune attunes us to ideals and teaches us about our illusions. Pluto carves out deep emotional growth and power dynamics.

One of the advantages of astrology is that it is a multilevel art. You can pay attention to everyday reality, while using the poetry, meaning, and essences of the planets to inform yourself about the cosmic harmonies in the world. If you are open to all experiences, then the planets help you to interpret and plan ahead for your personal development.

JUPITER ♃

Let's look at Jupiter. Jupiter's meaning is the principle of expansion, and he is called the *greater benefic*. Jupiter has always been associated with the more joyous aspects of life, a positive attitude, and all manner of optimism. Astrologers breathe easily with Jupiter aspects and transits because that is the good-news department of the chart. At the least, Jupiter can help give you a positive outlook, which goes a long way to plowing through some of the tough stretches of life.

Jupiter offers us the possibility of deep philosophical and spiritual wisdom as well. He not only indicates good times, but also helps define our outlook on life and the philosophy behind our actions. Whether or not we are conscious of them, we all have beliefs that inform our choices. In addition to our astrological character traits, we have beliefs that come from our upbringing and from the society around us. Some may be carried over from past lives. Jupiter also defines our religious views, whether they are part of an organized religion or an individual spiritual practice.

Presently, American society is adamantly materialistic, yet we see people yearning for some philosophy, activity, or belief system that takes them out of the malls and brings meaning, peace, and joy to their lives. Jupiter's position in a chart expresses where we will begin to investigate this spiritual basis for our lives. When people feel connected to a larger philosophy and are working to improve the planet, they feel rooted and patient.

JUPITER IN THE SIGNS

The sign placement of natal Jupiter is a clue to your basic orientation in life. Remember that Jupiter originally ruled both Sagittarius *and* Pisces. Although now Neptune is Pisces's ruler, it is always important to remember the ancient rulerships. The next time your dreamy Pisces friend has a scheme to begin an animal shelter or give away all his or her money to the poor, you will be able to recall that Jupiter definitely influences Pisces. That original rulership is important in understanding and interpreting the nature of Jupiter. Both Pisces and Sagittarius have philosophical interests. Pisces, however, is the more mystical sign and Sagittarius the more philosophical. Pisces quests through feelings and dreams; Sagittarius quests through enthusiasm and philosophy.

The word *enthusiasm* is derived from the Greek *entheos*, which means to infuse with *theos*, or God. When we are enthusiastic, we connect with an energy that can move us forward effortlessly. We have more power because we are eagerly anticipating the next chapter of any project. People whose charts are strongly influenced by Jupiter have a concentration of Sagittarius or Pisces planets, Jupiter in an angular house, or Sagittarius or Pisces rising.

When Jupiter is in a sign antithetical to his nature, we can expect that the Jupiterian buoyancy and optimism in life do not come as easily, or his gifts are squandered and mishandled. Jupiter in Gemini is a good example. This placement emphasizes mental and verbal activity so much that a person can talk away all their good intentions and plans and throw their positive energy to the winds. Excess is part of Jupiter's exuberance and enthusiasm, but other signs have an easier time balancing Jupiter's excesses. When Jupiter is in Capricorn, Saturn's sign, for example, a person can seem either overly cautious or prudently optimistic. The sign placement of the planets always leaves room for your individual temperament and choice.

JUPITER'S NATAL ASPECTS

When Jupiter trines or sextiles or conjuncts a natal planet, it gives ease to the expression of that planet. With the hard aspects, the square and opposition, Jupiter offers protection to those planets and mitigates difficulties.

RETROGRADE JUPITER IN A NATAL CHART ♃℞

When Jupiter is retrograde in a natal chart, a person usually emphasizes the more philosophical and internal meanings of Jupiter. The person's value system may be more concerned with intangible accomplishments than material accomplishments. Many traditional books interpret Jupiter retrograde to mean that a person cannot attract the money he or she needs. This isn't necessarily true. The retrograde position could mean, however, that a person values satisfying but not particularly lucrative occupations and endeavors. Jupiter retrograde sometimes indicates that a person chooses to emphasize nonmaterial goals.

JUPITER IN THE HOUSES

When you examine Jupiter, pay special attention to his natal house position as well as his natal sign. The house position will show the area of life that receives Jupiter's buoyant and optimistic influence. This can be either through a person's own efforts or by what they attract in life. Jupiter in the Seventh House of marriage, for example, means that that person will attract a marriage or marriages that will benefit them. When Jupiter is in the Second House of money, students often say, "Oh great, Jupiter in the Second House. That means you'll be rich." It *could* mean that. However, I have seen many clients with that Jupiter placement who attract money but cannot hold on to it. A better interpretation for Jupiter in the Second House would be that you have a free-flowing, optimistic attitude toward money. Without looking at the details of Jupiter's house placement, you can say that wherever Jupiter is located you will have blessings and optimism.

JUPITER TRANSITS

When Jupiter changes from one house through his transit to another, you will find there is a shift in emphasis in your life. It is as if Jupiter leaves one country, and in going to another, he brings his light to that area of life for the next year. If you have an intercepted house, then Jupiter will remain in that area for longer than a year. Applying your knowledge of the house meanings, you can readily identify which area of your chart Jupiter is enlivening. Where he will be traveling next can inform your decisions of where to place your emphasis. Since Jupiter aspects your planets for longer periods of time, it is worthwhile to note what his aspects are to your natal Jupiter, Saturn, Uranus, Neptune, and Pluto. Jupiter conjuncting any of these planets gives an energy boost and emphasizes a positive expression to that planet. As always, with Jupiter, it can also indicate excess. During a Jupiter conjunction to Neptune, you may be extremely sensitive to your dreams or daydreams. The phrase "head in the clouds" is particularly appropriate at this time. A Jupiter or Neptune transit encourages flights of fantasy, but this is also the time to check in with Saturn to make sure your dreams can be brought down to earth.

The trine facilitates Jupiter's energy with your natal placements. The square lets you know that there is a challenge with the two aspect energies; the square will tell you that now is not the time to spend money or energy imprudently. The opposition means that you have to balance the seesaw and pay attention to both planets. When you are interpreting transits, concentrate on the major aspects. Examining the uncommon aspects will give finesse and refinement to interpretations, but it would be rare for a semisextile, quincunx, or quintile to be the harbinger of a major event.

JUPITER RETURN

A Jupiter cycle takes about twelve years to complete. Every twelve years Jupiter returns to your natal position. That means at age twelve, twenty-four, thirty-six, forty-eight, sixty, seventy-two, eighty-four, and ninety-six, that person will have a Jupiter return. It is always interesting to track developments in a person's life to see if these years correspond with honors, recognition, or fortunate life events. A Jupiter return is only one cycle operating in one's life. If a chart is strongly attuned to Jupiter, these years will resonate more clearly. Watch your own chart and see what occurs during these times.

Jupiter's twelve-year cycle means that every twelve years, a person experiences a Jupiter return. This is when Jupiter returns to the sign and house of his birth. It means that during the past twelve years Jupiter has gone through all the possible aspects with the other planets in your chart and has now completed one part of a journey. For the year that Jupiter stays in your natal sign and house, you can expect the meanings of the sign and the house that Jupiter is located in to bring blessings and fruition. If other parts of the chart are taking you through muddy waters, the Jupiter return will give you a direction for joy and aid. During a Jupiter return, for example, one client was offered a full-time job and then found out that because of another employee's manipulation, the job was for only six months. He was crushed, but took the part-time position. Shortly after Jupiter was making his return, my client was promoted to another position and then paid for the entire year.

TRANSITING JUPITER RETROGRADE

The retrograde of Jupiter usually occurs once a year. Check your ephemeris, astro clock, or app to note when Jupiter goes retrograde. As you have seen with the other planets, the retrograde time internalizes the meaning of the planet. When Jupiter is retrograde, his normal flow of optimism is more inward. In the world, the stock market may slow down; money and philanthropy could be tight. Individuals usually hold off on purchases. Jupiter is gathering steam, and when he turns direct, material and spiritual life flow. The major activity to avoid during a Jupiter retrograde is beginning or opening a business or any endeavor designed to make a profit. You will find that either your expectations are too high or the business doesn't flourish.

SATURN ♄

Saturn is our taskmaster. Contrary to Jupiter's expansiveness, Saturn represents the principle of contraction. Saturn reins you in and forces you to structure life and be concrete about your dreams and plans. Considered the Lord of Time, Saturn was the farthest planet that could be seen with the naked eye in ancient times. When Saturn and his natural sign, Capricorn, dominate a chart, you know that this person is determined and diligent and must cultivate humor and lightness. A team of Saturn and Jupiter people can accomplish a lot if they don't drive each other nuts by the very different thrusts of their natures. This planet is not cheery, and describing a person's temperament as saturnine means that he or she is cautious, slow, sometimes worried, and very aware of consequences. If you need to plan for any eventuality on a camping trip, consult your Capricorn friend. Capricorn will effortlessly bring gear for all types of weather and make sure you have the latest equipment in working order. Capricorn will plan the route, so relax and enjoy the scenery knowing that everything is well organized.

Saturn is the planet of hierarchy. Saturn tells you that you must proceed step-by-step. Jupiter's danger is in excessive exuberance; projects aren't accomplished, because boredom sets in. Saturn's danger, in contrast, is overcautiousness, keeping everything in the planning stage, not moving ahead.

Saturn also describes the way the world works. Society is conservative and not always friendly to people or activities that go against its institutions. The placement of Saturn in your chart describes how you address these areas. Surprise successes do happen, but usually when you have laid the groundwork. Saturn is the reality check, and you should revel in his expertise, though it may not always feel pleasurable. Saturn suffers from a bad rep because we all tend to worry when we have difficult Saturn aspects or transits. It is important to remember that Saturn is exalted in Libra, which is the sign of balance, fairness, partnerships, and sociability. Enjoying good times and sharing jokes about the enormity of life's possibilities is one way of gracefully addressing Saturn in your chart.

SATURN IN THE SIGNS

Look at Saturn to see how easily a person can integrate this sign's gravity and structuring energy. The four elements help to immediately identify how easily Saturn can express himself. In Capricorn and Aquarius, we know that Saturn feels at home. Remember, while Aquarius is ruled by Uranus, Saturn is also a strong influence. This tone will be part of the sign's makeup. In the earth signs, Saturn facilitates orderly and concrete expression, which is consistent with his mission—the mission to keep life's experiences within the framework of your soul lessons. Saturn in the air signs creates order in a person's thinking. In today's society, where our concentration span is challenged daily by media assault, being an orderly thinker is a challenge but can lead to effective action. Saturn in fire is an uneasy fit. Fire wants Jupiterian enthusiasm and Saturn says, "Go slow." Saturn in fire can accomplish a great deal of work, but fire wants to burn freely and feels smothered by Saturn's demands. Their temperaments are not a harmonious fit. Lastly, Saturn in water signs is an easy fit only when a person's feelings flow naturally toward structure and dependability. This is usually not the case, so people with Saturn in water resent the hierarchy and lack of spontaneity that Saturn encourages.

SATURN'S NATAL ASPECTS

When Saturn conjuncts any planet in your chart, this is where you feel serious, grounded, and measured. Saturn delays the expression of the planets he conjuncts, but he does not necessarily deny their benefits. When Saturn trines your planets, then you feel easy with the demands of those planets. For example, Saturn trine Venus brings social and romantic encounters that are very traditional. Saturn trine Venus may also mean that you feel comfortable with older people both socially and romantically. When Saturn forms a sextile with a planet, it means there will be opportunities in life that will come your way to enhance your psychological and material development. When Saturn opposes a personal planet, the message is clear: Whenever you try and behave in an irresponsible way, Saturn will pull you back and require you to check things out more thoroughly.

Lastly, let's consider the uncomfortable Saturn square. This is a powerhouse aspect because of the challenge it offers a person. The planets squaring Saturn rub, chafe, and fight for expression. This is the aspect that drives people to persevere even when they believe they have tried everything. It also delays gratification for a person's efforts. Natal Saturn square Mars, for example, is a tough aspect because Mars wants to assert himself and Saturn keeps putting on the brakes. When you consider the squares in your own chart, or that of others, you can feel compassion because you can see so clearly how people fight to realize their abilities. Saturn will take you where you need to go, and the aspects tell you how much difficulty you will encounter along the way. The secret is always to enjoy the ride.

RETROGRADE SATURN IN A NATAL CHART ♄℞

Saturn is a slow-moving planet, and he retrogrades for around four or five months every year. This means that many people are born with Saturn retrograde. The usual interpretation of a planet's energy being internalized is not useful with Saturn, because no one has an outgoing, exuberant Saturn. It is antithetical to the nature of the planet. When we see a retrograde Saturn in a natal chart, it can be a clue to some health condition that needs to be monitored or a tendency to blocking emotions and walling up. Basically, the most important feature of a natal retrograde Saturn is the year it turns direct in the chart. This will be discussed more closely in Chapter 5.

SATURN IN THE HOUSES

Saturn's natal house has a large impact on a person's life direction. The house in which Saturn is located will tell you where you will encounter delays and frustration, and where you need to proceed in a structured, measured way. Saturn in the angular houses gives a Capricorn feeling to the personality. One woman with Saturn in the Seventh House married for the first time at age forty-four to a Capricorn man who was in his mid-thirties. Do you see how Saturn in the Seventh House describes perfectly her marriage and marriage partner? Saturn in the Twelfth House usually means that much of a person's expression in life is hampered by unconscious currents that could be from a past-life influence. When Saturn is in the Second House, attracting material abundance will be challenging. Saturn does not always have a negative interpretation. Saturn has to be somewhere in a natal chart, and what you are learning is the subtlety of how each of the planets informs and describes a person's life.

SATURN TRANSITS

Saturn spends approximately two and a half years in any sign. This means that all aspects that transiting Saturn forms in your chart will endure for at least a year. It also means that the house that Saturn is transiting will be very important in terms of understanding which areas of life need organizing and serious attention during that transit. For example, when Saturn is in the Sixth House, you may need to pay more attention to your health and to work very hard, sometimes without proper appreciation. When Saturn is passing through the Tenth House, a person can receive recognition for long service—or encounter delays and frustrations in realizing his or her career.

In addition to transiting Saturn's house position, note in your personal chart transiting Saturn's aspects to all your planets. While Jupiter expands the nature of the planet he aspects, Saturn contracts it and puts a lid on that planet's expression. For example, Saturn transiting in hard aspects (square or opposition) to Mars means that your vital energy is cramped. This is a time to do gentle physical exercise, because when Saturn puts the lid on Mars energy, the resulting tension can lead to injury. When Saturn forms a hard aspect with Venus, don't expect a lot of social activity. When Saturn forms a hard aspect with the Sun, life feels heavy. During a Saturn conjunction to your Moon by transit, you may find that personal relationships are ending. Saturn in hard aspect to Mercury deepens thought, but may lead you to brood on depressing topics and life.

Once you have scoped out transiting Saturn's aspects to the personal planets, make a list of his aspects to Jupiter, Uranus, Neptune, and Pluto. Saturn in a hard aspect to Jupiter forces you to plan; Saturn in easy aspect says you have the realistic grounding necessary to play well with Jupiter's benefits. Saturn in a hard aspect to Uranus is not comfortable. Uranus says to explode; Saturn says to contain. Find some activity that will appeal to your sense of adventure, but keep a watchful eye for danger or chaos. Transiting Saturn in hard aspect to Uranus reminds me of when I was a child and my sisters and I would get wound up and crazy during whatever game we were playing. As the noise grew louder, we could count on my father's voice booming: "Someone's going to get hurt. Calm down!" We were Uranus, and he was Saturn. Saturn's hard aspects to Neptune can be productive because Saturn's realism tempers Neptune's idealism. The soft aspects facilitate our dreams and spiritual concerns. If you have a tendency to become involved with fraudulent or overly idealistic projects that could involve your time and money, Saturn in hard aspect to Neptune will help you think twice about such opportunities. Saturn-Pluto aspects represent power struggles with authority. In this section I have elaborated on Saturn's hard aspects because they are the difficult ones.

When transiting Saturn is making easy aspects in your chart, this is the green light for proceeding with whatever projects you have in development. You could also take a break and relax.

THE SATURN CYCLE

The aspects between transiting Saturn and your natal Saturn are particularly important. Saturn squares your natal Saturn at age seven, opposes it at age fourteen, squares it again at age twenty-one, conjuncts it at ages twenty-nine or thirty (the first Saturn return), forms another square to it at age thirty-seven, opposes it at age forty-four, and squares it yet again at around age fifty-one. The second Saturn return occurs at around ages fifty-eight or fifty-nine. Let's also look at the soft, or easy, aspects. At age five, you have the Saturn sextile to your natal Saturn; at age ten, the trine; another trine at age nineteen; and a sextile at age twenty-five. During these years, you incorporate and enjoy the growth you have accomplished during the harder aspects. For Saturn cycles we use the broad strokes of the basic aspects. If you are interested in tracking Saturn's semisextile, semisquare, quincunx, and quintile, you might find interesting subtleties in your chart and life's events.

Notice that the years of a Saturn cycle correspond with definite developmental stages recognized in popular culture. The *seven-year itch* is a phrase used to describe a time when people are restless in their work or relationship and in need of a change. Every seven years, Saturn squares or opposes your natal Saturn and knocks on the door to see if you are going where you need to go. In the Bible, Joseph interpreted Pharaoh's dream about the seven full ears of corn and the seven withered ears of corn to mean there would be seven lean years and seven fruitful years of harvest. This was Joseph's intuitive understanding of Saturn's cycle...or perhaps he was also an astrologer.

One popular saying in the 1960s was "Don't trust anyone over thirty." It perfectly reflected the Saturn return because people over thirty at that time had left behind their freewheeling, hippie lifestyles.

Once you are thirty, you have completed the first Saturn return and have begun to incorporate ideals with practical considerations. You now have your two feet on the ground and can choose what you are going to do with your life. With the amount of education and material comfort many people in the US have available, the Saturn return is a fitting age to declare maturity. Although twenty-one is the legal age for many things in the US, more people are making major life decisions after their Saturn return.

TRANSITING SATURN RETROGRADE

Saturn retrogrades once a year and, as previously stated, stays retrograde for about four or five months. That means that whenever Saturn is making an aspect by transit to a planet in your natal chart, you could get three knocks before the transit finishes. This can be interpreted as the wake-up call, the attitude adjustment, and the finishing of the job. Look at Chart 3 and see if you can track with your ephemeris when transiting Saturn formed his first conjunction to this person's natal Saturn. The first time was on March 14, 1988, which would have been the wake-up call. Saturn moved on and retrograded on April 11, 1988.

You can see in the ephemeris that Saturn's degrees then got smaller, and on May 9, 1988, this person had a second exact aspect with transiting Saturn. This is the attitude adjustment. Ideally, between March and May, the person would have begun to look at what was not working or could work better in her life's plan. Saturn then continued to retrograde and, by the end of August, went direct to make his last conjunction (or finishes the job) on November 30, 1988. This person had finished the Saturn return and would not encounter it again until age fifty-eight.

The retrograde motion of Saturn also applies to all other aspects. If you pay attention to your ephemeris, you will see how many exact aspects Saturn makes and you can chart your progress accordingly.

SATURN RETURN

I want to write a bit more specifically about the Saturn return because it is the first major astrological cycle that a person experiences in life. It occurs around age twenty-eight or thirty and is always completed by age thirty-one. The cycle means that transiting Saturn returns to the position he was in when a person was born. The Saturn return is the first astrological diagnostic tool you have to see if a person's life is on course. If you experience a great deal of tumult and change around age twenty-eight or twenty-nine, the purpose is to move you in a direction more in keeping with your inner nature. If, at that time in your life, you continued moving in the same direction with some added responsibilities such as a marriage, children, or work responsibilities, then you can conclude that your actions and life are in harmony with your chart. If Saturn return experiences are difficult, the best approach is to realize that you may have been a little cavalier in your attitudes and may not have been paying attention to consequences.

Ask yourself this question: Am I where I want to be in all phases of my life? If not, what do I need to change to get there, and how can I plan that route step-by-step? The Saturn return is not the time to daydream that one day you will miraculously find yourself with the job, partner, friends, career, and children that you want. The Saturn return is the time to say, "I am here, in the driver's seat, and this is where I am going in my life."

The best antidote to Saturn's weight is silliness. Seek out silliness and you will feel lighter during your Saturn return or when Saturn makes tough aspects in your chart.

THE OUTER PLANETS

Before you learn about the outer planets—Uranus, Neptune, and Pluto—it is a good idea to adjust expectations. Consideration of these planets requires a different mind-set than when addressing the personal and transpersonal planets. To begin to understand the outer planets, you should think wide. The outer planets tell us about generations of people and states of spiritual evolution. Not everyone will respond to aspects with the outer planets in the same way. Most people are concerned with their own circle of life and not interested in too much outside of it. Astrology students, on the other hand, are interested in exploring different ways of knowing. Intuition, right-brained thinking, clairvoyance, ESP, dreams, and all the occult subjects are ways to approach life, and are experienced in a nonlinear, nonquantitative fashion. The influence of the outer planets, especially Uranus, is very strong among students of astrology. In her book *Astrology: A Cosmic Science*, Isabel M. Hickey uses the term *higher octave* for Uranus and Neptune. Uranus is the higher octave of Mercury, and Neptune is the higher octave of Venus. The octave is a note that is the same as a lower note, but it has twice the vibrations.

As people develop psychologically and spiritually, they change their vibrations. Students of meditation find that after periods of study, they sometimes can intuit or sense people's thoughts. This experience is the higher octave of communication. For example, speaking is the regular range of communication, and having an intuition or a flash of insight into something when you understand without words is a higher-octave communication. With these thoughts in mind, let's look at the outer planets.

URANUS ♅

Uranus is called the "higher octave of Mercury" because the kind of mental agility and electrifying nature of Uranus in a chart is Mercury at warp speed. Isabel M. Hickey states: "Mercury is intellect and Uranus is intuition." Mercury can think through a problem, but Uranus can intuit the problem and leap to a solution immediately. For example, many doctors are good and careful diagnosticians. They look at tests and conclude what the medical problem is. An intuitive doctor or a healer with a strong Uranus influence can make a diagnosis based on his or her insights, while the more cautious Mercury-influenced doctor cannot understand how that doctor leapt to such an instinct-led diagnosis. Frequently, intuitive thinkers themselves have no clue how they reached their goal. Uranus is uncontrollable. When someone falls in love at first sight, gets married after three days, and then divorced after two months, Uranus's influence is probably at work. Earthquakes and natural disasters are Uranian in nature. Sudden strokes of good fortune belong to Uranus's surprising energy. Winning the lottery or encountering a fast business deal with a lot of activity and not much staying power are also Uranian events. The nervous system is ruled by Uranus. People who have a strong Uranus influence must take care of their health. They can blow a fuse if they encounter too much stimulation or stress.

When Uranus is strong in a chart, people are highly individualistic and even eccentric. They enjoy shaking up stereotypes and pursuing their own idiosyncratic path. Uranus sparks our interest with out-of-the-blue, unusual thoughts and possibilities. Uranian influences also give bursts of creativity that are unexplainable. There can be a manic quality to these bursts, as if a person were possessed by energies from another dimension, but Uranus can also usher the person who experiences this to another plane of consciousness.

More commonly, Uranus's influence shakes up routines and prevents us from falling into a rut. In terms of spiritual development, Uranus helps us detach from our everyday habits and embrace being centered in the present. We learn with Uranus's influence what we can or cannot control.

Uranus has been particularly noteworthy in the last thirty years as he heralds in the age of Aquarius. There is disagreement in astrological circles about exactly when this long astrological cycle began, but whether you believe we are at the end of Pisces or at the beginning of Aquarius, clearly the present time offers unprecedented technological advances, social experimentation, and challenges to long-held beliefs and institutions. The rapid expansion of information and technology that we see now has been changing many of our ideas about family, society, fertility, and the nature of life itself. Cloning, stem cell research, and other medical procedures that press against the boundaries of what we assumed to be "life" are all under the aegis of Uranus.

URANUS IN THE SIGNS

I'd like to change the format for examining Uranus in the signs, because it is more important to see how Uranus operates in the chart instead of categorizing Uranus as comfortable in one element or sign and not another. Uranus is Aquarius's ruler, and all the other air signs express the rapid mental connections and mind changes that typify the planet's energy. Uranus is said to be in detriment in Leo because typically the warmhearted and personally dramatic sign of Leo is not comfortable with a detached mental planet. Leo, however, also represents personal will. If Leo can begin to turn his self-will over to the higher will, then Leo can align himself with Uranus's cosmic significance, and illumination is the result. In the other fire signs, Uranus usually can express himself well. The enthusiasm and internal energy of fire signs support Uranian energy. Can you see that Uranus operates differently according to a person's spiritual development? Uranus in water signs leans toward acute emotionality and gushes of feeling. Lastly, the earth signs contain some of the wild Uranian energy, but no one sign can tame the uncontrollable.

Due to the fact that Uranus stays in a sign for seven years or more, the sign position of Uranus also characterizes a large group of people. Like the other two outer planets, Neptune and Pluto, Uranus is a generational planet. Uranus's sign in a natal chart will give you indications of how an individual relates to their society and what contribution to the planet's development they can make.

URANUS'S NATAL ASPECTS

The planets that Uranus aspects in a chart will give you the best way to interpret the Uranian influence in a person's chart. When there are close Uranus conjunctions to a planet, that planet will behave in a surprising and unique manner. Uranus in aspect to any of the personal planets gives an abrupt, uncontrollable feeling to the way the planet functions.

When Uranus aspects Venus, unusual fashion and love affairs are in evidence. Mars and Uranus combinations are explosive, and channeling that energy is very important. Uranus in hard aspect to the Sun and the Moon usually signifies that a person seeks a higher spiritual vibration in life. They may be interested in meditation or have flashes of intuition that defy conventional understanding. The generation of people born from 1963 to 1968 had Uranus conjunct Pluto in their charts. Some of these are the people of dot-com riches. Uranus describes the technology that brought forth these riches—and the suddenness of companies opening and succeeding or opening and failing.

Uranian events lack staying power, and the initial sudden prosperity bubble of Silicon Valley burst around the year 2000. Beginning in 1998 and continuing through 2003, Uranus and Neptune were both in the sign of Aquarius. It is possible that babies born at this time had many extrasensory abilities and now that they are mature, these abilities are accepted as alternative ways of knowing. Prior to this conjunction, Uranus and Neptune were conjunct in the sign of Capricorn. The people born at that time may have a very different approach to institutions and societies' structures and will most probably prepare the way for the Aquarian future. As with all aspects, the hard ones can be challenging and the easy ones facilitate life. Uranus's energy is basically beyond our control, but we can learn how to react positively to this fascinating and energizing planet.

URANUS IN THE HOUSES

Needless to say, the house position of Uranus will be a major influence in your life. Wherever he is located is an unpredictable area of life. When Uranus is angular, especially in the First and Tenth houses, your entire character will have a Uranian or Aquarian tone to it. Your personality will be unconventional, and career matters will change quickly and be involved with Uranian fields such as media, technology, or avant-garde occupations. When Uranus is in the angular Fourth House, frequently there are untimely separations through death or divorce of one of the parents. In the Seventh House, Uranus usually makes conventional marriage a dicey proposition. The couple needs lots of individual space, and living together may be better than getting married. As you examine your own chart and the charts of others, focus on what sign Uranus is in and where he is located. You will begin to see how this out of-the-blue planet operates.

URANUS RETROGRADE AND TRANSITS

Like Saturn, Uranus spends about five months retrograde every year. Many people are born with a natal Uranus retrograde. I do not interpret this retrograde position as particularly significant unless Uranus turns direct in a progressed chart. You will learn more about this in Chapter 5. It is hard to apply the usual astrological rules to Uranus because there is no way to internalize Uranus's energy. Since Uranus spends seven years in a sign, the planets he aspects will receive his enlightening energy for a good long time. The house that Uranus is transiting through will also be a significant area for the time Uranus is there, and frequently you will notice a dramatic shift when Uranus changes houses. One client related that, after years of trying to conceive a child, as soon as Uranus moved into his Fifth House, his wife got pregnant. Uranian transits sometimes manifest through people we are close to as well as ourselves. This is important to remember when we look at chart comparisons and synastry.

The entire Uranus cycle takes eighty-four years. This is when Uranus returns to his natal position. Now that people are living longer, completing a Uranus return is more common. In the Uranus cycle, there are two important ages: twenty-one and forty-two. At twenty-one, transiting Uranus squares your natal Uranus position. Before it was lowered to eighteen in most places, this was the age of majority, which in the legal system indicates that people are of age. Remember that Saturn squares your natal Saturn at age twenty-one.

At age forty-two, when Uranus opposes your natal Uranus, there is a tendency to want to break loose from the lifestyle you were living. Some people call it a midlife crisis. It is common at this time for people to change careers, address health or healing issues, divorce, or make radical decisions about how they want to live. Some couples who for career reasons have put off raising a family decide to have children at this age. Many of the fertility techniques that exist today are definitely Uranus influenced.

At age sixty-three, there is another square, and people retire or find an occupation or interest that will take them into their old age. Uranus is the planet of divine discontent, and whenever he makes a hard aspect to your natal planets or to natal Uranus, you will not feel complacent. Of course, Uranus also forms trines and sextiles to natal Uranus and other planets in between squaring, opposing, and conjuncting the planets in your chart. The tempo of Uranian events now slows, and this is a time to enjoy the awakened insights you have gained.

NEPTUNE Ψ

Neptune, the dissolver, is the next outer planet. It is considered to be the higher octave of Venus, and, among other things, it pertains to divine love rather than personal and romantic love. In ancient Greek there is a difference between *agape*, which means the cordial and deep regard one person feels for another, and *eros*, which means romantic and sexual love. Neptune can be difficult to describe because the energies are ineffable and slippery. The true meaning of Neptune is the dissolution of the ego, but here on Earth you cannot really do that. With this in mind, I will give you an impression of Neptune.

Neptune clouds your judgment and promotes self-sacrifice and sometimes martyrdom. She is, as you know, associated with Pisces. When Neptune is prominent in the chart, a person lives on different planes. This could be in the realm of artistic imagination or escapism through alcohol and drugs. The entire art of cinema is ruled by Neptune. Here, we see the heights of great imagination that have stirred our hearts—and we see many casualties among film stars and actors who are unable to differentiate between fantasy and reality. Neptune rules medicinal and recreational drugs. Oil, liquid, and natural resources are also Neptunian. Neptune does not have solid boundaries. It is Neptune that gives us a feeling of religious awe and oneness with God or a deity in mystical experiences, and it is Neptune that rules all cults where an individual is swept away by an ideal, guru, or mission. Poets, saints, and visionaries are all Neptunian. For those who are touched by this planet of higher love, negotiating the world of appearances and tangible realities can be difficult. We all need escapes and places to renew ourselves, but the trick is always to take the journey and then return to reality, living with all the imperfections and hubbub that life encompasses. Other words used in reference to Neptune are *illusion* and *idealism*.

Mother Teresa was a Neptunian figure who worked among the poor of Calcutta. She was a tough bargainer, a fierce warrior for her cause, and a divinely practical person regarding getting food and goods for those who were disadvantaged. Her mission was Neptune; the way she got there was Saturn. On an everyday level, you will not notice Neptune's effects unless you are involved with illusionary schemes. When people are in business deals together and share Neptunian aspects, one or the other will feel that something is not clear or that there are currents that are subtly undermining the partnership, but it is difficult to pinpoint these currents because they are vague. These partnerships end in fraud or misunderstandings. If two people are involved in a Neptunian project—such as a religious retreat or a conference to build understanding—and their hearts are attuned to a spiritual cause, then Neptune can promote harmony because she dissolves ego concerns and promotes working together.

Isn't it interesting to see how studying astrology can lead you into large thoughts about the kind of world we live in and how we exist on the planet? A belief system can be very individual and no one can dissuade a person from those beliefs. Neptune's influence can fine-tune your views and ideals.

For example, one of the greatest American trance mediums was Edgar Cayce, who was born March 18, 1877, and lived until 1945. He had a stellium of the Sun, Mercury, Venus, and Saturn in Pisces.

Neptune was his ruling planet, and all of his readings were done while he was asleep, a Neptunian activity. He could not consciously control his gift and did not remember what he said while he was in a trance. His secretary wrote down Cayce's words and passed them on to the people who requested readings. He created a center in Virginia Beach, Virginia, where people could heal based upon his readings. Cayce was also an excellent example of a scrupulous man who never refused to do a reading for someone in need even if they could not pay. Today there are numerous centers throughout the world that study Cayce's readings and try to implement his simple and healthful cures.

Psychics and channelers who are usually strongly influenced by Neptune are becoming more accepted, but it is also important to realize that people only eager for profit are not necessarily attuned to the higher value of divine love. When a healer charges an outrageous amount of money for readings, it is a misuse of the healing energy. People who are interested in developing their Neptunian side need to think about what they are doing when they follow someone who purports to have powers to translate words from inspired masters, or another galaxy.

NEPTUNE IN THE SIGNS

Neptune spends fourteen years in a sign and, as with Uranus, the sign she is in will define a large group of people. Neptune rules Pisces, and she is comfortable with all of the water signs. The detriment and fall position for Neptune are Virgo and Capricorn, respectively.

Neptune feels contained and dull in the earth signs. They are simply too concrete a vibration for Neptune. Neptune in the fire signs can express enthusiasm, but the fire signs may feel doused by the watery nature of Neptune. Fire signs are usually intuitive, and this suits Neptune, but they are also egotistical, which is contrary to the Neptunian vibration. Lastly, the air signs give a mental emphasis to Neptune and can communicate in words some of Neptune's more positive traits. In an individual's chart, pay attention to the element occupied by Neptune; try to understand what kind of experiences that person undergoes in relation to that element. The highest purpose for Neptune in a chart is to loosen the restricting bonds of materialism and possessiveness so we can swim in an infinite sea of love.

NEPTUNE'S NATAL ASPECTS

When Neptune is in a hard aspect (square or opposition) with any of your personal planets, you will find a battle between heightened reality and concrete reality. The Sun conjunct Neptune gives a person great optimism and faith that can move mountains. But there is a fine line between faith and naiveté. Neptunian people must constantly check and see whether their faith is leading them well; the essential quality of faith is belief, and when you have that quality, it is difficult to recognize that devotion to ideals may cloud your judgment. The hard aspects challenge a person's blind spots and teach them clarity and discernment.

Flowing Neptunian aspects give an easy trust that life will unfold as it should. These people are usually extremely generous and pleasant to be around because they give so much.

NEPTUNE IN THE HOUSES

Wherever Neptune is located is where a person's highest ideals and human weak points are located. Neptune leads us forward with her vague, hazy promise of growth but usually makes us come in contact with experiences that force us to ground our ideals—and not be swept away by them. Neptune longs for the skies and for transcendence but needs to have grounding in order to reach them.

If Neptune is angular, a person tends to be attracted to activities that will involve service and generosity. If there are not enough Saturn influences in the chart, the person could also be involved with criminal or illusionary activities that create difficulties, to say the least. In Neptune's positive expression, a person may have a calling for the medical or social work fields. Angular Neptune could also mean a person is involved with the film world.

When Neptune is in the Fourth House or Tenth House, there was something hazy in the home during a person's developmental years. Sometimes, Neptune in the Fourth House means that the mother was addicted to alcohol or involved with drugs. People drink or take drugs because they want an experience beyond everyday reality. Usually these people are very creative, but they get mixed up and believe that dampening their senses will lead them into the oblivion and pleasure they seek.

When dealing with Neptune in a person's chart, you should consider whether a person is an "old soul," indicated by the number of aspects with the outer planets, or a soul beginning its spiritual journey. This will give you the correct interpretation for Neptune effects on the chart. One person's illusion is another person's meditation. Neptune is subtle, and trying to pin her down is like holding on to water.

NEPTUNE'S TRANSITS AND CYCLES

Neptune spends fourteen years in a sign; her transits are long and subtle. If you have determined that Neptune's influence is strong in your chart, then you can expect that Neptune's transits will register strongly with you, but don't expect big events. That is more Uranus's department. When transiting Neptune is forming any hard aspect with planets in the Sixth or Twelfth houses, you can expect that you will be very susceptible to toxins in the environment or challenges to your immune system. This is always a time to pay attention to drinking high-quality water and avoiding junk food and anything else that weakens the body. When Neptune is in a harmonious transit to or from planets in the Ninth House, you should pay attention to your dreams. If you do this, you may develop the ability to have prophetic dreams. The entire cycle of Neptune takes 168 years. Although longevity is increasing, so far no one has had a Neptune return. The opposition occurs at age eighty-four, which is also the age of a complete Uranus cycle. The most common Neptune aspect is Neptune squaring natal Neptune, which occurs between ages forty-one and forty-two.

In Chart 2, this person experienced a Neptune square at age forty-one. She began living at an ashram where she concentrated on practicing yoga and meditating. She confronted some of her past drug and alcohol addictions and spent a great deal of time healing herself. Neptune's transit helped her with her spiritual pursuits.

A retrograde Neptune in a natal chart is quite usual and, as you can probably understand, does not dramatically change the interpretation of the planet. Neptune's energy is internal, external, and all around us. It is our reaction to this different energy and plane of consciousness that we can notice, but the planet itself is boundless.

PLUTO ♀

Astrologically, Pluto is a new planet; astrologers have been studying him since 1930. In terms of the cosmos, that is very recent. When I first started reading about Pluto, authors used a word that I found mysterious, intriguing, and powerful: *chthonic*. Pluto is a chthonic planet. The word, which derives from the Greek *chthonios*, is defined as "pertaining to the deities, spirits, and other beings dwelling under the earth." Metaphorically, the word suggests that Pluto's effects are deep and hidden, and can offer riches if they are properly unearthed. Sometimes the riches are monetary, and sometimes they are psychological and spiritual. In Greek mythology, Pluto ruled the underworld and death. Pluto is the planet that carves out or mines the riches that an individual generation offers to the planet for further evolution. In this case, evolution pertains to the development of expanding consciousness that forces humanity to penetrate its depths and clear away what is not favorable for human advancement.

Pluto is powerful, but in order to fathom his depths and heights, you must think in terms of the balance of generations and what humanity is trying to learn. The outer planets (Pluto, Neptune, and Uranus) are energies that our consciousness can see only in a limited fashion.

With Pluto we are called on to see that, despite human frailties, life must move toward the preservation and development of a humane and just society for all people.

Scorpio, the sign Pluto rules, is vitally interested in transforming darkness into light. Pluto is neither moral nor immoral, neither good nor bad: It is the application of his power that determines whether his results are positive or negative. Newton's third law of motion states that for every action there is an equal and opposite reaction. This law of physics perfectly describes Pluto's effects. When Plutonian power is used to further hate, anger, and destruction, it will eventually bring forth an equal and opposite good, but it will take time. Pluto's rulership of Scorpio is a perfect description of the planet's importance in the cycle of life and death and rebirth. When something is created, something is destroyed; and when something is destroyed, something else is created. The balance of power in the world today represents Plutonian struggle between the forces of light and dark. It takes a long time to bring all these conflicting needs into balance to move civilization forward.

PLUTO'S NATAL ASPECTS

People with strong Pluto aspects or influences are magnetic and charismatic. They fascinate others like the snake charmer and his cobra. They can be powerful healers and orators, religious figures, revolutionary businesspeople, and power-mongers. You have learned that Uranus is the higher octave of Mercury, and Neptune of Venus, and our last planet, Pluto, is the higher octave of Mars. This is also why Pluto rules Scorpio. Aries is Mars's sign on a day-to-day basis, but since Scorpio delves into the very mysteries of life, it is fitting for Pluto to be her ruler. The high-er-octave planets mean that the energy is in the service of changing and advancing a person's consciousness. It also means that Pluto concerns the use and abuse of power often on a global scale.

In keeping with Pluto as Scorpio's ruler, Pluto has a lot to do with sex. When Pluto is heavily emphasized in a chart, sexual expression may take many forms, but whatever form it takes, the energy will always be intense. There can be an emphasis on power struggles within a relationship that can indicate a submissive/dominant relationship. Some people are vitally interested in exploring intense passions and consider them essential to their life. Astrology does not judge or moralize these inclinations in a person's chart. If the chart indicates that a person has potential for certain types of sexual expression, that is where that person can explore further. A good astrologer will, however, urge people to move through any Plutonian manifestations that are harming or challenging their lives. When Plutonian energy is balanced, the result in terms of sexuality can be intense and transforming. Pluto's very nature encourages an exploration of power, and these experiences can be seductive.

The aspects Pluto forms in a chart are critical in informing you whether a person is especially attuned to Pluto's vibration. When Pluto conjuncts a personal planet in the chart, you must add a Scorpio tone to the interpretation. Pluto intensifies any planet that he touches. When Pluto conjuncts the Sun or Moon, this person will have charisma and a deep need to promote his or her own significance. Such people are magnetic and can be manipulative in having their needs met. When Pluto and Venus are together, a person usually has a lot of sex appeal and a tendency toward passionate and sometimes difficult love affairs. With Pluto and Mars, it is obvious that you have a double Scorpio effect, and these people will brook no interference in their pursuits and pleasures.

When you consider the outer planets, it is very important to understand that these planets do not just indicate traumas and difficulties, but also other areas of life. Most of the world's population is involved with fulfilling basic life requirements such as food, shelter, jobs, and the raising of a family. Some people have the luxury or the necessity to study and develop their talents and skills for their own pleasure and development. Aspects and emphasis with the outer planets usually indicate an old, experienced soul growing in a spiritual dimension. In these sections on the outer planets, phrases like "Neptunian people" have been used, or we have talked about people who are "strongly influenced" by particular planets.

How do you know when these planets are strong in a chart? The first clues are whether or not any of the outer planets are in angular houses. When you learned the strength of the different houses, this was for the purpose of evaluating where a planet is stronger and where it is weaker. Examine whether there are tight or close aspects with any of these planets. Aspects with the Sun or Moon mean that the very core of a person is attuned to Plutonian energies, and they will have the challenge of dealing with these energies. When Pluto squares a natal planet in your chart, your challenge is to keep from becoming fascinated with your internal stress and difficulties while you create your life. Pluto square Venus often means that a person has deep and sad experiences with love. Usually these experiences are karmic and meant to teach a person that his or her own integrity and wholeness comes from self-nurturing and love rather than romantic love. Pluto in hard aspect to Mars means issues with power and authority will not ultimately be successful. A criminal or person with deep problems who asserts his or her power in a destructive, antisocial manner can often have Pluto and Mars in difficult aspect. The soft or easy aspects with Pluto, such as the sextile and trine, give a person a fascinating edge according to the planet involved. Pluto trine Venus usually means that a person has a subtle, indescribable power. Even if they are not involved with hypnosis or mind-control techniques, they effortlessly influence people. For example, have you ever had a friend who always manages to get his or her own way? Even when you say to yourself, "Today, I am going to do things my way," you end up following your friend's plan. It usually seems more interesting, but you feel that you have been led down a path that you didn't consciously choose. I suspect Pluto aspects here. Pluto fascinates and manipulates.

Consider Chart 7, with the heavy concentration of Scorpio planets square Pluto in Leo. According to our maximum orbs, the aspect to the Sun and Mercury is not a square. This stellium, however, is so concentrated that there is a "spillover" effect with the Sun and Mercury even though they are technically out of orb. This person is devilishly charming. He projects a very strong image, and he has been very successful in life; however, he always tries to top anything you say. If you mention a success you have had, he will steer the conversation around to his recent and more stellar success. Once you admire him for his wit or accomplishment, he is willing to be an equal, but all communication must be on his terms.

PLUTO IN THE HOUSES

Pluto's house location tells you where a person's deepest desires lie and where that person will have the hardest struggle to realize his or her desires. When Pluto is angular, the chart, as a whole, will have a Plutonian emphasis and we can say that Pluto informs the whole chart. Pluto in the First House means that a person's will and self-expression are essential to them. This person attracts experiences in life to allow them to dig into their soul for real power. When Pluto is in the Fourth House, conditions with one of the parents will be complicated by power struggles and feelings of alienation. In the Seventh House, the person will learn most of their life lessons through partnerships and the balance of power in relationships. In the Tenth House, Pluto offers career success, and frequently such a person is remembered long after their death; a member of this person's family might say they "cast a large shadow" when describing their personality. Pluto in the Tenth House can also mean a person is so driven to succeed that they neglect other parts of their life. Accordingly, they are perhaps not comfortable with the success created. When Pluto is in nonangular houses, he still has a strong influence upon the house. It isn't as if he can be tucked away in a benign house and forgotten. Pluto is a fascinating planet, and studying each person's battleground gives you insight and compassion into their lives.

PLUTO TRANSITS

Pluto transits last a long time. When people are in the midst of heavy Pluto transits, they are living on a mundane level as well as another level where they must follow Pluto's transforming energy. When Pluto entered Scorpio in 1983, I told a Scorpio friend, "You're taking a trip through the underworld until 1995." Now that I'm more experienced, I don't think I would be so blunt, but in fact, the years the Scorpio transited his Sun *were* difficult. He had many personally upsetting experiences in love, was mugged in New York City twice within a two-week period, and had to place his mother in a nursing home. But he also began psychoanalysis and started to examine his personal underworld. At the end of this journey as Pluto left Scorpio, he completed his PhD in psychology, married, and found a job working as a psychologist with veterans. He survived his battle and was in a position to help others in their quest for wholeness and balance.

Because Pluto transits last a long time, we need to look at general trends rather than specific events. As you have gathered, wherever Pluto is located in the houses or by transits, that area of life will be intensified. A complete Pluto cycle takes 248 years. So far no one has completed one. The only significant aspects between your natal Pluto and transiting Pluto will be the square or opposition. The square is an important time as there will be a challenge between power that is expressed and power that remains latent and rumbling in the subconscious. When considering Pluto transits, always check your ephemeris, as Pluto's eccentric orbit means that the age at which a person has certain Pluto aspects will vary. Those who receive aspects from Pluto will be involved with their personal transformation and be part of their generation's contribution to the Earth's development.

Pluto does retrograde for approximately four or five months each year. He will retrograde from April 25 to October 4, 2020, and from April 27 to October 6, 2021. Pluto retrograde in a natal chart is a subtle feeling and requires sensitivity and patience. The best way to describe it is that growth is hibernating.

PLUTO TRANSITING ANGULAR HOUSES

When Pluto crosses into any of the angular houses, his strength and presence will be felt. This is especially true when Pluto crosses from the shadows of the Twelfth House, over the ascendant, into the angular First House. This can be a dramatic transit, and some people may not be prepared for the challenges of carving out a new personality and addressing all their problems. Not everyone will experience Pluto crossing their ascendant in their lifetime, but for those who do, and who learn to master Pluto's power, there will be great rewards in terms of strength and self-confidence.

It may take awhile for a person to digest this energy and see how to use it. For example, the person in Chart 4 experienced Pluto crossing the ascendant in January 1998. As noted in Chapter 2, this person lives in a precarious balance between creative and self-destructive impulses. When Pluto crossed the First House cusp, he came face-to-face with many of his demons, mostly centered upon volatility and the use of power. A tamer example happened to a client who was not pleased with her figure. She became obsessed with her body image, and when Pluto crossed her ascendant, she finally decided to get breast implants. These are two slightly different transformational choices, but both fall under the umbrella of Pluto's desire to transform and re-create the self.

PLUTO'S GENERATIONAL MARK

In this section, we will take a look at how Pluto offers gifts and challenges to various generations according to their Pluto placement. Since Pluto remains in a sign for a significant amount of time, we can group generations according to the sign Pluto was in at their birth. These generational markers are the following: Pluto in Leo, Virgo, Libra, Scorpio, Sagittarius, and Capricorn. Each generation plays a part in the planet's evolvement as well as the personal deep transformation of its individual members.

Pluto in Leo

Pluto in Leo ranges from 1939–1958, which covers the baby boom generation. The baby boom generation has also been called the "me generation" because baby boomers concentrated on their personal development. Leo energy is focused on self-expression, and Leo rules the theater, film, and TV worlds, and these industries became a focal point for many people in this generation. The self-help movement that helped people develop their unique personalities arose during the Pluto ingress through Leo.

The gift that Pluto in Leo souls offered us all was enormous creativity in the arts. We still enjoy the great rock and soul hits that Pluto in Leo people gave the world. The integration of the hippie and transcendent dreams of the baby boomers into society was, however, not realized. That will be the work of future generations. The Pluto in Leo generation's gift is explosive creativity, and their challenge is avoiding self-centered indulgence.

Pluto in Virgo

The generation of Pluto in Virgo souls born between 1959 and 1972 has been called Generation X. It concentrates on service and self-sacrifice. Virgo has an innate interest in health and healing, and many of the alternate healing modalities we use today came about while Pluto was in Virgo. As a whole, the Pluto in Virgo generation is pragmatic and contributes to building an orderly and safe world. They are also prudent about money and making a living, more so than many of the baby boomers who were adults through the hippie era and who postponed many life decisions. The Pluto in Virgo generation's gift to the world is discernment and practicality, and their challenge is overcoming narrow-mindedness and their tendency to overly criticize others.

Pluto in Libra

In 1971, Pluto moved into Libra and remained there until 1983. This was a short transit of Pluto through a sign—only twelve years.

It was also the first time that Pluto was in a sign that emphasized the self in relationship to others. This generation deeply influenced the institution of marriage; they invented the ideas of *codependence* and *needing boundaries*, and the beginnings of modern questioning of gender stereotypes began. Libran idealism and the search for balance forged new ways of being in relationships. Their gift to us all is the attempt to bring honesty and balance to relationships, and their challenge is overly idealistic ideas about how people relate and interact.

Pluto in Scorpio

The millennials (those born between 1981 and 1996) are, for the most part, the Pluto in Scorpio generation. Pluto entered Scorpio in 1983 and left the sign in 1995; it was also a relatively short transit (twelve years). Pluto in Scorpio brought in a profound interest in transformation and exploring what is hidden and often taboo. Spiritual regeneration is important to these souls, but in the wake of religious abuse scandals, traditional organized religion has become a less popular way to find spiritual comfort and practice. Belief and interest in astrology in many instances has become the millennials' spiritual practice. The millennials are seeking truth and powerful experiences, often of a sexual nature. Gender fluidity and de-emphasized traditional sexual roles are now prevalent concepts in the Western developed world.

In the wake of the many possibilities to express sexual desires, the Pluto in Scorpio generation also witnessed the AIDS epidemic. The government and medical response to AIDS was woefully inadequate and narrow-minded. But, true to the transformative meaning of Pluto's work, people began to look at medicine and healing in a different way; this was the positive transformation that benefited society and the Earth's evolution. Again, we see the theme of transformation through intimate contact and the testing of limits. The Pluto in Scorpio generation's gift is total and deep transformation; their challenge is to avoid extremes and destruction in the process.

Pluto in Sagittarius

Pluto moved to Sagittarius in 1995 and remained there until 2008. The generation dubbed Generation Z is breezy. With an emphasis on traveling and staying on the move, Generation Z is interested in technology as a way to bring a wider sense of connectedness that defies physical space. Social media became a way to communicate to and from anyplace in the world during this time. Computer fluency and the expectation that there must be an app for anything they need is part of their worldview. Pluto in Sagittarius is also well aware of the expanse of the global village. Those who can travel often just hit the road and see where it takes them (Asia is a favorite destination of this generation). And after they see the conditions in developing nations, they become more acutely aware of the interaction and interdependence between all people on the planet. Education (both practical and theoretical) plays an important part in this generation's expectations.

Pluto in Sagittarius is extremely aware of climate change and the possible devastation of natural resources. This generation and subsequent generations will apply their technical skills to solving these complex energy problems. I believe they will lead us into a more balanced future.

The Pluto in Sagittarius generation are also religious, spiritual seekers. This may be through a private spiritual practice or organized religion. The Sagittarian search is for philosophy that answers the big questions of life: What is my purpose? What does it all mean? This search took a personal transformational approach in millennials, but in Generation Z it is more societal and global. The Pluto in Sagittarius generation's gift is absolute honesty, and their challenge is squandered focus and lack of perseverance.

Pluto in Capricorn

And finally, the current astrological generation is Pluto in Capricorn. They are the children born in the period from 2008 to 2024. It is interesting that as Pluto moved through Capricorn, the banking and loan crisis deepened. Capricorn rules structure, and this generation will build on the experience of the millennials, the philosophical pursuits of Gen Z, and their own ability to restructure energy sources, banking and monetary concerns, infrastructure, and hierarchy.

They are extremely pragmatic. The Pluto in Capricorn generation will be particularly noteworthy for changing structures in the US. In the US chart, Pluto is in Capricorn, and as a nation, it will experience a Pluto return in 2023. The confusion and chaos that many people currently feel will give rise to deep, fundamental planetary change. It will take time. Pluto in Capricorn souls will take action and create a plan to minimize the difference between the haves and the have-nots, get aid where it will truly be effective, and take action on finding new sources of energy. This generation vitally realizes that we sink or swim together. Their gift is effective structure and infrastructure; their challenge is rigid government control.

PLUTO, PARENTS, AND CHILDREN

Before leaving the topic of generations and Pluto, an important factor is how the Pluto in Scorpio, Sagittarius, and Capricorn generations energetically work with their parents. It is an interesting dynamic. Many of the children born with Pluto in Scorpio, Sagittarius, and Capricorn are older souls and may be stronger in terms of soul development than their parents, who were born with Pluto in Leo, Virgo, and Libra. These newer generations are incarnating at this time to help the Earth and humanity develop and refine its energies.

Every new generation builds upon the achievements and expectations of the previous generation. In former times, the frontiers we explored were physical and land-oriented, but now the frontiers are technological and spiritual. We will continue to develop technological expertise, but in conjunction with new inventions and machines, people will start to adjust their sensibilities and psychology to resolve social problems in a different manner. Psychic abilities may become commonplace, and people's view of the interdependence between ecology, health, psychology, and spirituality will grow.

What is considered New Age and mystical now will be grounded in day-to-day experience to create a less toxic and more harmonious world. The Pluto in Leo, Virgo, and Libra parents of these vanguard generations will have to provide a nurturing environment for their kids even if they themselves are not particularly psychically attuned. In the coming years, this may be challenging as some members of these newer generations may exhibit abilities and sensitivities that are unfamiliar and feel strange to their parents.

To conclude: Pluto in each generation has done and will do his work. The younger generations will find their way and make major contributions to the expansion and health of the planet. I take comfort in the fact that the planets are always moving and that the evolution of each individual and our planet will contribute to both changing and preserving life on Earth. With these cycles of the transpersonal and outer planets in mind, let's go to the next chapter and take a look at predictions.

CHAPTER FIVE
PREDICTIONS

Predictive astrology conjures up an image of a mysterious woman telling fortunes with a crystal ball. As you have learned in the preceding chapters, astrology and the prediction of the future with astrology are more complex matters. Using all the knowledge you have acquired so far, you have a good idea of how to maximize decisions in life based on understanding your personality and character, the transits of the personal planets, the transits of the transpersonal and outer planets, and the cycles of these larger planets as they make their periodic returns.

What else can you do to look into the future for yourself and for others? It is a heady question, and many astrologers shy away from prognostication. Everyone is aware of the mind-body connection and no one, least of all an astrological counselor, wants to create a self-fulfilling prophecy by making predictions that will overly influence a person or cause anxiety. But when you are asked a question and if the signs point to an event, you can't remain silent or pretend that nothing will happen. What you can do is give a gentle warning to take the necessary precautions to mitigate the effects of planetary duress. A good counselor can also offer options to a client. Some people may fear difficult transits, but others will greet them with enthusiasm. Even if it is a happy event, that, too, needs a gentle approach. Expectations can sometimes lead you to disparage positive events because you expected something bigger than what actually occurs.

Another factor to consider in making astrological predictions is that, as you study astrology, your intuition becomes stronger with time. In *How to Be an Astrologer*, you are learning a method to funnel hunches, inspirations, and intuitions and see patterns that no other study offers a person. Your intuition may surprise you, but remember, planetary motions are 100 percent predictable; events are not as predictable. However, you do have a better chance of seeing the future than those people who have not studied astrology. Psychics and tarot card readers also have a better-than-average chance of predicting what's to come. But no one is always right. Sometimes people's fate or outside events supersede a prediction and then astrologers, like all people, have to accept what cannot be changed.

Fate can be an elastic concept. In *The Astrology of Fate*, by the wonderful astrologer and author Liz Greene, the example of King Henri II is cited. Born in France in 1519, he received a prophecy from two prominent and well-respected astrologers that in his early forties, he would die of a wound to the head. The king continued with his life, and in the summer of his fortieth year he was killed by a lance wound to his head during a jousting match. The astrologers' prediction and its fulfillment were not thought to be extraordinary. However, this period of history was more oriented toward faith and belief than today's society. Greene goes on to explain that she has seen similar aspects and transits in modern charts to those of King Henri II's; however, no one's life ended from a lance wound to the head. Interestingly enough, one of these people, undergoing the same transits as King Henri II and with a similar chart, suffered terrible migraine headaches, and another person had a concussion. They received medical treatment and went on with their lives. Other people with similar transits and aspects did undergo profound changes but on an inner and psychological dimension. The position of the stars did not change, but the fabric of society and societal beliefs had changed. Those changes even colored how the astrological transits manifested. Our expectations and the world around us do influence what we find significant and what actually transpires.

DEATH IN THE CHART

The touchiest area of prediction is death. As an astrologer, you may be asked this question. Some astrologers feel strongly that this is an unethical issue and should not be addressed. I believe that astrology should not make such a prediction, but considering the issue of death as it is reflected in the chart can elucidate some of the questions concerning a person's life. It is essential to remember that *when* someone dies is not nearly as important as *how* he or she is living. No matter how much astrology you learn, it is extremely difficult to accurately predict your own death. It is also difficult to predict death for people close to you. The answer about when a person dies is within each soul. I believe there are many points and transits during which a person may feel they are ready to cross over, but most people are not consciously in control of this event.

Nevertheless, it is my belief that people can *subconsciously* influence the timing of their death date, and in retrospect, you can see that the astrological transits reflect something about both the manner and timing of a person's death. It is common in families for a person who is sick to wait for a holiday or significant family occasion to occur before they die. Or, a person waits until family members have had a chance to say goodbye. This can frequently heal old wounds and help the people left behind live more fully after the person's passing. Sometimes death is sudden and shocking. Perhaps the person who died quickly had a fear of aging and needed for his or her personal development to make a swift exit. This is harder for the people who mourn, but for that soul it may be appropriate and positive. The death of a child or young person is also mysterious and extremely difficult. If you are a parent, your chart may indicate reasons you had to bear that burden, or perhaps the child's chart may suggest that they had come to this plane of existence for a brief time to perfect some aspect of their development.

In whatever way a death occurs, each soul is eternally connected to the people who love them. Astrology can provide some answers and perhaps help in the grieving process. In short, there are many factors to consider when considering death in a chart. Older books will tell you there are formulas to follow, but my advice is simple: Don't go there. Living well is a full-time job, and death will come when it will come.

PROGRESSING THE CHART

A major tool for working with predictive astrology—in addition to transits to the natal planets—is called *progressing the chart*. There are two ways to do this. The first method is called *secondary progressions*, and the second method is called *solar arc progressions*. Let's discuss secondary progressions first. You need to put your mathematical brain back in gear because secondary progressions can be hand-calculated—or, of course, done with your software program.

SECONDARY PROGRESSIONS

The basic method of progressing a chart is known as the *day-for-a-year* method. This means that each day after a person is born represents a year in their life. Look at the tenth day after your birth date in the ephemeris; the planets on that day represent the astrological influences you felt at age ten. This holds true for any age, whether it is thirty days for age thirty or eighty-four days for age eighty-four.

If you take the planet's positions directly from the ephemeris, you will get a noncalculated reading of a person's progressed planets. It is noncalculated because, as discussed, the ephemeris gives the planetary positions for GMT, which is derived from the Royal Observatory in Greenwich, England. All time zones and longitudes are also measured from this location. Unless you live there, your own progressed planets will be slightly different. A progressed chart is based on the planetary motion of approximately 1 degree per year. If you start with the Sun at 10 degrees of Libra and count forward twenty days, for twenty years of age, you will see that the Sun has moved into Scorpio. When you calculate the entire chart for this progressed date, you will get a new chart, which influences the natal chart. In a secondary progressed chart, all the planets will move forward; however, you will see the most change with the personal planets. The personal planets will actually change signs. The outer planets in secondary progressions move slowly, and their signs and degrees will not change very much in a lifetime.

To calculate a progressed chart using your astrology software, look in the menu for secondary progressions. Change the location from the birthplace to where a person currently lives. The result will be a progressed chart. First, analyze the progressed chart to see what new planetary colors are in your life. Where is the progressed Sun? Where are progressed Mercury, Venus, and Mars? The progressed chart does not supplant or cancel out the natal chart. It is an overlay, a new set of influences. As you mature, different colors and attributes become more important to you. A shy, retiring Cancerian becomes more extroverted as his or her Sun moves into dramatic Leo. Does this progression mean that a person acquires an entirely new personality? No. This person is simply able to express parts of his or her personality that may have been dormant in the natal chart. Next, compare the progressed chart to the natal chart and note the aspects between the natal and progressed charts. You can do this by creating a bi-wheel with your software, which puts the natal chart in the center of the screen and the progressed chart in a large circle around it. You can also take a copy of your chart and manually put the progressed planets outside the wheel in their appropriate houses. It is sometimes convenient to use a different colored ink. You should also include the progressed midheaven and ascendant and see how they both aspect the natal chart. Basically, you want to see what all the aspects are between a natal and progressed chart. You don't have to get fancy with minor aspects. Stick to the conjunction, sextile, square, trine, and opposition.

TRANSITS TO PROGRESSED AND NATAL CHARTS

Once you have a good sense of the interplay between the progressed and natal chart, look at the current transits and how they affect both the progressed and natal charts. When you see a concentration of transits involving a planet, you know that signs are pointing toward an event during the period of time that the transits exactly aspect that planet or planets. If Uranus is involved, the event will be surprising. If Saturn is involved, it will be a serious event and one that you usually have worked hard for. Jupiter usually indicates good fortune. Pluto will deepen any of the planets that he aspects. Look at the houses involved and you will begin to see how these progressed planets and transits play out. You know the parameters of your life, so you can fill in the specifics of likely outcomes.

If you are using two wheels on the computer, it is easy to become bleary-eyed with all the information. You need to isolate the transits both to the natal chart and to the progressed chart. A simple worksheet is the most practical way of doing this.

Make five columns and write down Jupiter, Saturn, Uranus, Neptune, and Pluto in that order at the top of each column. Fill in the transits to the natal planets for whatever day you are considering; then fill in the transits to the progressed planets on that date. Note the transits to the progressed planets by putting the letter *P* by the planet. You would write ♄ transiting P♀, or Saturn transiting PVenus, and know that means progressed Venus, not your natal Venus. As you fill in these columns, you can see how the evidence stacks up. The progressed planets for Chart 3 for December 21, 2003, are noted in the Table of Transits to Natal and Progressed Planets for Chart 3 at the end of this book and are formatted under the five columns for Jupiter, Saturn, Uranus, Neptune, and Pluto.

Look at the transits of the planets on December 21, 2003, from the ephemeris and examine their relationship to Chart 3's natal and progressed planets. The position of the progressed planets is found on the table. Can you determine which are the crucial transits to the natal planets? I would say that the most important aspect is Jupiter crossing the midheaven and initiating a period of career expansion and perhaps a career change. Why didn't I focus on Saturn conjunct the Moon, which is potentially a more disturbing aspect? First, you know that Saturn conjunct the Moon can mean changes in the structure of a relationship. But Saturn in 2003 was located at 10 degrees of Cancer and wouldn't conjunct this person's Moon until June 2004.

Perhaps this person is having relationship difficulties but no action or event is indicated yet. The other transit that needs to be addressed is Uranus square Mars. However, this square aspect has passed its exact degree. The exact square was in December 2001, but since at that time Uranus was still influencing Mars, this person might have been cautioned to drive their motorcycle carefully. No hard-and-fast predictions would be made.

Now you have to blend the transits into the progressed chart. A different story unfolds here. Draw up a progressed chart and place these progressed planets in the natal wheel. To save you the trouble, the calculations are as follows: Sun 17 Pisces, Moon 15 Pisces, Mercury 5 Aries, Venus 15 Aries, Mars 12 Gemini, Jupiter 1 Sagittarius, Saturn 5 Capricorn, Uranus 12 Leo R, Neptune 6 Scorpio R, and Pluto 2 Virgo R (the R stands for *retrograde*). For the sake of brevity, the minutes are not indicated, but on your calculated progressed chart you would see them.

The key event in the progressed chart is Pluto squaring the progressed Moon and Sun in Pisces in the Fourth House. Saturn is active by squaring progressed Venus and opposing the progressed ascendant. The Pluto square to the progressed Sun and Moon is a significant aspect, as it indicates deep changes to one's self and one's emotions. As you know, the Fourth House pertains to a parent, or home, or real estate, among other things. In this chart the progressions indicate that the relationship with the parent may change. I knew this client's father had been sick, so I applied the meaning to that parent. If the client had asked, "Will my father die soon?" I would have said that it looked like he was weak. I would not have given a specific date for death, because I was not totally sure when or if he would die. All an astrologer can do is confirm the seriousness of a situation or say it will improve. With Pluto squaring these two planets in the Fourth House, it doesn't look like the situation will get better.

This illustrates how transits highlight matters that need tending. The best way to practice with a secondary progressed chart is to look at events that you know occurred in the past and compare the transits to both the natal and progressed chart. These comparisons can reveal a lot of information. You will learn a great deal about astrology by researching past known events. I always marvel when an event is so perfectly described by astrological symbolism.

SOLAR ARC DIRECTION

Solar arcs are a different method of moving the chart forward into the future. Some astrologers swear they are the best method to use, while others prefer secondary progressions. Learn and experiment with both techniques. The advantage to the solar arc method is that the outer planets advance as well as the personal ones. On your computer, progressions using a solar arc method are called *direct* or *directing the chart*. Directing the chart is easy to figure out mentally. The approximate daily motion of the Sun is 59 minutes and 8 seconds. This is called the *major arc*. You can round this figure off to 1 degree. Following the same day-for-a-year method, if you want to find what your directed chart would be at age twenty-five, you would add 25 degrees to each planetary position and this would give you a solar arc directed chart. To draw up a solar arc wheel, you would add 25 degrees to all house cusps as well.

Note the aspects between a directed chart and your natal chart. Do not consider the aspects between a secondary progressed chart and a directed chart. This is like comparing apples and oranges. All progressed methods are to help inform you about potentials that are usually indicated in the natal birth chart. As one of my favorite astrologers, Ivy Goldstein-Jacobson, said: "No promise made, no promise kept." If the potential is not in the birth chart to begin with, no transit or progression can make it happen.

SYNTHESIZING PROGRESSIONS

Let's put all these techniques together and clarify what you can do with this information. First take your natal chart, the secondary progressions, and the solar arc directions. You can organize all of this on paper by noting the natal chart in one color of ink, the secondary in another, and the solar arc in a third. You now have a multilevel chart and can see where the astrological evidence is piling up. You can also erect a tri-wheel using your software and put all these rings on the screen. You can also take a separate sheet of paper and write down the most noteworthy aspects and connections.

Place the current transits on the outside of this entire circle of astrological data. You want to see what aspects might trigger the most heavily concentrated planets. Are any of the transits forming a grand trine with progressed planets or natal ones? Is there a T-square that is activated by transiting Mars? Look for the patterns you have learned as well as the aspects and then muse on the potential meanings of the planets. If the aspects are easy, you can expect fortunate events. If the aspects are tough, it could be a bumpy ride. It is up to you to utilize all the planets' energies, because you are the best creator of your life.

THE PROGRESSED MOON

The progressed Moon tells you immediately where a person is in relationship to his or her feelings about life's events. People react in different ways, and how you feel about life can determine how prepared you are to take action. Because the Moon moves so quickly, I recommend drawing up a special sheet for it. The sheet I am going to teach you is based on directing the chart. This system is called the radix system. Ivy Goldstein-Jacobson drew up the following table for what she calls the Minor Moon; it is taken from her book *Foundation of the Astrological Chart*.

TABLE OF MINOR ARCS		
YEAR	SIGN	DEGREE/MINUTES
1	0	13:11
2	0	26:21
3	1	09:32
4	1	22:42
5	2	05:53
6	2	19:03
7	3	02:14
8	3	15:25
9	3	28:35
10	4	11:46
11	4	24:56
12	5	08:07
13	5	21:18
14	6	04:28
15	6	17:39
16	7	00:49
17	7	14:00

YEAR	SIGN	DEGREE/MINUTES
18	7	27:10
19	8	10:21
20	8	23:32
21	9	06:42
22	9	19:53
23	10	03:03
24	10	16:14
25	10	29:25
26	11	12:35
27	11	25:46
28	0	08:56
29	0	22:07
30	1	05:18
31	1	18:28
32	2	01:39
33	2	14:49
34	2	28:00
35	3	11:10
36	3	24:21
37	4	07:32
38	4	20:42
39	5	03:53
40	5	17:03
41	6	00:14
42	6	13:25
43	6	26:35
44	7	09:46
45	7	22:56

YEAR	SIGN	DEGREE/MINUTES
46	8	06:07
47	8	19:17
48	9	02:28
49	9	15:39
50	9	28:49
51	10	12:00
52	10	25:10
53	11	08:21
54	11	21:32
55	0	04:42
56	0	17:53
57	1	01:03
58	1	14:14
59	1	27:24
60	2	10:35
61	2	23:46
62	3	06:56
63	3	20:07
64	4	03:17
65	4	16:28
66	4	29:39
67	5	12:49
68	5	26:00
69	6	09:10
70	6	22:31
71	7	05:31
72	7	18:42
73	8	01:53

YEAR	SIGN	DEGREE/MINUTES
74	8	15:03
75	8	28:14
76	9	11:24
77	9	24:35
78	10	07:46
79	10	20:56
80	11	04:07
81	11	17:17
82	0	00:28
83	0	13:38
84	0	26:49
85	1	10:00
86	1	23:10
87	2	06:21
88	2	19:31
89	3	02:42
90	3	15:53
91	3	29:03
92	4	12:14
93	4	25:24
94	5	08:35
95	5	21:45
96	6	04:56
97	6	18:07
98	7	01:17
99	7	14:28
100	7	27:38

First you need to determine the Minor Moon's position and locate the age that you want to examine. Let's say it is age fifty-four in 2019. The chart tells you that the sign is 11 and the degree is 21 degrees and 32 minutes. For certain astrological calculations, the signs are numbered, which makes addition and subtraction easier. The key to numbering the signs is the following chart: Aries=0, Taurus=1, Gemini=2, Cancer=3, Leo=4, Virgo=5, Libra=6, Scorpio=7, Sagittarius=8, Capricorn=9, Aquarius=10, and Pisces=11. So at age fifty-four, according to the Table of Minor Arcs, add 11 (Pisces) 21:32 to the natal Moon's position. This will give you the Minor Moon's position on the birthday at age fifty-four. For example, in Chart 1, take the natal Moon 28 degrees Sagittarius 6 minutes and add the minor arc to it.

The math looks like this:

$$
\begin{array}{rrrr}
 & 8 & 28 & 06 \\
+ & 11 & 21 & 32 \\
\hline
= & 19 & 49 & 38 \\
\end{array}
$$

You need to subtract 30 degrees from 49 because no sign has 49 degrees. That leaves 19 degrees and 38 minutes. Add 1 for the one sign—which equates to the 30 degrees—you subtracted to get 19, giving you a numerical value for the sign of 20, and then subtract 12 from 20 because there are only twelve signs. Your Minor Moon position is 19 degrees Sagittarius 38 minutes. It is a good idea to keep handy the Table of Minor Arcs. It will make calculating the Minor Moons easier.

Now you are ready to plot the motion of this progressed Moon's position and see what it means in the chart. At the end of the book is an example of the form I use for the progressed Moon (see Table of Progressed Moon, Radix, or Minor Moon Systems for Chart 1). On the left-hand side, write down the twelve months of the year. Then draw a grid for each of the planets. For Chart 1, let's look at 2019, the year my client was fifty-four. List all the months, beginning with January on the left, and in the square under February (her birth month), place the position of the Moon 19♐38 minutes. Then add the monthly motion of the Moon, which is 1 degree 6 minutes for each month. For the sixth month, add 1 degree 5 minutes to make the total motion of the Moon (13 degrees 11 minutes ÷ 12 months) even.

Once you have plotted all your information, you can fill in the aspects between the Minor Moon and the natal planets. Use only the major aspects for this: the conjunction, square, opposition, trine, and sextile. When you have completed the grid, you will see whether easy or hard aspects dominate or if there is a mixture of both. Basically, flowing aspects mean a green light: Go ahead. Hard aspects mean a red light: Stop. And a mixture means a yellow light: Caution; look both ways. This simple interpretation can answer numerous questions you might have and give you advice about how best to proceed.

Also note the aspects between the progressed Moon and the current planetary transits. These aspects will tell you whether the outer world is giving you a hard or easy time. The aspects between your Minor Moon and natal chart tell you how you are feeling about life. The aspects between the Minor Moon and the current planetary transits tell you how the world is reacting to your endeavors. Keep this worksheet and watch the progressions and see how they indicate events.

What do you think the year 2019 was like for the client in Chart 1? Bumpy and very emotional, I would say. Four squares and the Minor Moon conjuncted her natal Moon. There was only one sextile with Venus, which could sweeten the year. The red light for the year: My client needed to take it slow and be very mindful of how she dealt with obstacles. The progressed Moon and transiting Neptune also likely presented some challenges. She is a Pisces, ruled by Neptune, and her chart showed a square to her progressed Moon. The year was apt to be confusing, and she may have been overly sensitive to her environment. Jupiter does help with a conjunction to the Minor Moon, so according to her chart, she was protected from major harm. You can also use the progressed Moon from a computer-calculated secondary progressed chart and place it in the grid the same way you plotted the Minor Moon. Usually the secondary progressed Moon's degrees are a little later than the Minor Moon, but experiment and see which aspects reveal the most for you.

SATURN WHEEL

The progressed Moon tells us about our feelings about life. Saturn, as you know, tells us about the structure of life. An unusual technique for examining the structure we are building or need to build is called a Saturn wheel. This is not an event-oriented predictive technique but a good indication of the structure you are creating in your life. It is very simple. First draw a basic astrological wheel with the twelve houses. Place the current position of Saturn in the ascendant position and then go around the wheel placing each succeeding sign on the house cusp. Use Saturn's degree for each cusp. If you want to look at past dates, just fill in Saturn's position for any time period you want to examine. For example, on December 21, 2003, Saturn was located at 10♋37. Therefore, the sign on the Second House would be 10♌37. Place your natal planets in the wheel according to where they fall with this new ascendant. This is where you are creating or need to create structure. In Chart 4, this person was looking for work and trying to make sense of his financial life in 2003. His Moon/Pluto conjunction in Leo fell in the Second House of the Saturn wheel. It is a perfect description of what needed his attention.

This technique is astrological shorthand, but it works very well. According to the houses that your planets fall in on the Saturn wheel, you can pinpoint where you should concentrate your energy to move forward.

PLANETS CHANGING DIRECTIONS

Another very simple and often illuminating predictive technique is noting when a planet changes direction in a progressed chart. In this instance, changing direction means going from retrograde motion to direct motion or vice versa. Look at your ephemeris for ninety days following a person's birth. As you follow the planetary motions through the ninety days, there may come a day (i.e., a year) when a planet moves from being retrograde to direct. For example, in Chart 2, using your ephemeris, you can see that twenty-nine days after birth, at age twenty-nine, both Saturn and Mars moved into direct motion by progression. This is a significant year as these two malefic planets turning direct could influence this person's life more overtly and get the issues and difficulties they describe into the light of day. When the planets turned direct in her chart, this client felt as if "a burden had been lifted and there was some hope in her life."

On a worksheet, note the year that the planets change directions. When Mercury goes retrograde in a progressed chart, a person often becomes more meditative and may start writing thoughts and feelings down. When Venus retrogrades, a long-standing relationship or marriage may break up. When Venus has been retrograde since birth and goes direct, a person may find that he or she can more easily attract romantic relationships. Mars going direct often means that a person can assert their will outwardly and achieve goals. One client who was born with a retrograde Jupiter was surprised to learn that when Jupiter went direct, she was receiving an inheritance. Watching the years that planets change directions in a chart can give you a very quick and oftentimes accurate predictive technique. Look at your own chart and see if there were events during years that planets changed directions. Astrology offers 20/20 hindsight; by studying the past you can teach yourself about the future.

SOLAR RETURNS

A *solar return* is the astrological term for your birthday, but, more specifically, it is the exact moment each year that your Sun returns to the same sign, degree, and minute where it was at your birth. Sometimes it is on your birthday, and sometimes it is the day before or after. The easiest way to calculate this chart is to look for the "returns" options on your astrological program's menu and then select "solar return." There also are options for a lunar return as well as for all other planets. Examine these returns to see if you can make any correlations with your own chart and past events.

Always remember, though, there is a wealth of data available with which to make predictions. The skill is zeroing in on which pieces of information are significant. When you draw up a solar return, it will give you a snapshot of the year ahead. You will see which houses are emphasized and what your ascendant will be for the coming year. This chart is used in conjunction with a progressed chart and transits. It further defines areas that are active in the chart and can guide you to see specific areas in your life that need attention.

For example, in Chart 2a, the solar return for 2003 was erected for Boston, Massachusetts, the person's then place of residence. This is the solar return for Chart 2. The time for this chart was for 8:51 p.m. because that was the time the Sun was located at the same degree and minute as when this person was born. Take a quick look at this chart. Will this be a year that marriage or a business partnership is likely? Saturn is in the house of partnership; unless an older person comes into this person's life, it is unlikely. Will this person be moving? Look at the Fourth House. No planets are there, and the only aspect is between Pluto and the Fourth House cusp. A move is not indicated. What will happen? In the Second House, you see Mars and Neptune, two difficult indicators for financial matters. Mars means that there will be strife with money, and Neptune shows there is some illusion or lack of clarity about money matters. Also note the Sun is in the

Sixth House of work. That indicates a focus on work-related matters. This client lost a job under stressful conditions and had to face some very difficult financial problems. Eventually she found another job and began to look at her finances with an accountant. When Neptune is influencing any kind of financial matters, a person needs to consult someone who is very clearheaded.

The Fifth House emphasis is interesting, as it shows some creative projects or interaction with children. If this person were thirty years old, I might have predicted that she would become pregnant. As I knew that she was past childbearing age, my prediction might have been that some creative projects or perhaps a quick romantic encounter could come her way. Why do I say "quick"? Venus in Aries usually does not indicate a long-term romance, because Aries is much too impetuous to stick around.

Can you see how the solar return will help you zero in on events for the years? By checking the progressed charts and the transits, you can see if the themes you note in the solar return are reiterated in the other charts.

THE LUNAR RETURN

Every year, you have a solar return, when the Sun returns to the exact degree and minute of the Sun sign when you were born. Each month, there is a lunar return when the Moon returns to the position she was in at your birth. Calculating a lunar return chart is an interesting way to view the emotional tides of the upcoming month, as the ascendant and the distribution of planets will be different each month. The lunar return is not a major predictive technique, but it does add finesse and subtlety. Once you are in tune with the transits of the major planets and see what the current period of time indicates for you or your clients, zero in on the lunar return to see where emotional connection will be felt. The areas governed by the house holding the lunar return will be focal points for that month. Also note any planets or the ascendant that are in the same degrees as your natal planets. These will be prominent and influential for that month.

To calculate a lunar return, you can draw up the chart for the month and determine when your lunar return is in that month. Even without calculating a chart, you will know yourself when you are in emotional harmony or emotional distress about some part of your life. I don't recommend calculating thirteen lunar charts for the upcoming year—that's too much information! A better practice is to study the lunar chart for each month, perhaps at the new moon, and see how to focus your activities. For example, for Chart 4, the lunar return for August 2004 placed the Leo Moon at 22 degrees exactly conjunct the Sun in the Sixth House. This person had been looking for a job at this time and was emotionally challenged by being unemployed. The outlook was positive, however, because in addition to the lunar return in the Sixth House, if you look at the transits for August 2004, you will notice that Jupiter was passing over the midheaven, which initiates a new cycle of positive career focus. The lunar return outlines a short-term emotional focus, and the longer-lasting transits indicate where action needs to be taken.

ECLIPSES

The final predictive technique in this chapter you need to learn concerns eclipses. These solar and lunar events have amazed people since ancient times. If you have ever watched the Sun or the Moon be totally covered by an eclipse, it is impossible not to feel awe at the workings of the heavens. Eclipses happen every year and always happen in pairs. They are not visible in all parts of the world, but they are always potent indicators of influences and events if the degree of the eclipse falls on a significant degree in your natal or progressed chart or forms a tight aspect with any of your planets. If you look in your handy celestial guide or ephemeris, you will see the eclipses listed. The most convenient way is to look in your astrological calendar or app because it lists all the eclipses for each year. As you look at the eclipses, note the degree of the eclipse. For example, the eclipse that occurred on July 12, 2018, was a solar eclipse at 20 degrees ♋ 41 minutes.

Using the charts in this book, can you find which one would be most affected by this eclipse? The correct chart is Chart 4. You can see that this July eclipse conjuncts the natal Sun and occurred the day before his solar return (birthday). It is a strong indication of changes and stress regarding the home and family. In fact, this year marked the beginning of this person dealing with challenging family dynamics.

If an eclipse does not aspect any position in your natal or progressed chart within an orb of plus or minus 3 degrees, it should not be used for predictions. Also be aware that when the eclipse aspect goes into effect depends on how tight the aspect is. Keep track of eclipses in your own chart and you will be amazed by how many events were heralded by eclipses.

ORGANIZING THIS INFORMATION

There are many techniques to use when looking for predictions and trends. You should experiment with all of them and record your observations. Looking at events in hindsight is a very good way to sharpen your skills. Whether you use the secondary progressions, directions, a Saturn wheel, or solar return, you must consider the progressed Moon. It is a primary indicator of the major and minor changes in life. It is also important to find the clearest way for you to isolate pieces of information so that you can interpret them; if you use *all* these techniques, your worksheet or wheels can look as if they have been attacked by linguini. Go through each progression methodically and write down your thoughts. If you keep trying this method, you will internalize the predictive techniques and be able to assess charts in a more intuitive manner.

It is as if with all your study you have been programming your mental computer and then one day the connections are so fast that you see "the answer" without knowing how you got there. If you see a serious problem or upcoming major planetary duress, your astrological studies and intuitive development should prepare you to communicate to your friend or client in a compassionate and sympathetic manner. Try to avoid spelling out worst-case scenarios and concentrate on expressing the energies that the planetary motions indicate. You also want to mention where there is relief in the chart. By also focusing on easier transits or joyous parts of a person's chart, you can help that person mitigate times of tension and stress. This practice also applies to you when predicting your own chart. It is easy to panic when you look at upcoming aspects for your chart. If you become obsessed with doom and gloom, please consult an astrologer. It is always good to have a second opinion, since we are often not the best interpreters of our own lives.

Lastly, there is a practice in astrological circles that any major prediction, positive or negative, must have three solid indications in the chart. Even if you believe your intuition is absolutely keen, do the astrological homework and study the transits, progressions, and solar returns for evidence and to confirm what you have intuited. Some astrologers may downplay the intuitive part to this art and work strictly on the astrological evidence. I feel that is shortsighted and denies the cumulative and subconscious experience an astrologer gathers from working with many people and many charts. Astrology is a Uranian study, and this planet often heavily influences astrologers. This means we can have flashes of insight that are psychic and may be true. If you ground yourself in the study of transits, progressions, and returns, you will be able to support your insights.

CHAPTER SIX

ASSESSING COMPATIBILITY BETWEEN CHARTS

The most common area of interest for friends, family, and clients visiting an astrologer is relationships. In addition to examining two individuals' charts, there are many ways to do chart comparisons. The term for chart comparisons in astrology is *synastry*, which comes from the Greek word *synergia*, meaning, "working together, cooperating, and synergetic." By comparing one chart with another, you can gain wisdom and insight into the avenues of connection between two people and the areas where they will face challenges. Synastry is useful not only for romantic relationships, but also for relationships with parents, children, coworkers, and siblings. A chart simply describes how you relate to someone else's chart without judging one person or the other. The aspects between charts affect both charts and define an exchange and dynamic between two people. For example, if your Mars is conjunct another's Saturn, you both will feel the effects of this combination. With what you have learned so far, you might wince at this particular combination. It is a tough aspect to have between people. The Mars person always feels thwarted by the Saturn person, and the Saturn person always feels challenged and ticked off by the Mars person.

When you compare two charts, as you did when you analyzed your natal chart, look for the problem areas and areas of relief in the chart. Many marriages and partnerships with difficult aspects have survived because the couple has concentrated on the positive aspects of their union. Concentrating in this way defuses the negative. Most Sun sign columns and beginning astrology books concentrate on the relationships between Sun signs and reduce a subtle and complex set of factors to "Aries doesn't get along with Taurus," for example. You have learned, however, that there are many ingredients that go into making up a chart, and these ingredients can be crucial in determining whether a relationship is problematic or easy. To compare two charts, you need to focus on the signs of each person's Sun, Moon, Mercury, Venus, and Mars. For fine-tuning, we examine Jupiter and Saturn. The outer planets are important when they aspect a personal planet in one person's chart. For chart comparisons between parents and children or between two people of very different ages, the aspects between the outer planets in both charts will be significant.

THE ELEMENTS IN CHART COMPARISONS

Before you analyze the aspects between two charts, look at the elements of the personal planets in each person's chart. Grab a piece of paper and draw two columns to make a worksheet. Label them at the top with the names of the two people you are comparing. Then write down the elements of the Sun, Moon, Mercury, Venus, and Mars in each column. When you see compatible elements across a row, you know that there will be sympathy between the two people in those departments of life. When the elements are incompatible, two people speak a different language and will have to learn to translate for each other.

SUN AND MOON

When the Suns are in the same element, there is a basic easy understanding. But perhaps in this same relationship, the couple's Moons are not in harmony. For example, a Virgo Sun and a Capricorn Sun share the earth element, but if their Moons are in Leo and Taurus, respectively, the elements of their Moon signs are not compatible. This means that although their personalities (the Sun) have similarities and compatibility, emotionally (the Moon), they have very different requirements. The Leo Moon needs constant attention and interesting, dramatic ways to express himself, and the Taurus Moon needs calm, sensual, and solid emotional contact. In this area these two people do not connect with each other.

MERCURY

Continue your analysis with Mercury. Mercury's elements describe how two people communicate. Since difficulties in most relationships are in regards to communication, this is a very important planet to examine. Mercury in the same element means that the two people speak the same language. Mercury in complementary elements means that the two people stimulate each other's thoughts. Have you ever had a conversation with someone and noticed that you think more clearly, with ideas flowing effortlessly? If you look at the other person's chart, note the Mercury aspects between you and the individual. Mercury will probably be in the same element or in a compatible one.

Perhaps the Mercury positions between two people are in incompatible elements; in this case, talking about a problem usually does no good. Writing your feelings down can help, though. Possibly the toughest Mercury combination is fire and earth. Fire wants to enthuse in his speech, and earth wants to organize or arrange the specifics. These are two different views of life, and both partners can leave any kind of discussion feeling that the other person doesn't understand or won't make an effort to understand. Mercury in air and water, although they are in incompatible elements, tends to be easier. Water wants more emotional closeness than air can usually give, but air can be mentally vague and water emotionally vague, so the two people do not irritate each other. In addition, note if one person has Mercury retrograde and the other's Mercury is direct. The person with the direct Mercury will have to compromise, since the retrograde Mercury partner finds it difficult to understand that his or her method of communication is unique. With Mercury retrograde people, try phrasing a question negatively, such as "Don't you want..." or "You wouldn't want to do such and such..." It usually allows them to say yes rather than refute your request.

VENUS

Next, look at the Venus aspects and list them on your sheet. Venus describes affections, such as how a person feels romantically and also what gives them pleasure. Venus in fire wants to be on the go and entertained all night. Venus in earth may like to go out once in a while, but prefers more steady comforts. Venus in air needs to talk and say sweet things to a beloved and will enjoy mentally engaging activities. Venus in water must express feelings and feel protected and safe in their environment. These are just a few examples of how to compare two people's Venus elements.

Usually when people are enjoying themselves, conflicts between elements are not as evident. If there is a bond of friendship or love between two people, the couple can take turns doing any activity that they enjoy and the relationship works out. The one area of Venus controversy can be spending money. Venus frequently indicates a person's attitude toward money. If one person is more free-spending (as air and fire signs tend to be) and the other (usually the earth signs) is more cautious, there must be a compromise. Remember to look at the chart as a whole.

MARS

Here you find the major arena of conflict and passion. How a person expresses their Mars energy describes a lot about their relationship with the world. Traditionally, men have had an easier time expressing their Mars nature, and women have sublimated their assertive energy or lived vicariously through the men in their lives. This equation is changing, but some remnants of these behaviors remain for some people. Many couples—practically or energetically—still hold on to a stereotype of one strong, protective provider partnering with a softer, more nurturing mate. In the US, men and women are trying to free themselves from gender stereotypes so that they can develop their individual yin and yang energies.

Those efforts can still be challenged by society, however. For instance, if a man embraces his yin energies, he may be accused of being weak. As astrologers, you can look past these stereotypes and understand how each person is trying to express all parts of their personality.

Mars intrinsically means conflict, and when two people have Mars in incompatible elements, conflicts have little hope of resolution unless each person can honor the other person's feelings and point of view. Mars in fire gets over insults quickly; Mars in water holds every mean remark and cannot let go. Mars in air can argue vehemently but dispassionately and is easily distracted when a more interesting topic comes along. Lastly, Mars in earth handles conflict in a very practical way. The Mars in earth person may say or feel, "I hate you at the moment, but we have to work or live together, so let's get on with it." Mars also describes sexual passion. Any adult in good physical health, regardless of Mars's element, can find a way to express his or her sexual nature. Issues of sexual compatibility can come into play in long relationships where the thrill may have worn off, but the sexual energy can still be released.

There are a lot of books on astrological sexual chemistry and how to please your lover by knowing his or her sign, but comparing the passion levels between the signs can create competitive scenarios and work against each sign's sexual expression. Sex is best left to the feeling parts of our natures rather than the mental department.

ASPECTS BETWEEN CHARTS

Once you have gleaned the nature of the elements between two charts, then you will want to zero in on the aspects between the charts. This will tell you exactly how flowing or nonflowing the energies are between people. On your worksheet, write how one person's planet aspects the other's. Let's call Chart 6, Jack, and Chart 5, Jane. At the top of your sheet, label the columns Jack and Jane. Jack's Moon at 00♐39 squares Jane's Moon at 7♓52. You would write that as ☽□☽ or Moon square Moon.

Continue to fill in your sheet with all the aspects between the two charts. Pay particular attention to the number of squares and oppositions, and the number of sextiles and trines. When you have finished, add up the number of hard aspects and the number of easy ones. If there are more hard aspects than easy aspects, the relationship is challenging; if there are more easy ones, then there is a flow of energies between the two charts.

This is a quantitative analysis. We also need to look qualitatively at how the relationship is difficult or easy. You know that aspects between the malefic planets are going to be more difficult than aspects between Venus and Mercury, for example. Concentrate on the aspects between Mars, Saturn, and Uranus. The presence of Uranus aspects in a relationship may be exciting but very chaotic because it is a malefic planet. Difficult aspects involving Pluto in synastry means that there is a strong element of control and domination present in the relationship. If there is one tight Pluto aspect and everything else is easy, the relationship can be very dynamic. However, when there are too many problems between charts, no matter how great the attraction, a wise astrologer will counsel someone to let this one go. If the two people involved live for drama, then the astrologer can point out the pros and cons and allow a client to exercise free will.

Frequently, Mars in a woman's chart will tell you the kind of yang (traditionally male) energy she seeks or loves. Venus in a man's chart will delineate the yin energy that he seeks.

To consider aspects between Jupiter and Saturn and the outer planets, also analyze the aspects between the personal planets and the outer planets. This will give you more pertinent information about how the two people react to each other. If their Uranus is conjunct the Moon, then the relationship will be surprising and full of erratic behavior. It will also be tremendously exciting.

THE CONJUNCTION

In synastry, the conjunction is a very important aspect. When two people's planets conjunct each other in a synastry chart, that conjunction creates a synergy between the two. This can create a symbiosis, which lasts for as long as the two people are in sync. It is difficult to change or break these bonds.

When the yang partner's Sun conjuncts the yin partner's Moon, the yang energy partner dominates the relationship. If the yin partner's Sun conjuncts the yang partner's Moon, then the yin person will dominate the relationship. In either case, a Sun/Moon conjunction indicates a past-life marriage and a deep bond. If the nature of the relationship in the present lifetime is that of friendship, or parent and child, the Sun/Moon conjunction can mean that there is also a deep and probable past-life connection between the two people.

When any of the other personal planets are conjunct each other, such as Mercury conjunct Mercury, Venus conjunct Venus, and Mars conjunct Mars, there is a great deal of sympathy between the charts. When Saturn and Uranus in one person's chart conjunct another's Venus or Mars, then there is a struggle between the two charts. Neptune conjunctions can give a very sweet and dreamy contact in two charts, and, as you may surmise, Pluto conjunctions lend themselves to fascination and power dynamics.

THE ASCENDANT AND DESCENDANT

Usually, in marriages, committed partnerships, and romantic relationships, the ascendant and descendant are intimately involved. The descendant, or the sign on the Seventh House cusp, rules the house of partnership. It is a good indicator of a long-lasting relationship when one person's Sun falls in the other person's Seventh House or the Moon falls in the partner's or spouse's Seventh House. When the personal planets are also in harmonious aspect with each person's ascendant, they can build a life together because their outlook is similar. In examining two charts, look to see what the aspects are between the personal planets and the ascendant/descendant axis. This will also tell you a lot about how the two people function in their relationship to society.

FRIENDSHIP

In addition to examining the elements and aspects between friends, which will tell you how easily they relate to each other, look at the Eleventh House and which planets are located there. The Eleventh House will tell you how easily a person makes and keeps friends. If one person has several personal planets in the Eleventh House, then friendships will be significant and will help this person throughout his or her life. If Mars or Uranus is in the Eleventh House, then there will be quarrels and many separations between friends, or the people involved will have an amicable sparring relationship where they like to argue. If Jupiter is in the Eleventh House, then prominent and influential friends will come into this person's life.

When considering friendship in the chart, it is also good to evaluate the entire chart to see what qualities a person brings to a friendship. After all, you choose your friends, and unlike family, there are no obligatory bonds holding the two people together except that of mutual regard and support.

PARENTS AND CHILDREN

If parents studied astrology, they would be able to gain insight into their relationships with their children. Of course, knowing something and implementing it are different activities, but certainly understanding astrology is a good place to start. Astrology is based on the belief that we choose our parents and incarnate to learn lessons that the soul needs in order to grow. The important question is how to deal with this complex and fundamental relationship. A parent has in their child's astrology chart a clear guide to what experiences the child needs to have and what activities will best suit his or her talents. Free will is always there but needs guidance. By studying the synastry chart between parents and children, a parent can see what his or her strengths are in regard to raising children. Look at the elements. Parents who know astrology maximize their abilities to help nurture their children simply by recognizing that each child needs a specific atmosphere in which to grow.

In addition to considering the elements between parents and children, it is important to see how the child learns so that a parent knows the best way of approaching him or her. This is also important in terms of schooling. A parent can easily look at their child's Mercury and Moon placements to discern this. Not all children respond to the same kind of education. With a little guidance, the parent can determine what individual experts, like teachers and doctors, are advising and whether or not that approach will be good for their child.

Also, it is important to know that from birth to age seven, children may typify their Moon sign more than their Sun sign. Children grow into their personalities and need the emotional security dictated by their Moon. All children need lots of cuddling and assurance. Which element would need that the most? If you answered water, you are correct. Children with lots of air in their charts need to be talked to and read to as much as possible. The fire signs need to run around, blow off their exuberance, and have someone to mirror their enthusiasms. The earth signs need time to construct, hold, and create structure in the world. They also need cuddles almost as much as the water signs do.

The relationships between the parents' and child's astrology charts will illuminate what kind of nurturing suits each child. And the beauty of astrology is that in learning about your children, you will also learn something about yourself.

COWORKERS AND BOSSES

The relationships people have at work are an important part of being successful in their careers. The workplace offers people the opportunity to work together in an impersonal way, yet it is the interpersonal dynamics that determine the quality of that experience. To understand how to get along with your boss, you would look at a comparison of the elements and aspects as you have done for other synastry charts. You may not know your boss's birth time, but you can erect what is called a *solar wheel* for anyone without knowing the individual's time of birth. You do need to have the date and place of birth, but with a little careful sleuthing, you can probably discover this information. If the atmosphere in your workplace is extremely private, you may want to be cautious about asking personal questions. In that case, observe your boss and coworkers and see if you can intuit their signs. This may be an interesting astrological exercise for you. To draw up a solar wheel, place the person's Sun on the ascendant position. Then continue around the wheel in order of the signs to create the house cusps. In Chart 6, the ascendant would be 12♋50. The Second House cusp would be 12♌50, and so forth. When you have set up this wheel, place all the planets in the appropriate houses and read the chart as if it were a natal chart. The most important planets regarding a relationship with a boss or a coworker are Mars, Saturn, and Pluto. These planets will tell you how a person asserts their authority and what standards they expect on the job. The Sun sign will, of course, let you know a boss's personality. If your Sun sign is at odds with your boss's Sun sign, look for other ways that you can relate to him or her. As an employee, your job is dependent on how well you can keep your personality in harmony with the demands of your job and your boss's expectations.

Your Tenth House will also give you information about the relationship between you and your boss. If his or her benefic planets fall in your Tenth House, then you can expect that your relationship will be encouraging for your career. If the malefic planets are in your Tenth House, the relationship will be tough. It may be the kind of antagonistic relationship that spurs you on to achievement, or it could just be aggravating. The rest of the chart's aspects will clue you in to the dynamics between you and your boss. If most of the connections between your chart and your boss's chart are in the Sixth House, then your relationship is simply that of employer and employee with little emphasis on mentoring.

You can look at relationships with coworkers in the same way. Examine the aspects, house cusps, and any planets in the Sixth House for information on the relationship between you and your coworkers. Usually when people irritate us, they magnify some fault or aspect of our own personalities that we prefer to keep hidden. Astrology's gift is that when you are annoyed with someone, you can look at your charts and see exactly what irritates you about that person. If you choose to work with the astrological information available, you will have an unparalleled guide to increasing your understanding and compassion for people.

THE MARRIAGE CHART

A useful and interesting way to look at marriages is to draw up a chart for the date, time, and place the marriage took place. This represents the event of legally joining two people, and it can be used—in addition to the transits and progressions of each person's chart—to understand how the state of the union is moving. Use your astrology software program for this chart, or hand-calculate it. If you are not exactly sure what time the vows were spoken, you can use an approximate time or erect a solar wheel. This chart is a good indicator of how the marriage functions. In addition to charting the ebb and flow of relationships, a marriage chart is also a good way to look at times when the couple is in a good astrological condition for having a child. Using the marriage chart for predictions, however, is not totally reliable. Predictions are better indicated in each person's natal chart.

THE COMPOSITE CHART

A composite chart combines two natal charts into one and in effect creates a new natal chart for a relationship. This can be a relationship between any two people who have to cooperate or live together. The composite chart takes the same planet from each chart, adds them together, and divides the sum by 2 to reach what is called a *midpoint* between those two planets. The midpoint is the halfway point between the same planets. If you look at Jack and Jane's charts and want to know the composite Sun, you would add (using our numerical system for the signs: 3 for Cancer and 6 for Libra) each Sun's position and divide by 2. The math looks like this:

$$
\begin{array}{rrrr}
  & 3 & 12 & 50 \\
+ & 6 & 25 & 59 \\
\hline
= & 9 & 37 & 109 \\
- &   & 30 & 60 \\
+ &   & 1 & 1 \\
\hline
= & 10 & 08 & 49 \\
\div & 2 & 2 & 2 \\
\hline
= & 5 & 4 & 24 \\
\end{array}
$$

4 ♍ 24
(4 Virgo 24 minutes)

You can proceed in the same way for all the planets as well as the house cusps, or you can press a button for a composite chart under "synastry" on your astrology software program and get the whole chart immediately. You should enter the location where the two people are living at the time of the chart's calculation.

This composite chart will also tell you what affects the couple. Noting the transits to the composite chart helps to see what is affecting the relationship as a whole. You could progress a composite chart, but I don't feel that the progressed composite chart gives enough information to be of value. A more realistic method is plotting the transits to the composite chart and seeing how they describe the ups and downs of any relationship.

THE DAVISON CHART

British astrologer Ronald C. Davison pioneered another type of composite chart. He combined two charts based on the exact midpoint in time between the two birth dates to create a new chart, or birthday, for the relationship or marriage. The Davison chart should be included in your software program and is located under the menu for "synastry." If you like, you can calculate the chart yourself. For example, if one individual is born on July 1, 1990, and the other on September 1, 1990, the Davison chart would be calculated for August 1, 1990. The Davison chart is another way to examine the dynamics of a couple's life together. As with the composite chart, it is not the most reliable indicator for predictions. Examining transits to the Davison chart will give you a sense of the ebb and flow of the couple's feelings.

ANALYSIS OF JACK AND JANE

With all you have learned in this chapter, let's look at Charts 5 and 6 and analyze this relationship at the point at which their charts were read. First, the elements:

JACK'S AND JANE'S CHARTS		
PLANET	JACK	JANE
Sun	Water	Air
Moon	Fire	Water
Mercury	Air	Air
Venus	Fire	Water
Mars	Fire	Air
Jupiter	Air	Water
Saturn	Air	Air
Uranus	Water	Water
Neptune	Fire	Fire
Pluto	Water	Water

COMPATIBILITY BETWEEN CHARTS

Did the total absence of earth from both of these charts catch your eye? If you total Jack's elements you should have three water, four fire, three air, and no earth signs. Jane's total is five water, four air, one fire, and no earth signs. The element that is unbalanced between the two charts is fire. Jack has a lot and Jane has very little. All the attributes of fire will need to be balanced between these two people. Jack would have to tread carefully on Jane's watery feelings (which he can do because of his water planets), and Jane would have to increase her enthusiasm and joys to match Jack's fire. This would be harder for her because she lacks fire. Both people lack earth. That means their natures are primarily thinking and feeling. There is a lot of easy flow in that part

of their lives. You might think that these two people have money problems, but they do not. Jane was born fairly wealthy, and Jack makes a
ton of money from his own business. Money is not an issue between
them. In fact, if you look quickly at Jane's chart and see Jupiter in the
Second House, you can interpret that she is able to find and attract
money easily and enjoys all the benefits of a comfortable lifestyle. Also,
Jack's Pluto and Sun in the Tenth House means that he is ambitious
and driven to succeed in his career and make a mark on the world.

JACK'S AND JANE'S ASPECTS

Now let's examine the aspects between the two charts. There are a
lot, but they are listed so that you can get the hang of identifying them.

JACK	ASPECT	JANE
☉	△	☽
☉	△	♀
☉	△	♅
☉	☌	♀
☽	□	☽
☽	✶	♂
☽	✶	☿
☿	△	☉
☿	△	♄
☿	□	♅
♀	✶	☉
♀	✶	♄
♀	☌	♆
♀	□	♃
♂	□	☽
♂	✶	☿
♂	□	♅

JACK	ASPECT	JANE
♃	☌	☿
♃	☌	♂
♃	□	♀
♄	☌	♂
♄	☌	♀
♅	☌	♅
♅	△	♃
♅	△	♀
♆	☌	♆
♆	✶	☉
♆	□	♃
♆	✶	♄
♇	△	☽
♇	□	☿
♇	□	♂
♇	△	♀
♇	△	♅
♇	☌	♇

Now that you have all the aspects between Jack and Jane, let's see what they mean. First, notice that there are many contacts between these two people. They have a basis, good or bad, for a relationship. When there are few aspects between charts, two people don't have much to offer each other. If you total up the aspects, you have ten trines, seven sextiles, nine squares, and nine conjunctions. The hard aspects win! I am counting the conjunction as a tough aspect, although some of the conjunctions are quite positive.

To understand *how* this couple interacts, you want to look at the tough aspects and then point out where they will find relief.

Since most people learn astrology to get perspective on difficulties an individual may be experiencing, let's start with the bones of contention. There are two whoppers that jump out from looking at these charts. The first is Jack's Moon square Jane's Moon, and the second is Jack's Saturn conjunct Jane's Mars. When the Moons are square in a marriage or romantic relationship, there is no easy flow of feelings. The two people anger each other often. This is true in this couple's experience. Jack is a noisy fighter, as fire wants to express himself dramatically, and Jane is a weepy protester, because her watery Pisces Moon feels put upon and martyred. The fighting, however, allows each person to express a lot of feelings, and that creates an emotional bond between people. The next tough one is Jack's Saturn conjunct Jane's Mars. Jack, being the male and slightly older, takes the lead in the relationship (the marriage also occurred in the fifties when a man was expected to dominate the relationship). Even disregarding the cultural stereotypes of that time, however, Jack's personality squelches many of Jane's assertive feelings. Had Jane been born in a different time, she may not have been exclusively a mother and homemaker.

Her Sun in the First House indicates that she is vitally interested in expressing herself in the world, but her Mars in the Twelfth House shows that she has hidden fears about self-expression. Jack cannot help her assert herself. He frequently acts like a father to her, but not an encouraging one.

Jane also suffers from depression as indicated by the Sun/Saturn conjunction in the First House. Jack, with all his fire planets, thinks depression is part of her weepy character, and he is neither helpful nor tolerant. His Pluto/Sun conjunction means that he is interested in expressing his power, and anyone who lags behind is out of luck. But his energy may, in fact, have helped her cope with her depression. From Jack's perspective, Jane is not a warm nurturer for him or their children. Jane's ambition to be prominent in social circles—as indicated by the number of planets in Libra and Mercury in Libra conjunct the ascendant—interferes with Jack's feeling of family togetherness indicated by his Cancerian emphasis. Additionally, Jack's need to be appreciated by an enthusiastic partner is continually dampened by Jane's needs and personality. The chart indicates Jack is also a very nurturing parent (Sun in Cancer), and had he lived in a different time, he might have spent time at home educating and raising his children. His motivation to succeed would be strong no matter when he lived, but he might have more balance in his life and be happier if he could have more opportunity to express his caring impulses.

Another challenging aspect is Jack's Mars square Jane's Uranus. Here we see one reason the couple stayed together and the very same reason that the relationship was not peaceful. They both like to fight! Even if Jane feels weakened by Jack's strength, she does enjoy standing up for herself and expressing her anger. Remember that Libra is the sign of relationships and is frequently most comfortable expressing feelings within the structure of marriage or partnership. The aspect is challenging because Mars and Uranus in a square relationship is tough on the nervous system. These two people often needed time away from each other so they could regain their individual rhythms. Jack traveled for business, and that afforded the couple a good break.

THE ASCENDANTS

One of the clearest indicators of compatibility between these two charts is the Libra ascendant for both Jack and Jane. Their combined outlook on the world is social and charming, and filled with a desire to please others. They enjoy their friends, and hosting company is a great pleasure for them both. Which person might sometimes feel less social? Jack, of course. His Cancer Sun is not in an easy relationship with his Libra ascendant, and he needs to retreat periodically. Jane, however, with her Libra Sun is always ready for social events. The Libra ascendant also gives both people Aries on the Seventh House cusp. Mars is Aries's planet, and again we see the theme of conflict as part of the marriage contract and the lessons to be learned from this relationship.

EASY ASPECTS

The smooth parts of these two charts are indicated by all of the trines from Jack's Sun to Jane's Moon, Venus, Uranus, and Pluto, and the sextile between Jack's Venus and Jane's Sun and Saturn. He genuinely loves parts of her personality and has a good time with the way she expresses herself. She enjoys his ambition and the adventure of being with a man very different from the people she grew up with. There is also a wide-orbed sextile between Jack's Neptune and Jane's Sun. In their peaceful moments, they share a spiritual harmony that makes up for much of the strife. They also love many of their differences. Here is where knowing a person's background makes a difference in understanding astrology. These two people came from different social backgrounds. He came from a poor immigrant background, and she came from an upper-middle-class background. She is very religious, and he is blasé about organized religion. Jack enjoys Jane's social standing, and Jane enjoys the more emotional and less mannered way Jack and his family view the world.

When you are interpreting synastry charts, apply the meaning of the aspects to the background and personality of the people you are dealing with. When you consider all the factors that go into creating a person's chart, you need to ground the astrological information in the reality of the lives involved. This is the difference between knowing astrology and applying astrology. A person and a relationship are always greater than the sum of their astrological parts.

JACK AND JANE'S COMPOSITE CHART

If you calculate a composite chart for Jack and Jane, some very interesting placements occur. The composite Sun is Virgo, and together their composite Moon is Capricorn. Both these signs are earth signs and compensate for the lack of earth in their individual natal charts. That means that together these two people are well grounded in the material world and can be very successful financially. Jane and Jack's marriage was very successful financially, and this helped keep them together. The most interesting pattern in the composite chart is a water grand trine between Pluto, Mars, and Uranus. The composite Mars is in Scorpio, Pluto in Cancer, and Uranus in Pisces. If you remember what you learned about chart patterns, the grand trine is a fortunate pattern indicating a great deal of feeling but difficulty in communicating it. Perhaps this is the best description of Jack and Jane's marriage: There are many feelings, but it is difficult for them to always communicate them positively. The emotional intensity kept them connected but encouraged drama and storms.

In looking at chart comparisons, you will often find that people come together to master some part of their own personality. In the case of Jack and Jane, one part of their "mission" was to let feelings flow without indulging in ego and power plays; with Pluto part of the water grand trine, this was indeed a challenge. Now that you have learned some of the truly interesting ways of looking at relationships, you are well equipped to explore life and love from an astrological perspective. The next chapter will help you understand the hidden chart and ways to interpret past-life influences.

CHAPTER SEVEN
THE HIDDEN CHART

You have learned many astrological techniques that can improve your life as well as help friends, family, and clients. In this chapter, you will examine what I call the *hidden chart*. The hidden chart will help you find ways to understand karma and your life purpose or the life purpose of someone else. In some ways the entire astrological chart is a karmic map. When you examine questions concerning your life's purpose and inherited tendencies from past lives, your perspective must consider the metaphors that the chart suggests rather than hewing to hard-and-fast rules. You cannot skate through your life's karma in the same way that you can ameliorate retrograde Mercury. There are no rules for studying karmic astrology that will give you the secret of life, but the information that the chart points toward is invaluable for understanding the underlying foundations of a person's life. Karma and past lives are topics for which there can be no empirical study. Although many people have had near-death experiences, and mediums and others have reported about what happens when someone passes over, we earthbound beings cannot verify the information, nor can we easily assimilate and use these perspectives in daily life. Also, if a person spends all his or her time thinking of the life to come, it will be difficult to focus on the tasks of *this* life. All groups, no matter how spiritually oriented they are, must contend with earthly matters and the here and now.

In many astrology books, you can flip to the sections on karmic influences and identify karmic burdens according to certain planets, signs, and aspects. This is not, in my opinion, the way to approach the occult meanings of karma and past lives. A person tends to look at these descriptions like a checklist: "Well, I am going to be lonely... check. Ill-health, what a pity...check. No money, tough luck...check." The net result is a passive life filled with no growth or attempt to move things along. You cannot avoid karma, but you can transmute karma by deeply understanding the planetary messages and choosing the higher road or more responsible actions, even when you feel naturally inclined to a different direction. In fact, the very purpose of life may be to work with your karma to purify your soul. There are astrological clues and indications for karma in a chart, and this is what you will learn about in this chapter.

If you find as you study astrology that your intuition increases and you are receiving pictures of what you believe to be past lives in your dreams or meditations, try to understand the qualities and lessons to be learned rather than getting caught up in the story. For example, clients have told me they believe they were Joan of Arc in a previous lifetime. It is doubtful that they were, but the qualities of martyrdom and sacrifice, and the sense of having a mission, are all valuable lessons. Many people may be refining these aspects of their life and learning about feelings of victimization by choosing the image of Joan of Arc as personally relevant to them.

People rarely say that they were a power-hungry ruler or peasant in other incarnations. We prefer to think of ourselves as great and worthy characters. This is good for the ego, but it may obscure parts of the personality that are less impressive. All people are capable of every human quality, from the highest altruism and love to the lowest depravity and deceit. It is possible that each of us has at times lived an ignoble existence, and as we progress through various lifetimes, we aspire to a more noble life. It can be difficult to keep this very compassionate and high-minded concept in your mind when you are cleaning up a big mess, arguing bitterly with your wife or husband, battling for your job, or resenting your kids because their lives are not in your control. It is only in reflection that we can touch these truths and notice how we might have reacted differently or simply note that there is a repetitive pattern to our difficulties. This is where knowing something about your past lives and karma is healing and useful. As you become familiar with your lessons and successes, you develop a personal code and shortcut to understanding yourself and any tendencies that may be karmic in origin. Understanding is the first step to clear away debris and energy blocks that hinder you. Let's now define karma and examine its indicators in the chart.

KARMA

The concept of karma originated in the Eastern religions of Buddhism and Hinduism; it describes the ever-ascending wheel of life where deeds, thoughts, and actions from the past draw experiences to a person's present life in order to grow and perfect his or her soul. It is the law of cause and effect, or in more colloquial terms, "What goes around comes around."

Karma has positive dimensions. The gifts and talents of our current lives come from benefits accrued in other lifetimes. Self-esteem and the ability to go through life successfully is due in part to a life that has been worked for in prior incarnations. Sometimes, when people have a seemingly easy life, they are reaping benefits from other, more difficult lifetimes. Also, people with relatively stress-free lives may be resting for another growth spurt in a future lifetime. A challenging life may mean that your soul is ambitious for growth and knowledge.

A good image for the spiral of karma is walking through a maze in a garden. There are many ways through the maze, and when you reach the end, metaphorically speaking, there is another maze at a higher level of consciousness to go through. You will keep the knowledge gained from the previous maze, knowing the twists and turns, and learning the dangers you faced there as well as the joys and pleasures. These successes become part of your tool kit for future journeys. You will repeat any experiences that you shirked or neglected in a previous incarnation until you have completed that bit of development.

These lessons and incarnations are your soul's choice. The choice does not come from the conscious mind but from the deepest part of a person; in effect, it means "as you sow, so shall you reap." Karma does not mean a person deserves trauma and difficult experiences as punishment. But, in moments of contemplation, if you are in the midst of a painful period of life, you might take comfort in the belief that your difficulties are there to further your knowledge and personal development.

Karma, however, is not like a cosmic score sheet where each bad thought, sin, or action is noted down. This idea would paralyze our ability to act and put us all in psychological and emotional straitjackets, breeding more guilt and misery. How then do you emphasize sowing positive seeds and reducing the creation of additional difficult karma? *Gracefully* is the word that comes to mind. There is no way to live perfectly, but the effort to understand your life and how you can grow is perhaps the only way to fathom the twists and turns that life takes. Doing your best and cheerfully considering others' feelings may be the best guide to working with your karmic challenges, and your good intentions will in turn sow good karma for future lifetimes.

The following are some of the astrological indicators for tracing and understanding a person's karmic legacy. I have also included some possible past-life scenarios that may have given rise to these karmic indicators. Lastly, I have included some meditation and therapeutic techniques for addressing past-life conditions in your chart. Chart 1 and Chart 2 are excellent examples for study, as these people were very mindful of finding and living their soul's purpose.

THE MOON'S NODES

There are two positions in a chart that I have not mentioned. They are called the *nodes of the Moon*; they are not physical bodies but points on the ecliptic of the Moon's orbit. There is a north node, which is the point of the ecliptic where the Moon passes from south latitude to north latitude. This is called the *dragon's head*, the *north node*, or the *ascending node*. The symbol is ☊. The dragon's tail, descending node, or south node, whose symbol is ☋, is always the same degree but in the opposite sign from the north node. In an ephemeris, you will find only the north node listed. Most astrology programs calculate both positions. In Chart 1, the ☊ is 19♊, so the ☋ would be 19♐. In Chart 2, the ☊ is 26 degrees ♒; and the ☋ is 26 degrees ♌.

The nodes are a key ingredient in Vedic, or Hindu, astrology and are also important in identifying life lessons in Western astrology. Vedic astrology is a branch of astrology used in India and is based on the Moon's position. By contrast, the Sun's position forms the basis for Western astrology. In Hindu mythology, Rahu was a demon with an appendage to his body that resembled a dragon's tail. Rahu made himself immortal by stealing the elixir of divine life. This angered Vishnu, one of the major creator gods of the Hindu pantheon, and when he could not take away Rahu's eternal life, Vishnu cut him in half: The demon's head was called Rahu, and his tail, Ketu. Vishnu threw Rahu into the sky where he became part of the constellation Draco.

Using his dragon's tail as a weapon, Rahu waged a war on the Sun and the Moon gods by swallowing them during an eclipse. Other names for Rahu and Ketu are Caput Draconis (dragon's head) and Cauda Draconis (dragon's tail). The polarity described by the Moon's nodes is one of the primary karmic and past-life indicators in the chart. The south node tells us about subconscious patterns and ingrained patterns from the past. The north node outlines new lessons and characteristics to which a person aspires in the present lifetime. Of course, achieving the promise of your north node takes a lifetime of learning. Some astrologers simply look at the nodes as the dichotomy between Saturn and Jupiter. They consider that the north node has the quality of Jupiter and the south node the quality of Saturn. This is too narrow and needlessly reductive to express two new astrological concepts in terms of other planets. Regarding the north and south nodes, Isabel M. Hickey states it best in her book *Astrology: A Cosmic Science*:

> *The ancients said the north node was benefic and the south node was malefic. Not necessarily so. When we cling to the past and refuse to go into the future or into the new and untried experiences, we retard our growth and development.*

Crystallization is not evil. It is merely stupid....
The north node represents the new work to be done, the new
faculty to be developed. The south node is the line of least
resistance and operates with ease because it has become a
repetitive pattern. The north node is the new channel to be
made; the new challenge and the point of spiritual fulfillment.

When interpreting the nodes, you will see that they always express a continuum of experience. Instead of saying the north node is in Aries and the south node is in Libra, try to think of the Aries/Libra experience. Most simply stated, this would be the emphasis on *I* (Aries) and the emphasis on *we* (Libra). The idea of the continuum is true for all the other nodal positions. The two houses containing the Moon's nodes will be where these karmic indicators play out the lessons and successes for life.

The following is a brief description of the major thrust each nodal pair outlines. Remember that the south node highlights what you are leaving behind and the north node outlines the knowledge to which you are aspiring.

ARIES/LIBRA

The Aries/Libra axis outlines challenges in self-assertion compared to the need for compromise and harmonious relationships. When the north node is in Aries, a person is developing the ability to stand on their own as an individual. The south node indicates that a person has been too self-assertive at the expense of other's viewpoints. For Libra's north nodes, that person is reaching toward harmonious partnerships and balancing their individual desires with the demands of cooperation. A Libra south node indicates that a person has been too accommodating and "other" oriented and must focus on maintaining a balanced center in relationships.

TAURUS/SCORPIO

The Taurus/Scorpio axis concerns accumulating and disposing of material possessions and harnessing energy for creative rather than destructive purposes. When the north node is in Taurus, a person can attract resources and has the ability to be very practical and share their success. With the south node in Taurus, a person has overly emphasized possessions and will have to relinquish control. The north node in Scorpio outlines the use of creative power beyond selfish interests to serve others and society. When the south node is in Scorpio, a person has been primarily interested in manipulating others.

GEMINI/SAGITTARIUS

The Gemini/Sagittarius axis outlines different approaches to communication and the accumulation of knowledge. The Gemini north node indicates versatility and an optimistic attitude toward life. The south node in Gemini shows that the mind was too restless and superficial and communication was not directed to sustaining projects. The north node in Sagittarius points the way to a person developing a personal philosophy and code of values. When the south node is in Sagittarius, that person has had a tendency to indulge in rash tendencies and flee from responsibilities. The proverb "a rolling stone gathers no moss" comes to mind.

CANCER/CAPRICORN

The Cancer/Capricorn axis outlines the influence of emotional nurturing at home compared to the discipline needed to deal with the demands of working and thriving in the world outside the home. The Cancer north node shows a person developing strong nurturing and sympathetic traits so they can mother themselves or others. The south node shows a tendency for perpetual emotional chaos and self-centeredness that must learn to yield to caring for others. In Capricorn, the north node indicates that a person has executive ability and can methodically work toward their goals not only for their own success but to redeem and assist others. The south node in Capricorn indicates past habits of selfish ambition and a tendency to dominate others.

LEO/AQUARIUS

The Leo/Aquarius axis concerns personal glory and the public good. When the north node is in Leo, a person has a great deal of self-respect and can lead others with wisdom and generosity. The south node in Leo means that in the past, that person has overdeveloped their ego and misused their power. The opposite nodal point, Aquarius for the north Node, shows a person who effortlessly gives service to a group that works for the benefit of society. The south node in Aquarius shows a person who has had a tendency to both become a law unto themselves and refuse to work with others.

VIRGO/PISCES

The Virgo/Pisces challenge is to moderate the tendencies toward critical, analytical detail and total unqualified acceptance; it is considered to be difficult, as Virgo/Pisces tests the rational mind with faith. The difficulties of these nodal positions from a karmic point of view are considered modified because of the service to others that they usually indicate. The north node in Virgo shows that a person has mastered discrimination without judgment. When the south node is in Virgo, a person must become aware of their tendency to criticize and judge people harshly. The north node in Pisces is considered a "high calling," for it means compassionate service to all people. A person with a Pisces north node is learning about faith. The Pisces south node indicates that a person has indulged in escapist tendencies and senses and now must assume responsibility for their actions.

READING THE NODES

These are brief sketches of the nodal positions. The two houses containing the Moon's nodes will tell you where the karmic indicators play out the lessons and successes for life. There are many books that interpret and detail what the node's positions mean, but some of them are needlessly harsh. You should read them with discernment.

Most people who consult astrologers are in the midst of dealing with problems. It is a very good practice to examine and interpret charts of people who are quite content with their lives. Whether someone is happy or sad, or whether they consider themselves a failure or a success, everyone has the Moon's nodes and everyone is living out karma. Studying many people's charts will help you apply these concepts to others' lives rather than seeing people as the sum of bad or good karma.

Of course, you should also pay attention to transits to the nodes. Positive transits to the north node tend to smooth life's events. Challenging aspects to the south node can feel bleak, as they can wake up patterns and feelings from past lives. Transits to either of the nodes can also bring about events with karmic resonances. My advice is to deal with what you can and laugh at the rest.

The nodes point out a trajectory and describe lifelong patterns. As you study astrology, you will become more attuned to accepting what your chart and life offers you: the good, the bad, and the ugly. Acceptance and working with all the material you've got means you are running the show as much as you are able to, and this takes the sting of victimization away. You cannot control everything. You cannot escape your karma, but you can take on your life with good grace and faith.

THE MOON

The Moon indicates habitual and emotional responses to life. The Moon sign dominates in childhood and can also indicate deeply ingrained patterns of response that may have been built up over many lifetimes. These ways of reacting have become comfortable to each of us and offer the first line of defense that a person has in dealing with the world around them. When the Moon is harmoniously aspected, a person can easily project a self-image that helps with getting along well in the world. When the Moon is adversely aspected, a person can be in an emotional left field and unable to communicate feelings.

When considering karmic questions, the Moon indicates subterranean emotional currents that a person brings to the present life. Rather than describe each Moon position, I think considering the elements brings questions of general karma into good focus, as each of the Moon's elements describes the way a person defends his or her own turf. Learning how that defense is effective or where it is outmoded can describe a karmic debt or inheritance. Moon in fire is likely to react with anger and dramatic flourishes. Moon in earth reacts with endurance and fortitude. Moon in air reacts with rationalizations, discussions, or arguments. A watery Moon reacts by retreating, or with emotional outpourings.

If you meditate on these simple explanations and consider that a person has chosen his or her Moon sign to master an automatic reaction pattern, then you have some information on the karmic lesson involved with the position of the Moon. It is reductive to say, "Oh, you have Moon in Cancer. You must have been an overemotional mother in a previous lifetime." Likewise, to say a person with Moon in Leo was probably very dramatic is too simplistic. It is more important to recognize the quality of emotional energy that a person uses to interact with the world. As you understand the positive ways your Moon position can influence your life, you'll begin to master a good portion of your karmic assignment.

SATURN

You have already learned a lot about Saturn in Chapter 4 and elsewhere. In ancient times, Saturn was called the Lord of Karma because this planet stood for the passage of time and lessons learned in this lifetime and other lifetimes. In addition to the way Saturn informs your daily life on Earth, consider the sign and house position of Saturn as an indication of specific karmic lessons for you this time around. With your knowledge of the signs, it is easy to identify the basic thrust of your plan according to Saturn, but living your karmic plan takes a lifetime to master. Fortunately, we have many lifetimes to get it right.

These are brief notes on karma and Saturn's position, but you are the best judge of what your own life needs to balance and purify. I have included a small description of a possible scenario of Saturn's position in each sign. This is an imaginative view of Saturn positions to give you an idea of how to understand karmic placements.

ARIES

With Saturn in Aries, a person has challenges in expressing outgoing energy and dealing with authority. Courage and the natural verve of Aries have become crystallized and stiff. This position lends itself to either a person who makes a big show out of everything or someone who pretends to be meek. Saturn in Aries indicates karmic links with authority figures. In a past life, the person may have been a warrior who turned from a battle when it was important to fight.

TAURUS

Saturn in Taurus addresses the challenge of holding on to, and possessiveness in, material goods, ideas, or values. In terms of earthly success, Saturn in Taurus may be very good in real estate or commerce, but the acquisitiveness that this sign placement implies also holds a lesson for the soul, which is to be able to let go. If you worship gold and possessions, then your material world runs you and can lead to inflexibility that discounts other life experiences. There can be a fear of poverty with this sign placement. In a past life, a person may have been a merchant or landlord with many responsibilities and riches but little joy in living. Saturn in Taurus can bring karmic links with debtors or those in financial positions of authority.

GEMINI

Saturn in Gemini offers the test of concentrated thought rather than scattered and ineffectual energy. A person with this placement could be experiencing how to learn or how to focus the mind. The mind can have a negative, rigid cast, and learning the power of optimism is part of Gemini's life lesson. Saturn in Gemini may also be learning to communicate thoughts and find value in personal ideas. Saturn in Gemini can indicate karmic links with brothers and sisters or members of the extended family. In a past life, this person may have been a messenger or scribe who had difficulty in reporting messages or vital information accurately. This lifetime demands that a person with this position speak optimistically and truthfully.

CANCER

Saturn in Cancer offers the karmic test of releasing past emotions that cloud present reality. A person with this position can cling to family values regardless of their suitability or advisability. Emotion for emotion's sake is an exhausting choice, and always going with the flow can lead to lack of foresight and planning. The karmic links with this position are with family members, usually the mother. Those with Saturn in Cancer must also learn to release hardened emotions and develop empathy with other people. In the past this person may have held tightly to family and squelched others' individuality because of his or her own fear of loneliness.

LEO

Saturn in Leo people are learning the lesson of giving and receiving. It is difficult when Leo's abundant egocentric solar energy is the challenge, because Saturn in Leo people want the limelight. People with this placement will learn that they cannot receive everyone's undivided attention all the time, and they may experience loneliness and lack of friends until the lesson of sharing, leading, and following becomes part of their life's path. There are frequent karmic links with children when Saturn is in Leo. "Pride goeth before a fall" is a good phrase for Saturn in Leo people. In a past life, this person may have been a ruler or leader who ruled autocratically and created dissension among his or her people.

VIRGO

Here Saturn enforces the lesson that criticism, analysis, and even gossip serve to demean others and can create a very judgmental streak. The very gifts of discernment and analysis that Virgo offers can be tests when Saturn is in Virgo. With this placement, a person must make distinctions among individuals, experiences, and events without labeling them good or bad. When the Saturn in Virgo person hews to a rigid idea of what is correct, perfect, or healthy, then everything that doesn't agree with that position becomes the enemy. With Saturn in Virgo, life's experiences will try and teach this person the validity of others' viewpoints as well as their own. Saturn in Virgo is apt to have karmic links with people through work experiences. In a past life, this person may have been a cold bureaucrat who stuck mindlessly to the rules regardless of the human situation.

LIBRA

Saturn is exalted in Libra, which is the cosmos's way of saying that fairness, sociability, cooperation, and relationships are essential parts of people's lives. The test here is proper responsibility in marriage and in partnership. The Saturn in Libra person will encounter relationships again and again where perhaps they neglected common courtesy and fair play. All karmic links with Saturn in Libra will be with a marriage partner. Competitiveness must be replaced with cooperation. In a past life, this position could have meant a deceitful marriage partner or someone who dodged the responsibilities of partnership at the last moment.

SCORPIO

Scorpio offers the test of desire and passion in the service of others rather than exclusively for pleasure. I would call this a lesson of "right desire" but not from a moral point of view. Right desire means that there are consequences to unleashing sexual energies. The character is usually very strong but may sink into vendettas and harbor negative feelings when his or her power is not recognized. Saturn in Scorpio has such strength that it must use it for creative purposes. There are usually karmic links with healers, doctors, and, sometimes, witches. Saturn in Scorpio may have been involved with magic and the occult and used that knowledge for ill or for purposes of manipulation.

SAGITTARIUS

Saturn in Jupiter's sign lends gravity and concentration to Sagittarius's at times reckless optimism. The lesson is to develop understanding. Saturn in Sagittarius offers the lessons of correcting blunt speech that does not regard another's feelings. This is a sign of a teacher or religious leader in the past, and there will be karmic links with educators. The present lifetime will invite experiences in which a person can share knowledge for everyone's benefit rather than for personal aggrandizement.

CAPRICORN

Under Saturn's rulership, this position indicates that a person has mastered many karmic lessons regarding responsibility and structure in life. This character has power and ambition but may have neglected sharing that power to increase joy and foster good relationships among people. When ambition without a sense of connectedness to others dominates, life can be dreary. There can be karmic links with the father or father figures. In a past life, this person may have been a strict disciplinarian in a religious community where silence and grim duty dominated. The spiritual values this person learned purified the soul, but now he or she needs to remember "my yoke is easy and my burden is light" (Matthew 11:30).

AQUARIUS

Saturn in Aquarius indicates that a person has been through many lifetimes and is now in a position to move from the everyday ego to the higher self. Not all people will heed the call, but this particular soul development is available to the person who does. Saturn in Aquarius offers the ability to teach others the value of detached wisdom through friendship and work with groups of people. There are karmic links with friends when Saturn is in this position. It is important for the person with Saturn in this position to speak out. In a past life, they may have been an innovator, to whom society was not ready to listen. Now, offering ideas and speaking about their visions and ideals may require effort due to their fear of being criticized or rebuked.

PISCES

Saturn in Pisces draws a person toward karmic lessons in letting go of emotions and keeping some distance in empathy. A person with this position can become so involved in other people's feelings that they cannot locate their own feelings. In a past life, this person may have been someone who neglected emotional and material needs because they were always offering a shoulder to lean on. Karmic links may involve spiritual teachers, gurus, and priests.

PLUTO

Pluto and Pluto aspects directly express energies and relationships that have a karmic basis. But, here, I want to emphasize the evolutionary dimension of Pluto's placements. Not all charts are strongly influenced by Pluto. Your first astrological task is to investigate how Plutonian a person is; then you will know something about the karmic issues with which a person is concerned. If there is a heavy emphasis on Scorpio planets, that person is strongly influenced by Pluto. If Pluto is angular, or if many of the personal planets are in tight aspects—positive or negative—to Pluto, then that person is working toward clearing up Plutonian issues. As mentioned in Chapter 4, wherever Pluto is located represents where a person's strongest desires lie, and what parts of life that person will struggle with the most to realize his or her desires. When Pluto is linked to a personal planet, the issues that need to be addressed will come from past lives. Daily life is affected by these aspects as well. Pluto conjunct the Moon or Sun is particularly indicative of a past life where the personality (the Sun) or the emotions (the Moon) used power inappropriately.

It is not useful to delineate all the Pluto aspects here, as there are many books that do this masterfully. Look at the resource list at the back of the book for additional information. The best advice is to examine Pluto in his Phoenix form. All Pluto contacts are like the Phoenix, destroying themselves and then regenerating from ashes. It is an intense process, but like the pursuit of the ancient alchemists, it can turn lead into gold.

RETROGRADE PLANETS

Retrograde planets in a natal chart almost always indicate past-life issues that come around again to be mastered. This is why the year that a natal retrograde planet turns direct can be very liberating. It feels as if a debt has been paid or a long-standing burden lifted. The more retrograde planets a chart has, the more patterns are coming up for review. A chart with no retrograde planets means that a person is reaping benefits in this lifetime. These people have direct access to all the planets' energies and a good chance of successfully moving along on their life's path. Of course, in addition to the retrograde planet's meaning, the house position will tell you where the challenges of these energies are.

When you examine someone's chart, it is never advisable to say, "Oh, you have a retrograde Mercury; that means that you couldn't communicate with anyone in a past life and now you are paying off your karma." You can't be glib with karmic placements, and you will not help your relationship with anyone by announcing that they have karmic debts. Gentle description is the best approach. The water signs—Cancer, Scorpio, and Pisces—are very receptive to psychic impressions and vibrations. They also can have thin boundaries and a difficult time discerning the difference between their own imagination and wisdom from a higher source. Also, charts with mutable signs on the angles remember every critical or negative word that is ever said to them. If you are counseling someone who is a water sign with mutable signs on the angles, tread carefully. If this describes your chart, then learn to listen with discernment, for you can be easily influenced.

Remember, no one has studied at your personal Karmic University, and advice from other people about past lives and the lives to come is highly speculative. But when you instinctively feel, "Aha, that's why I behave in this manner" or "That's why this happened," then that person or book has given you a real message on which you can build.

RETROGRADE MERCURY

Retrograde Mercury indicates that in many past lives, a person's manner of communicating was unique and often not clear to other people. They may have been liars or people who exaggerated the truth. These people must take special pains to say what they mean and mean what they say. Retrograde Mercury frequently describes a person with an impractical approach to life. Writing ability is indicated. This is a good activity for retrograde Mercury people as the effort to write thoughts down helps focus the mind and can clarify the person's true feelings.

RETROGRADE VENUS

Retrograde Venus in a chart reveals that a person neglected affections in a past life. They may have been personally cold or ignorant about expressing simple and genuine affection. This placement can also indicate austerity and neglect of some of the more refined aspects of life. The image of Scrooge comes to mind. Because Venus rules two signs, Taurus and Libra, the sign position will tell you what type of austerity and aesthetic neglect is emphasized.

RETROGRADE MARS

Retrograde Mars can indicate misuse of energy and passion in past lives. Perhaps the person was a coward when bravery was needed, or perhaps they dissipated their abilities by excessive timidity and insecurity. Proper assertion and sense of self is the test for this lifetime. Retrograde Mars can also indicate stockpiling anger and then exploding during inopportune moments. A person who has a retrograde Mars must learn to handle aggression effectively.

RETROGRADE JUPITER

Retrograde Jupiter indicates a test of expansion in life. In a past life, perhaps this person did not experience much of anything: They were content to stay in place and not explore the abilities and talents indicated by the chart. This time around, they are invited to taste different experiences and choose activities that will contribute to the soul's development. Retrograde Jupiter also frequently describes a person who is on a philosophical quest in life and one who searches for a homeland. On an everyday level, a retrograde Jupiter can indicate problems in attracting resources.

RETROGRADE SATURN

Retrograde Saturn offers a person lessons in addressing neglected responsibilities. Perhaps because of fear or laziness, this person gave up on marriage, business ventures, parenting, or leadership positions where people counted on him or her. The current lifetime will offer many of the same situations in the hopes that this person will take the chance to grow in self-knowledge by accepting life's challenges. In the body, retrograde Saturn can indicate rigid, defensive patterns that prevent the free flow of feelings.

THE OUTER PLANETS RETROGRADE

The outer planets—Uranus, Neptune, and Pluto—are frequently retrograde in people's charts. The impact of these planets is not always significant, as many people are not as sensitive to the effect of these planets. For a person on the path of self-knowledge, retrogrades of the outer planets mean that as that person grows in higher consciousness, issues of the outer planets become an essential part of his or her chart. Uranus retrograde is concerned with questions regarding freedom and obligation. Retrograde Neptune poses questions in the area of spiritual awakenings versus delusion and deceit. And our friend Pluto looks at the karmic debts of power abused.

ASPECTS AS KARMIC INDICATORS

You have learned about applying and separating aspects in other areas of chart interpretation. In terms of karma and the hidden chart, the number of applying aspects has special significance. The applying aspects and the planets receiving them are involved with the experiences you are attracting in this lifetime to create your blueprint for the next life. These aspects are sowing karma, and according to the quality of how you use them, you are planting seeds for the future. The separating aspects show what you have finished up and mastered. When there are more separating aspects than applying ones, you are in a "finishing up" lifetime.

When applying aspects dominate, a person is beginning with a slate that is almost clean. If you notice this in your chart, you might want to be as mindful of your actions as you can be, for the quality of this life will map out the quality of future lives for a long time to come. If, however, a person is a water sign or has mutable signs on the angles, this advice will inhibit and frighten them. It is better to give this person confidence for the future and let them do as they will.

It is also important to note whether aspects are in predominantly cardinal, fixed, or mutable signs. The cardinal signs are active and carry recent karmic energy from the previous life, which can be changed by constructive action. The fixed signs are definite and strong; the habits they describe are deeply embedded and acquired over many lifetimes. These take a lot of patience to change. The mutable signs are flexible and easier to work with. They have characteristics that are just beginning and can be changed more easily. When there are trines in a chart, these indicate talents and abilities that a person brings over from previous lifetimes. Such a person will never have to work hard to develop these gifts; they are part of the bounty that they achieved in the past.

PAST LIVES AND THE LIFE TO COME

In addition to revealing information on the present incarnation, an astrology chart includes information about past and future lives. Astrologers make the assumption that a person chooses his or her parents and the moment of birth so that the perfect chart occurs to direct this lifetime. When I tell clients that they have chosen their parents, many roll their eyes and shake their heads as if to say, "Why would I choose such bozos?" You can't query your karma; you can only live it and accept that there is a larger plan than you are aware of on a day-to-day basis. In the most difficult family relationships, there is growth, knowledge, and the opportunity to learn about your soul. Maybe next time around you will choose a harmonious family and spend a lifetime reaping the benefits of growth from *this* difficult life. Part of your job may be to understand what was not happy with your family and transcend it. Of course, the chart points out the right way for you.

If you have an accurately timed chart, the sign prior to the ascendant—or the sign on the Twelfth House cusp—was probably your ascendant for the previous incarnation. The lifetime before that corresponds to the sign on the Eleventh House, then the Tenth House, and continues around the wheel counterclockwise to understand all the past-life possibilities. For example, if you have Capricorn rising in this life, one part of your life lesson is to incorporate a seriousness and steadiness you may have neglected when Sagittarius (the sign on the Twelfth House cusp) was your rising sign. The lifetime before that was influenced by the sign on the Eleventh House cusp. Identifying these signs is only the beginning of tracing and understanding past lives. You can meditate on the meanings of each previous incarnation by noting the strengths and weaknesses of those signs.

When there are planets located in the Twelfth House, which represent the most recent prior lifetime, these planets indicate carryover lessons to this lifetime. For example, when the Sun is in the Twelfth

House, frequently the soul remembers much of the past life and has trouble shining in this life because the personality feels like it must travel a long way. The Sun here also means that the ego dominated in past lives and now the soul needs the experience of selfless service.

When other personal planets are in the Twelfth House with tough aspects, this is another indication of past-life residue. Use your knowledge of the core meanings of the signs and aspects to construct a picture of what these past-life indications could mean for you, your clients, or your circle of friends and loved ones.

SOUL MATES

Frequently, in romantic relationships and marriage, people who get together have been connected before in a past life. The term *soul mate* is used commonly to express having a relationship with someone where there is a special harmony, sympathy, or connection that goes beyond the boundaries of many love relationships. Sometimes this word is used casually because someone is in love and experiences the thrill of basking in that glow. Sometimes someone says the other person is his or her soul mate because they can't explain how deeply they feel for the other person, regardless of whether that feeling is returned and whether the other person is a good or suitable partner.

In addition to the general use of the term *soul mate*, there is a specific definition. This is when two souls have been connected before birth and are split into two different bodies. This is a rare situation. When or if you encounter this other soul, you will feel a sense of recognition and commonality, as if you have found a part of yourself. It is unusual, however, to form a relationship with this person, because your life path and lessons are similar enough that there is not sufficient friction and charge to create the situations that each person needs for growth.

There is also a term called *astrological twins* for people born on the same date, place, and time, but in different families.

If astrological twins meet, it is usually interesting to trace common themes and development, but interest wanes quickly because there is not enough new ground to cover. Astrological twins rarely form a romantic relationship.

The more common use of the term *soul mate* is to designate a relationship with someone with whom there is a very close bond and where there are connections that are mutually beneficial for each person's soul development. This is where karma and relationships can get sticky. People sometimes feel connected to others even when the relationship is extremely challenging. I know couples that have been married for a long time and are always on the verge of divorce. The popular term *codependent* may be the reason couples like this stick together, but it also can be a karmic lesson that both people need to work out before they can move on. The bond is made of love, but through habit and past-life remnants, the love has changed into a habitual pattern of unkindness. Usually the problem is a power dynamic; one person wields power and the other person feels dependent, resulting in an imbalanced relationship.

Does it feel like you are permanently trapped in a wheel of difficult love and romantic relationships? Will true love and romance ever be yours? Will people never give you what you want? Love is the generator for all of life. When a relationship must change because it no longer fits with a person's life path, the love doesn't evaporate; it goes in a different direction. The degree to which you carry a person in your heart will nourish your life. If you have to separate or divorce, try with as much strength and good grace as possible to accept that some part of your soul development called this situation for you both to grow.

The astrological indications for relationships that are karmically based between two people are a Sun/Moon conjunction, or Saturn or Pluto in conjunction, opposition, or square with another's Sun, Moon, Venus, or Mars. When these aspects appear, you need to examine each of the charts to gain a more complete picture of the person's karmic story. As with all astrological aspects, the closer the aspects, the more intense the relationship will be.

Karmic relationships between people do not necessarily mean that they were married or romantically involved in a past life. The relationship could be teacher and pupil, parent and child, siblings, close friends, or enemies. Frequently, a person was a different gender in a previous life and has incarnated as another gender this time around because it affords the best platform for understanding and realizing this person's karmic plan. As you look at your relationships, see if you can identify through examining the astrological correspondences what a likely past-life scenario might be. For example, in Jack's and Jane's charts with Jack's Saturn exactly conjunct Jane's Mars, it would make sense to imagine that in a past life, Jack was an authority figure, perhaps a father to Jane. In Jane's past life, however, she could have been a boy (Mars) who needed, but was unable, to rebel against his father. Now, in this present lifetime, Jane has another chance to assert herself, but this time as a wife. Jack still wields authority, but Jane is an adult and has abilities of her own to cope with the power dynamics. With practice you will be able to note similar scenarios to explain some of the puzzling and interesting facets of your own relationships and of those you read for.

KARMIC ASSISTANCE

Although you are the best caretaker of your karma, there are techniques and people who can help your evolution. People have different soul levels of development. An old soul incorporates many experiences and skills because it has lived longer than a new soul. Your chart can teach you some things about your soul level. When there are many separating aspects with the outer planets—Uranus, Neptune, and Pluto—a soul may have gone through many incarnations. If most of the aspects in a chart are between the personal planets, then the soul is possibly newly minted and is undergoing experiences that are putting it on a path toward spiritual evolution.

When you consult with an astrologer or reader of any kind and the subject of your karma or life lessons is discussed, it is important to intuit whether this person has something to offer you. By this, I mean that only someone who is more experienced and more evolved can assist you in your growth. That said, in addition to astrologers, there are talented practitioners who perform past-life regressions, energy balancing, and hypnotherapy. These practitioners can help you access information about your karma and past lives. Past-life regression with an experienced, reputable professional can clear out karmic debris and free up energy for the current lifetime. Channelers may also be helpful to you with this information. It can be difficult to find a qualified professional in channeling, healing, or astrology, so a client must rely on recommendations, thorough research, and personal intuition when consulting these practitioners.

Another technique that can be helpful to you is energy rebirthing. This is a breathing practice where a trained professional can help you resolve issues of birth in the present life or in any other life using only your breath. It may be very cathartic and help root out deep-seated energy problems. Look at the back of this book for some resources for you to find healers who practice some of these therapies mentioned.

Another time-tested technique is meditation. There are many systems and ideas of how to meditate, but they are all mostly based on the idea of focusing the mind on the breath or on one idea, word, or color. As the person begins to contact deeper areas of relaxation, integration from all past and present lives can occur. Meditation takes practice but will help you in all areas of your life.

Lastly, in thinking about working with your particular karmic issues, here is a helpful practice. It is a Tibetan or Tibetan Buddhist prayer for forgiveness. This prayer can help resolve relationship problems that have become intractable and seemingly unsolvable. Say the prayer, with an image of the person you need to forgive in your mind, for forty consecutive nights before going to sleep.

*I freely forgive*_____*for any wrongdoing he/she has done to me in this life or in any other, and I hope for*_____ *between us.*

The second part is perhaps more difficult.

I freely forgive myself for any wrongdoing I have done to _____ *in this life or in any other, and I hope for*_____ *between us.*

Try this and see where you can sow forgiveness in your own life. It can't hurt.

Karmic indicators can be the most elusive and interesting parts of a chart. As you grow in your astrological knowledge, this area of study may become more and more fascinating to you. It is one of the most fertile and rewarding areas of astrology and can lead you to contemplate many areas of life that no other study offers.

In the next two chapters, you will learn ways to refine and use all the information you have learned so far. Your understanding of the hidden chart can inform these techniques also. Astrology concerns all life: from the smallest query to the largest event.

CHAPTER EIGHT

REFINING YOUR ASTROLOGICAL KNOWLEDGE

In all the previous chapters, you have learned basic and advanced techniques to apply to the art of chart interpretation. There are even more clues that will help you understand subtleties in a chart and expand the way you apply your astrological knowledge. You can practice astrology to better understand yourself and those who are close to you, but at times a chart is puzzling, or you may need to make fine and subtle distinctions between charts. Or sometimes you look at a chart for a particular event and cannot find any obvious correspondences in either the transits or progressions. It is interesting to start digging to see if there is a planetary signature in some of the subtler areas of chart interpretation.

The following extras will further refine your knowledge. Please don't feel that you have to memorize a list of all the fixed stars, decanates, and asteroids. You can use this book (or any of the books I've listed at the back of this book) as a reference. It is important, however, to be aware of this facet of astrology.

CRITICAL DEGREES

Each of the triplicities has certain degrees that are considered critical. This means that any planet or house cusp located at these degrees registers strongly throughout a person's life. When a planet is located in a critical degree, pay attention to this planet. All transits and aspects involving that planet will affect the person more than a planet in noncritical degrees. The concept of critical degrees comes to us from Hindu, or Vedic, astrology and is based on the complete cycle of the Moon as she passes through the 360 degrees of a circle. The cycle is called the Mansions of the Moon. The entire use and meaning of these degrees has been lost, but what is used in Western astrology is noting the following degrees as having particular significance. The critical degrees for the cardinal signs are 0, 13, and 26 degrees. For fixed signs, the critical degrees are 9 and 21 degrees, and for mutable signs, they are 4 and 17 degrees. It is best to memorize these degrees and be on the lookout for them in any chart you are casting.

In Chart 7, Saturn is located at 8♌53. Technically, at 8 degrees and 53 minutes, it is almost 9 degrees, but it still falls within the parameters; it is in a fixed sign, which renders the degree critical. Saturn will influence this person's life strongly. This is positive for this individual because, with the heavy concentration of Scorpio and the potential for self-destructive behavior, Saturn is a calming and sobering influence. In Chart 4, Pluto at 21♌ is critical. Pluto in a critical degree and conjunct the Moon is a dynamic and dramatic combination. Pluto can be a dark planet, which promotes great transformation; this person will have a battle with impulses between creation and destruction. Pluto in critical degrees reinforces this planetary theme and alerts you to pay attention to all transits that aspect Pluto. In many cases, noting which degrees are critical highlights information that is outlined by other aspects.

FIXED STARS

In ancient times, a fixed star was so named to distinguish it from a wandering star or planet. The motion of the planets could be traced long before the advent of the telescope, but the fixed stars moved so slowly that they appeared to be stationary. Throughout the history of astrology, various interpretations have gathered around certain fixed stars. They are thought to be either extremely beneficial or malevolent. If you note a planet close to the degrees of a fixed star, the orb must not be more than 1 or 2 degrees. A conjunction with a fixed star highlights this planet, and if you have any planet exactly conjunct a fixed star, it means that planet has a special role to play in a person's life. Many of the names of the fixed stars, such as Algenib, El Nath, or Caphir, come to us from Arabian astrologers. Not all the fixed stars are considered relevant today, but I want to outline a few of the most prominent, which I have noticed do have interpretative value in people's charts. The positions of fixed stars have moved forward and are no longer at their original degree placement. However, there is interpretive value in examining any planet located on the original position as well as the progressed position. The following interpretations are for the stars as they were identified by the ancient astrologers.

One fixed star originally located at 19 degrees 19 minutes of Scorpio is called Serpentis. Ancient astrologers called this position the "accursed degree of the accursed sign." Lest you faint if you have a planet on this degree, rest assured I have known many people with this position who are living and thriving. The ancient description is needlessly dramatic. Serpentis does involve a person's use of sexual energy; this fixed star encourages people to lead with seduction. Such people are very aware of the innuendos and nuances of sexual energy between individuals and feel strongly about asserting their own sexuality.

Other malevolent fixed stars are Antares at 9 degrees Sagittarius, the Ascelli in 6 Leo, and the Pleiades in 29 Taurus. Older books state with the Pleiades that there will be something to weep about. Caput Algol in 24 Taurus is considered to be the evilest of all fixed stars. If you notice a planet in a chart at 24 Taurus, or Caput Algol's current position, it is worth taking extra safety precautions in life, because it can mean being more susceptible to accidents. Many of the ancient interpretations of the fixed stars read like a diary of doom. Here is a description of the fixed star Procyon located at 25♋41 taken from Nicholas de Vore's *Encyclopedia of Astrology*:

This position brings:

> *Sudden preferment, the result of individual exertion; yet eventually the activity it promotes brings sudden misfortune. Afflictions threaten trouble with and danger through liquids, water, gas, poison, or dog bites. When rising, said to inspire admiration for the canine species.*

If I noticed this star in a person's chart, I might ask if the person had any relationships with dogs, but I wouldn't be surprised if they said they hadn't. Investigate how these positions appear in charts and you will be able to temper classical interpretations with your own experience.

you can glean very good information about creating a supportive world for each sign. In addition to the Sun sign, look at the Moon and Venus. The Moon will tell you what atmosphere is comfortable emotionally, and Venus will tell you what kinds of luxuries and aesthetics a person likes to have around them.

Using astrology in this manner may not solve psychological or financial problems, but it can increase delight and joy in life, and that can go a long way to smoothing difficulties. The following is a brief description of each sign and their preferred environment. For more detail, take a look at my first book, *The Hidden Power of Everyday Things*. You also might want to look at my book *Instant Wall Art: Astrological Designs*. This book features three prints of different views of your sign and suggestions on how to decorate with the artwork.

ARIES

Aries loves red, other bright colors, and vibrant atmospheres. Noise doesn't bother him; in fact, he prefers any kind of music, traffic noises, or background sounds to silence. Fireplaces or outdoor barbecues are especially pleasing to this first fire sign. Spicy food or charbroiled meats appeal to Aries. Fashion accessories usually include caps or hats. Gems of importance to Aries are diamonds and malachite.

TAURUS

Taurus likes quiet sensuality in the home. Classical design with lots of soft fabrics and plush furniture give the Bull the right feeling. There is a pack rat tendency, as Taurus loves possessions. The kitchen is an area of focus, and many Taureans are very good cooks. The color palette is usually pale with an emphasis on turquoise or pink. Bronze sculptures may hold special appeal. Taurus enjoys sweets, rich foods, and anything with sauces. A scarf around the neck is a good accessory and prudent, as Taurus should always keep her throat protected.Taurus's gem is a clear green emerald.

GEMINI

Gemini loves windows, lots of space, and ceiling fans. Gemini needs to have a constant flow of air in the environment. Good colors for Gemini are pale blue and yellow. There are usually too many things going on in Gemini's life for him to worry about cooking, but if he had to choose, he would prefer milder-tasting foods. Clothes that are flowing and unrestrictive usually appeal to Gemini. Gemini's gemstones are blue zircon and aquamarine.

CANCER

Home, home, and more home is the focal point for Cancer. The style could vary, but it is the consistency of having a dependable home that Cancer finds essential. Usually Cancer prefers cozy spaces. She may feel most comfortable at night. Black, white, gray, and silver are soothing colors. A view of the water, an aquarium, or an indoor fountain keeps Moon children balanced. Salty foods and cheeses usually are appealing to Cancer. Cancer's gems are pearls and moonstone.

LEO

Leo wants a regal atmosphere at home with lots of sunlight. A large special chair is almost always featured. Oranges, yellows, and bright pinks contribute to a happy atmosphere for Leo. You will notice that most Leos spend a good deal of time grooming their hair; hair products are an essential part of Leo's environment. Leo usually likes spicy food and may have a special fondness for walnuts. Leo gems include ruby, cat's-eye, and amber.

VIRGO

Understated and classical is Virgo's style. No bright colors, but everything is usually expensive and well tailored. At home, there is usually a sense of quiet organization. When Virgo is messy, she still knows where to find whatever she needs. Due to a sensitive digestive system, Virgo needs basic and slightly bland food. Chili peppers are not her friends. Gemstones for Virgo are pearls and jasper.

LIBRA

Whatever environment Libra creates must be beautiful and symmetrical. Libra prefers pastel colors and nothing jarring in the environment. For clothing, Libras of both sexes love silk. Their favorite colors are pastel greens and lilac. Many Libras may have copper trays or decorative objects in their homes. No matter what tastes Libra enjoys, the important aspect of food is in its presentation. Even when pizza is for dinner, Libra will enjoy setting the table with china and linen napkins. Libra's gem is opal.

SCORPIO

Scorpio needs emblems of whatever she creates around her in her space. Her home is usually kept private and filled with possessions. Clear crystal and keepsake boxes may be objects that she particularly treasures. Scorpio's colors are black, maroon, chocolate brown, and white. Tastes range from very spicy international food to well-cured meats. A Scorpio cook is usually very accomplished. Scorpios don't usually follow fashion, although they may very well create their own distinct style. However Scorpios put themselves together, they will keep that style, refine it, and then when they feel they have had enough of it, change it. Scorpio gems are onyx and garnet.

SAGITTARIUS

Sagittarius needs a large uncluttered space with lots of light. Rich colors like blue, purple, and green suit Sagittarius, and he may have a particular fondness for velvet. Furniture or decorative objects tend to be large in the Sagittarian home. Preferred tastes are all the warm spices of winter such as cinnamon and nutmeg. Sagittarius may be too busy to cook, but if he slows down and focuses, the results are quite good and generous; a Sagittarian host will never be stingy with hospitality. Sagittarian stones are topaz and sapphire.

CAPRICORN

The Capricorn style is usually conservative and slightly formal. Capricorn favors ivory colors and earth tones with perhaps a few splashes of vibrancy. Capricorns tend to surround themselves with photographs of family members and even ancestors. Capricorn rules all rocks and stones. Marble or granite in the kitchen or a special rock garden would be very positive for Capricorn. Her gemstones are turquoise and amethyst.

AQUARIUS

The outrageous and unusual is common for a true Aquarian. Aquarians who are influenced by Saturn will tend to be more conservative, but the Uranus-influenced Aquarius will always have his unique style. Electric blue and multicolored garments suit this sign. He may also have a preference for large hats. In décor, Aquarius might have a very cluttered apartment or home and then throw everything out and have one camp chair. Tastes in food and fashion are eclectic. Aquarius gemstones are aquamarine and lapis lazuli.

PISCES

Dreamy, cozy, and private qualities typify Pisces's favorite environment. The home must offer a place to retreat. Colors for Pisces are sea green and purple. There is a tendency for Pisces to wear black-and-white combinations. A good music and home entertainment center is a focal point for Pisces, as music and films are a prime way to relax. Pisces really enjoys seafood and fish. Her gemstones are amethyst and sapphire.

I hope in this chapter that you have learned some creative and interesting ideas on how to use astrology in different ways. Next, we will thoroughly analyze a specific chart. This will give you an idea of how to apply what you have learned.

CHAPTER NINE

ANALYSIS OF A CHART

Now let's go through a chart that I haven't analyzed yet and see how astrology describes this person's life. We will use Chart 8, and, for the purpose of this analysis, call the native "Lina." First, look at the whole chart. The first thing that jumps out is the concentration of planets in the Twelfth House. Right away, we know that Lina is extremely empathetic and is likely involved in service to people who are less fortunate. The second planetary placement worth noting is her Moon in Taurus at the top of the chart near the midheaven. Also, notice that most of the planets are on the eastern, or ascendant, side of the chart. In hemisphere division, if the majority of planets are on the eastern side of a chart, that person has more control over the course of their life. They achieve their goals by direct action. When most of the planets are on the western side of the chart, events happen through the backdoor. In other words, a person may be going directly toward their goal, but in the end, something is accomplished by means of other people. Without examining any elements or planetary placements, we know Lina will be of service and will pursue her goals directly. In addition, with the Moon at the top of the chart, she will be involved in communicating and sharing her feelings with large groups of people.

ELEMENTS

Next, you will want to study the elements. The major element is earth with 5 points (2 points for the Moon, 1 point for the midheaven, and 1 point each for Venus and Mars), followed by fire, air, and water, with 3 points each. As discussed in Chapter 1, these calculations are made by assigning 1 point for each sign and giving 2 points to the signs that the Sun and Moon are in, and giving 1 point for the ascendant and the midheaven when analyzing the elements. This point system is for the elemental balance. For the quadruplicities, we use only the planets and their signs and do not include the midheaven and ascendant. This is a fairly balanced chart for the elements. The earth dominance tells us that Lina is a sensual person, is fond of good food, and is a concrete, practical, and Earth Mother type of person. The balance with her other elements supports her basic good health and steady energy. Next are the quadruplicities: She has four cardinal signs (4 points), 3 points for the number of fixed signs, and 3 points for her mutable signs. Now you need to do some refined astrological sleuthing. Her Sun is at the very end of Cancer, close to Leo, and both the midheaven and ascendant are in fixed signs. Although judging her chart strictly by the point system would seem to suggest she is a cardinal go-getter, we need to add a good dose of fixity, which indicates tremendous drive, steadiness, and a tendency to be stubborn. The mutable signs in Lina's chart give her some flexibility, which helps with the fixed signs' rigidity. Note the yin and yang balance: The chart has five yin signs (Moon, Saturn, Sun, Venus, and Mars), and four yang (Pluto, Mercury, Neptune, Jupiter). We do not give 2 points for Sun and Moon in yin/yang balance nor do we count the asteroids or nodes or part of fortune signs. She is equally at home with receptive and assertive energy. Next, look in the ephemeris for her prenatal eclipses, which are a solar eclipse at 6♋49 and a lunar eclipse at 23♏05. Note that these eclipse points fall in the Eleventh and Fifth houses, respectively, and will be important positions when planets transit them. There are always two eclipses, a lunar and solar eclipse, before a child is born. You should note these on your worksheet as they are sensitive points in a chart and if aspected by transiting planets or an eclipse they will be significant for that year.

PLANETS IN CRITICAL DEGREES

Next, turn your attention to any planets in critical degrees. The most important one is the Moon at 21♉. Also, Taurus is the sign of the Moon's exaltation. This further dignifies and emphasizes the Moon's prominence and influence in the chart. The Moon is the only planet in critical degrees, and there are no obvious fixed stars. Next, you want to judge the strength of the planetary positions. The Moon is exalted, Mercury is in his fall in Leo, and Venus is in her fall in Virgo. These two personal planets in fall means Lina will have some adjustments to make in communication and in expressing affection. The retrograde position of Mercury further emphasizes lessons in communication. Note that Mercury is the only retrograde planet and turned direct when Lina was twenty-one. For this and other astrological reasons that you have learned, twenty-one should have been a significant year. None of her other planets are retrograde, and no planet turns retrograde in her progressed chart. There are also no intercepted signs. This is all fortunate for Lina.

Pluto in the Twelfth House indicates that much of Lina's personal power is expressed by serving and helping other people. Her own ego may sometimes feel neglected because she is in the shadows of the Twelfth House, but she will grow in consciousness and in spiritual development the more she serves others.

Neptune in the Second House slightly mitigates the fortunate position of Venus and Mars in the house of money and personal values. Lina can earn and attract enough money for herself and her family's needs, but she may be a little hazy with investments or financial schemes. Neptune is also so close to the Third House of siblings and extended family that she may become involved financially with family matters that cost a lot of money and are a business and spiritual challenge. If I were speaking with her about her chart, I would tell her to keep her eyes out for any kind of business dealings with family members where there might need to be cooperation in money matters.

ASPECTS

Now let's fill in the aspectarian. Lina's chart has a total of twenty-three aspects, and most of them are soft and are either trines, sextiles, or semisextiles. In fact, the sextile is the most prominent aspect of her chart. This means that life will present her with many opportunities, and she will be able to take advantage of them because there is basic flow in her chart. Lina also has all of her planets on the eastern side of the chart; you may recall that this means that a person can directly pursue their goals without depending on intermediaries. The second most common aspect is the semisextile, which reinforces the friendly, neighborly dimension of Lina's personality. She doesn't get too flustered by everyday activities.

The two trines between the Moon and Mars and Jupiter and Uranus are interesting. Moon trine Mars in the earth element means that she is steady in her affections and feelings and that she can assert herself easily. Jupiter trine Uranus brings in a dimension of power and insight into her communication abilities and insights from the "higher mind." I would interpret this as part of her ability to pray and receive guidance and nurturing from her spiritual commitment. The hard aspects are three squares and three of the four conjunctions. Let's look at the squares, which show the tensions and action in the chart. The Moon is square Mercury and suggests tension in getting her message across and feelings of being misunderstood. Venus square Uranus is known as the divorce aspect, and Lina did divorce her first husband when she was quite young. The more challenging aspect is the close aspect between Mars and Uranus, two malefic planets. This is the central tension in the chart and betokens a strong temper and energy that can be expressed erratically and potentially explosively.

You will see when we look at the details of Lina's life that she has worked around people less fortunate than herself all her life. She has worked with violent criminals in prisons, and the square between Mars and Uranus could be interpreted as indicating a person who can withstand such an environment—and even thrive in it—because it helps balance her own energy. I do not mean that if she hadn't worked in a prison she would have become a criminal, just that this is an intense aspect and needs an equally intense focus in life to express itself. The energies that a chart indicates fight for expression, and the most interesting part of life is watching how people use the planetary gifts they have.

The conjunctions in Lina's chart are also intriguing. Venus and Mars are conjunct in Virgo, and this indicates harmony between her yin and yang energies. Virgo is also the sign of service, reiterating the career and spiritual path that she has chosen. The conjunction between the Sun and Saturn is the closest aspect. This lends seriousness to Lina's personality and means she could be prone to depression. One reason that she works so successfully with less fortunate people is that it helps her to place her focus on others rather than herself. The Sun is also part of a very wide conjunction with Pluto, and Pluto is conjunct Mercury. This is a powerful combination of planets and informs her entire chart. She is a strong communicator when expressing her spiritual beliefs. She also has the ability to help others transform themselves through her beliefs and commitment to service. For Lina, the very act of connecting with her religion is transformative for herself and other people. She may not receive the world's attention for her efforts, but she will have a lasting effect on others.

Lastly, there are eleven applying aspects and eleven separating aspects, a perfect balance between finishing up issues from past lives and sowing new seeds for the present and future. There are no aspect patterns.

ENERGY DYNAMICS

Once you have listed all this information, you will have a good idea what the energy dynamics of the chart are. Then look at the planets in the signs and which houses they are located in. We already discussed the prominent Twelfth House. To refine your understanding of Lina's life, you also need to look at the planets in the Second, Third, Tenth, and Eleventh houses as well as the signs ruling the empty houses. Empty houses do not mean a lack of activity therein; they do mean that to find out what is influencing that house, you should locate where and what the planetary ruler of that house is. That will tell you more about the influences for that house.

NODES

At this point in your analysis, look at the Moon's nodes, their house positions, and what they outline for this person's life lessons and karma. While you are examining karmic indicators, take a look at Saturn, the retrograde Mercury, and the Twelfth House. The south node is in Sagittarius and the north node in Gemini conjunct Uranus. The Sagittarius south node indicates lifetimes of restlessness and rash decisions that emphasized personal freedom rather than communication and focused concentration. Located in the Fifth House, Lina's children may not offer the solace and comfort that she would have liked, and they may pursue very different goals and ideals. However, the north node in Gemini points her toward communicating her learned optimism with groups of people and adopted family.

WAS IT ACCURATE?

Now, let's see if Lina's chart accurately reflects her life. Lina, at age seventeen, went on a religious retreat sponsored by her high school. She had an epiphany and realized that she "was called" to working with children and adults with disabilities. That sounds like a good description of the Twelfth House to me. Her first job was teaching in a boys' alternative school. After that, the majority of her working life was within the prison system, teaching convicts and then working as an administrator for other teachers within the state prison system. She said that she loved her work.

Lina then entered divinity school and studied to be a minister. She communicates the Word of God through her preaching and parish work. With this activity, she is both transmuting any past-life problems from the retrograde Mercury by dedicating her speech and thoughts to a spiritual source *and* using the power of her Tenth House Moon to share her views and feelings with groups of people.

The Third House emphasis is illustrated by her very strong connections to her sisters, brother, and extended family. She is the youngest of four children but is the diplomat of the family. Jupiter in Libra in the Third House describes her fair way of assessing each family member's point of view. The position of Neptune, which could be a warning of financial dealings with family members, describes, in fact, co-ownership with her sisters and brother of a family home by the sea. Neptune indicates the sea, and this home is the focal point for the entire extended family. So far, there have not been any financial problems or fraud between the siblings; thus, the meaning of Neptune in the Second House may be an indication that the siblings have a spiritual bond that requires a lot of communication and patience.

PERSONAL LIFE

We haven't said anything about Lina's personal life yet. With Aquarius in the Seventh House of marriage and Mercury opposite the descendant, a marriage with a lot of independence is the best type for Lina. Many times, Aquarius on the Seventh House indicates divorce. Lina married young for the first time in 1969 and divorced in 1971. The Venus square Uranus aspect reiterates the potential for divorce. In December 1972, she married again and has now been married to the same person for almost fifty years. That is a solid record. What do you think the chart indicates about children? First, Lina's Sun at 29 degrees Cancer is a cusp position. She has the strong maternal instincts indicated by Cancer and, with the Leo influence, is a leader within her family. The Moon in Taurus is a fertile Moon. Regarding the Fifth House of children, Jupiter, the ruler of Sagittarius, rules the cusp, and she has the south node in Sagittarius in the Fifth House. The south node is usually not a positive indicator for good fortune in any house, and Sagittarius is not usually a child-oriented sign. Also, you see the asteroid, Pallas Athena, in the Fifth House indicating creative abilities, through either having children or expressing artistic talents. Jupiter, the ruler of the Fifth House, is in Libra, and you know that Venus rules Libra and Taurus. So there is a positive connection between the Fifth House's ruler and Lina's Moon in a fertile sign, Taurus. Therefore, children are indicated in the chart. Lina and her second husband have three kids, and the only problem indicator as signified by the south node was that all the births were by unplanned caesarean section (she suffered no complications, and as this procedure is so common now, it almost does not merit mention).

Let's also look at the Eleventh House, where you see the north node conjunct Uranus. The Eleventh House rules adopted and foster children, and the coupling of Uranus (Aquarius's sign) with the north node means that Lina has a strong belief in extending herself to children. She and her family have frequently hosted kids from disadvantaged areas for the summer, and they have been involved with many groups of children throughout her life.

OTHER POINTS

Other points of interest in the chart include a love of travel, described by Aries in the Ninth House. A fire sign on the Ninth House always enjoys the stimulation that travel brings. Scorpio on the Fourth House cusp shows Lina's tenacity in maintaining family roots and traditions and the strong ties she has with her parents and extended family. Lina's parents divorced when she was quite young, but she and her brother and sisters keep in touch with her father's second wife and children and maintain a close relationship with her mother's second husband. She has expended a lot of effort to keep family ties strong. Her health picture is basically good, with Capricorn in the Sixth House, but with all those planets in Cancer and Leo, she must guard against eating too many sweets and gaining weight. When the Moon's position is applying to that of the Sun's, it is more likely for a person to put on weight easily. The Taurus Moon also predisposes a person to a sweet tooth. Lina has battled weight problems much of her life. She was also an active drinker in the past. The Twelfth House of the natural wheel is ruled by Pisces, and you remember Pisces can be interpreted both as indicating spiritual influences and escapist influences. Both are part of Lina's life, but in 1992, she worked on becoming sober and has been so ever since. Not drinking is also good preventive health. Both Venus and Mars in Lina's chart are in Virgo, which rules digestion and assimilation. As she gets older, she will have to take care with what she eats, as she will become increasingly sensitive to toxins. You now have a good basic understanding of Lina's chart and personality.

TRANSITS

Now, take a look at the transits for key events in Lina's life. I am only going to explore the relationship between the transits and her natal chart. If you also examine the progressed chart, you will see further confirmation for the meanings of these transits. I want to keep this simple so you can see that with the basics of natal astrology and transits, you can learn a lot and accurately perceive meaningful events in a person's life. If you want to do extended research on a chart, look at the progressions and transits.

Lina said on a winter retreat when she was seventeen that she felt strongly that she was called to work with children with disabilities. If you look in your ephemeris for December 1963 and note the position of the transpersonal planets and outer planets, they perfectly describe someone finding a mission and sense of purpose. Jupiter is at 9 degrees Aries in Lina's Ninth House at this time, indicating that she is expanding her philosophy and mental horizons. Also, Jupiter is moving toward an opposition with her natal Jupiter. The Third House is the everyday mind and the Ninth House, the higher mind. A feeling of "being called" is a religious experience and is part of the provenance of the Ninth House. Then you see that Saturn is moving up from the midnight, or nadir, part of the chart across the descendant and into the Seventh House of partnership. Frequently, when Saturn moves from below the horizon to above the horizon, a person feels drawn to activities that bring him or her into prominent contact with groups of people, mentors, or sponsors.

Uranus is moving toward a direct conjunction with Venus. This could be a sudden falling-in-love event, or in Lina's case, a revelation about how to express her love for kids who have disabilities. Neptune is at 16 degrees of Scorpio and opposite the Moon, which might describe a brush with divine love and spiritual feelings rather than personal feelings. And since Neptune was transiting through the Fourth House, these feelings took root in Lina's heart and soul and mapped out much of her future life path. Lastly, Pluto was moving to a conjunction with Mars. This is a powerful transit, and with Lina's natal Pluto in the Twelfth House, her revelation of working with people with disabilities definitely speaks to the way she can best express her power: in service to others.

There are many other transits and events that you could study in Lina's life and see how beautifully the astrological signatures reflect the meaning and timing of these events. Briefly, I want to show you the transits for the birth of her three children. The first, a boy, was born on December 28, 1974; the second, also a boy, was born on July 22, 1976; and the third, a girl, was born on June 14, 1984.

Her first child arrived at the beginning of her Saturn return (age twenty-eight), and the second child arrived when she was just finishing up this cycle. This is a clear indication of the increased responsibilities that a Saturn return can indicate. Also, the progressed Moon, according to the radix system, was for the first child at 00♊56 and for the second child at 26♊58. Gemini and its opposite sign, Sagittarius, are located in Lina's natal chart on the Eleventh and Fifth house axis indicating children. Interestingly, Lina had children only after Mercury, Gemini's ruler, went direct in her progressed chart. Her third child came when she was almost thirty-eight and in a different position in life. She and her husband had good jobs and had learned a great deal about child-rearing from their two sons. Lina's daughter also fit into the Fifth/Eleventh House axis, as she is a Gemini. In terms of the karmic lessons that Lina's nodes outline, her children have helped her develop her ability to communicate optimism and important values. If you examine each one of her children's charts, the sign of Gemini is prominent. Both boys have Gemini Moons, and the girl has a Gemini Sun. The ties with Lina's chart are very clear.

Lina's husband's chart also has very clear connections to each one of their children. In general, this is a very closely involved family. They may have their differences, but they have a strong clan feeling that is supportive and nurturing.

Let's look at what the later transits had in store for Lina. Lina completed her second Saturn return in June 2005. The first Saturn return at age twenty-nine or thirty establishes a person in terms of their own life. An individual is beginning to take responsibility for themselves and for their decisions. The second Saturn return occurs at around age fifty-eight or fifty-nine, and heralds the beginning of the legacy a person leaves to the next generation. This is not a monetary legacy and does not mean that a person is close to death. It is a new phase of life where a person shares the values, insights, loves, work, and achievement that they have accumulated up to this point. Sometimes, the Saturn return is accompanied with retirement from work, or a new work and career focus.

Lina's children were grown at this point, and she retired from her work in the prison system during her second Saturn return. She had pursued her theological studies, and on July 4, 2004, she was installed at her new church and officiated at her first service there. Let's look at the transits for that day and their relationship to Lina's natal chart and some of her progressed planets. The Sun and Saturn were conjunct at 12 degrees and 16 degrees respectively of Cancer. They also were both conjunct the progressed Moon at 10♋51 minutes. In addition, both the progressed Moon and the Minor Moon in Cancer conjunct Lina's prenatal eclipse. This is a definite indication that this event was "meant to be," and is important for Lina's spiritual development. In Lina's chart, all these planetary configurations were in the Eleventh House showing that this event pertained to new responsibilities with groups. With the presence of the progressed Moon, it also meant that Lina felt very emotionally connected to this event. Also transiting Jupiter at 14♍ was coming close to a conjunction with Mars and trine Lina's natal Moon. This is a blessing on the natal Moon/Mars trine with which she was born. Transiting Jupiter was also a few degrees past natal Venus in Virgo. The Moon's position for that July 4 was 26♒ and passing through Lina's Seventh House of partnership. She was, at that time, beginning a new partnership with her congregation, and, of course, Aquarius is the natural ruler of the Eleventh House, which holds transiting Saturn, the Sun, the progressed Moon, and the prenatal eclipse. Do you see how everything fits together?

As the fall of that year progressed, Jupiter would go on to move into Libra on September 25, and Lina would have had a Jupiter return the following September, specifically September 4–6. This may have been a very fruitful time for her work with her church congregation and may have also indicated the beginning of a writing project. In September 2006, Saturn would have completed his motion through the

Twelfth House and would have crossed the ascendant. This is usually a time when much of the spiritual growth indicated by Saturn's sojourn in the Twelfth House comes to light. Saturn crossing the ascendant and moving through Lina's First House emphasizes the seriousness and responsibility of the commitment she had to her church work. She will also come to be known as a wise person. We could also examine other transits, progressions, and the lunar and solar returns to glean more information about Lina's life and events the future held for her.

Lina has now retired from her parish and concentrates on enjoying her five grandchildren and rebuilt house at the shore. In 2012, Hurricane Sandy struck the Jersey Shore. A natural disaster affects people's chart in general, but it is noteworthy that the chart for Sandy (October 29, 2012) formed an exact square with Lina's Sun position. It was an emotional and life obstacle that she *did* overcome; as described by her Jupiter optimism in the Third House of siblings, she and her brother and sisters pulled together and rebuilt. The new house does not have the memories of the old one, but it is more convenient and remains a central location for all her immediate and extended family to gather together.

SUMMARY

This is a comprehensive analysis of Lina's chart. By outlining the major themes indicated by a chart, the astrologer has a clear indication of the strengths and weaknesses of any person. If you were working with Lina's chart, your basic understanding of her "cosmic recipe" would inform all your interpretations for transits and progressions. The most interesting part of astrology is to watch people develop and create their own unique life within the parameters of the chart with which they were born. In the next chapter, you will learn how to apply your knowledge to a variety of questions and to begin to think like an astrologer.

CHAPTER TEN

HOW TO THINK LIKE AN ASTROLOGER

You now have the knowledge to assist yourself, your friends, and your family in living life in tune with cosmic currents. In this chapter, you will put all the pieces together to synthesize your knowledge and apply it to specific questions. Sometimes people ask me if I really believe in all this stuff and if I use it myself. After practicing astrology for more than twenty-five years, and reading more than ten thousand charts, I think like an astrologer about *everything*. I always consider the motions of the planets in living and planning my life. I also consider the planetary placements for interpreting the world around me. When I notice a "vibe" in the air, I frequently check with my ephemeris or astro clock to see what the daily transits are. I consider people's signs in terms of my business dealings with them, and I observe when a professional relationship is difficult or productive to see how the planetary aspects between the two charts reflect this.

On an everyday level, I plan social engagements by looking at the Moon's position. I use astrology to plan trips, especially when traveling by plane. I use astrology for myself and to advise my family regarding health matters. I rest when the Moon is at the end of her cycle, and I never sign documents during retrograde Mercury. I try to be patient with myself when there are difficult transits and to take advantage of opportunities when the planets are forming easy aspects. I observe where the planets were when people told me that something unusual happened. Even people who are not my clients tell me about strange and interesting events. I look at their natal chart—if I know it—and at the transits for the day, and I note the correspondences I see.

For example, a woman called to tell me that on her fiftieth birthday, she decided to register with a matchmaking website. She had been thinking about it for years. She told me that her first response was from an extraordinarily interesting, kind man and that they had begun dating. I looked at their charts and saw that they have good potential for romance and friendship. I am not sure whether he's "the one," and I wouldn't give my opinion at the early stages of a relationship. Uranus, the planet of surprises, was strongly aspecting her chart, and this was a fortunate surprise. I was happy for her that her first venture into something that scared her was successful. I love to hear about people who make a bold decision and then see what planets are influencing them.

I also use astrology to let myself off the hook when I am angry and impatient that everything I want seems hopeless and out of grasp. I comfort myself with the thought that the planets will change. Saturn, for example, won't always be in a tough aspect to my Sun or Moon, and while he is bearing down, I try to be content with lots of work and responsibilities. Let's look at some specific questions and how to implement all the theory you have so diligently studied.

ELECTIONAL ASTROLOGY

One of the ways that you can pinpoint good times for certain activities is to erect a chart for the time you intend to do something and see in advance if the planets are beneficial. If it is an important event, then you should experiment with different times until the chart looks good. This is called *electional astrology*. This practice has been made immeasurably easier by a rectify feature on most astrology programs. Usually when we rectify a chart, it is to determine a natal chart when the birth time is unknown. For a birth chart, this can be a time-consuming process in which you examine known events in a person's life, and based on the timing of those events, you deduce the correct birth time. For an electional chart, the rectify feature allows you to draw up a number of charts for different times and eliminates the time spent in casting different charts. To select an advantageous electional chart, choose "rectify" on your astrological program or app and see what time suits your purposes.

For example, you might erect a chart for a meeting at 2:00 p.m. and note that the aspects don't look auspicious. With the rectify option, you can advance or reverse the time to easily find one that looks better for you without recalculating an entire chart. Then if you can, change the meeting time to a better one. There are some basic rules for the beginning of all activities and some specific rules depending on what you are planning. The following is a description of what to consider when planning many different life activities.

ASTROLOGY FOR TRAVEL

A very common question asked by clients is "Is this a good time to fly?" There are a few basic astrological indicators that ensure a safe and comfortable flight. We all know that day after day most flights reach their destinations safely. The few horrifying exceptions, however, have had specific aspects that were not favorable for travel. One of the greatest tragedies in recent memory was, of course, the World Trade Center terrorist attack. In the astrological community, I believe there was only one person who predicted some kind of terrorist attack during that time period in September, but no one predicted that terrorists would use planes as weapons. This event was unimaginable. However, if someone had asked me whether they should take a flight on the morning of September 11, I would have said no. The Moon was void-of-course, and as you learned in the section about the Moon, unexpected activities can occur at such times. The event on that morning was so unbelievable that it has marked an entire new chapter in US history, air travel, and, of course, thousands of people's lives. I would not have been able to say that there would be an unprecedented accident, just that in my experience a v/c Moon is not a reliable time to fly.

In considering travel charts, you want to erect a chart for the scheduled departure time of a plane, train, car, or boat. Calculate a chart for the time, date, and place of departure. These are the rules to follow for a safe, efficient travel experience:

1. The rulers of the ascendant and midheaven should not be retrograde.
2. The malefic planets should not be in the First House or Tenth House.
3. The Moon should be solidly in a sign and not void-of-course.

4. There should not be any planets in the same degrees as the Moon's nodes, no matter what the aspects or signs are. For example, if the Moon's nodes are located at 2 degrees of Scorpio, you should not travel if any planet in the chart is at 2 degrees, especially if it is the ruler of the midheaven or ascendant.
5. Avoid travel if the chart has a Yod or inconjunct aspect pattern.

These travel rules have served me and my clients well. You may find it unavoidable to observe all the rules, but if you have a majority of positive indications in the chart, it is safe to fly. As mentioned before, there is in astrology a practice called the "Rule of Three." This means that there must be three distinct indications to confirm an interpretation or prediction. If you have three of the described signatures in a travel chart, reschedule your trip. The issues may concern not only safety but convenience, pleasant travel, punctuality, and a feeling of ease. My one piece of advice is to draw up the charts before you make your reservations to avoid the difficulties of changing travel plans. These rules govern the beginning of a journey. If you must change planes or stop over at another location before proceeding, you do not have to recalculate the chart. The same astrological factors apply for a cruise or a long train or car journey. Certainly, it is not necessary to draw up a chart for your morning commute! If, at times, there is something unusual about the trip—such as a delay because a moose was crossing the road, stopping traffic—you might want to erect a chart and see if there are any strange indications. It is always interesting to see how the planets reflect events.

ASTROLOGY FOR BUYING AND SELLING REAL ESTATE

The Fourth House governs the home and all real estate. You can tell if a person will be happy as a homeowner or not by the sign on the Fourth House cusp. In this instance, an electional chart is not useful, because there are many steps along the way to purchasing or selling real estate. You need to examine whether a person has good judgment for buying or selling, which is indicated by the sign and its ruler on the Fourth House cusp. If a person has Pisces on the Fourth House cusp, that person may not be knowledgeable when handling a business deal regarding a home.

If this describes you, then you should find a reliable advisor to help you, as you may not be clear about the details of such a large purchase. The same would be true if Neptune were aspecting the Fourth House cusp or transiting the Fourth House. Where Neptune is located, we are open to deceit and illusion and need to take precautions. When buying or selling a home, look carefully at the transits to the natal chart and the progressed chart. For example, Saturn in hard or soft aspect to the Fourth House or to the ruler of the Fourth House is good for purchasing land or a home because he lends sober judgment to the question. It also means there will be delays. If you are buying during a Venus retrograde, the asking price will be too high, but if you are selling, you might receive more money than you had anticipated. Of course, avoid signing and finalizing papers in the Mercury retrograde.

ASTROLOGY FOR FERTILITY AND CONCEPTION

These topics have grown in importance as families in modern society are delaying having children. It is fascinating to me that astrology, developed in antiquity when people had only rudimentary knowledge about how children were conceived, is consulted for modern fertility methods. First, when considering questions of conception, you need to determine if children are likely according to the chart. This is influenced by the Moon's position, aspects to the Moon, aspects to the Fifth House ruler, and planets in the Fifth House.

There are certain signs that are considered more fertile than others. The fertile Moon signs are Cancer, Scorpio, and Pisces and secondarily Capricorn, and Taurus, and some astrologers claim fruitfulness for Libra and Aquarius. These terms are quite old and with today's modern methods of assisting conception, conceiving a child even with "less than fertile" signs is very possible. That being said, I know women with none of these Moon signs who have had children. Other indications must be present to show possible difficulties with having children. Interestingly enough, many of the ancient clues that indicate problems with childbearing are challenged today because of advanced medical techniques. Frequently, Pluto in the Fifth House means that there are problems with childbirth. I know many women who have successfully had children with this position, but the birth was a struggle, or there were other difficulties before having a full-term pregnancy. Women who, in the past, might not have been able to get pregnant can now conceive because of medical advances, but the astrological indicators will still show how easy or difficult the conception will be, regardless of the techniques used in conceiving.

Once you have determined that children are a possibility, then the question is how to use astrology to maximize your chances of conceiving a healthy child. The first piece of advice is that practice in the bedroom makes perfect. Second, use the Moon's cycle and notice any correspondences with the menstrual cycle. Ovulation at the time of the full moon aids conception. When Jupiter or Venus is transiting the Fifth House, it is a good time to concentrate on procreating. Lastly, each chart has a particular angle between the Sun and the Moon called the *Sun/Moon phase angle*. This can easily be calculated by looking at your chart menu under "returns," and noting the day of the month when the phase angle returns to the same angle formed at birth. If these times are harmonious with a woman's menstrual cycle, it is a good time for conception. The Sun/Moon phase angle refers to the number of degrees between the Sun and Moon as well as the phase of the Moon in which a person is born. The Sun/Moon phase angle return calculates the day each month that the angle reoccurs. It will not necessarily be in the same signs as at birth.

I have used astrology for clients who are trying to conceive in vitro, with surrogates, and through other advanced techniques. It is tricky to coordinate all the factors with the fertility clinic's availability, as well as the menstrual cycle, but using some basic astrological tenets helps the process. In addition to coordinating fertility techniques around these suggestions, you should not attempt fertility techniques during a void-of-course Moon or retrograde Mercury. There are too many variables to coordinate and if Mercury is retrograde, there is a possibility that confused communication will affect the outcome. The void-of-course Moon means that there is not sufficient lunar energy to aid conception and pregnancy. Following the Moon's motion and signs can be an invaluable tool for conceiving a child, either naturally or with assistance.

ADOPTION

The chart will give you information about adoption. Can you intuit which house rules adoption? It is the Eleventh House, native home of Aquarius, the sign of brotherly love and all groups. The Eleventh House is also opposite the Fifth House, which governs biological children. You could describe the entire 5/11 House axis as the area of the chart that concerns offspring. When there are good aspects to the ruler of the Eleventh House and benefic planets located in that house, the adoption process will probably be easy. If there is a preponderance of bad aspects and malefic planets in the Eleventh House, it is not advisable to adopt a child.

It is difficult to give advice to someone who wants a family. If the chart is not positive for adoption, the best you can do is say that it may not be an easy activity. If a person still wants a family, he or she may need for their development the experience of trying every avenue. It is not your place as a friend, or astrologer, to put the cosmic kibosh on such a fundamental desire. Here you run into the sensitive question of free will and astrological determinism. Love and determination can accomplish a great deal, and a person deserves support and encouragement, especially with regard to conception or adoption.

ASTROLOGY FOR STARTING A BUSINESS

We have covered many of the rules for starting a business in other chapters. One prime tenet needs to be reiterated: Do not begin a business during a retrograde Jupiter. You may lose your shirt. Another factor to consider is whether a person likes to work on his or her own. The two houses involved here are the Tenth House and the Sixth House. The Tenth House reveals information about a career path, and the Sixth House more about the day-to-day handling of business affairs.

If Venus is in the Sixth House, as it is in Chart 4, there is no way this person could possibly maintain his own business. Venus prefers artistic expression and being in a comfortable environment. This is not a good indication that a person can handle the demands of their own business. What do you think about Chart 7, with all of those planets in Scorpio in the Sixth House? This person must work on his own projects and call the shots in all endeavors. He can work *with* people but not *for* people.

In addition, when assessing the potential for someone in his or her own business, the transits affecting the Sixth and Seventh houses should be positive and Neptune-free. As you have learned, Neptune clouds the issues and will not be of help to a person who has difficulty clearly seeing the road ahead for a business. Neptune is particularly important regarding business partnerships. When there are conjunctions, squares, or oppositions between two business partners, there is the chance of deceit or dishonesty. One partner may not fully trust the other, and eventually the business could dissolve. Needless to say, you don't want to sign important business documents during a Mercury retrograde.

The Sixth House will also give you information about employees and whether you will be able to find reliable help. If you own your own business, look at the transiting planets through the Sixth House and you will see whether you will have success in hiring and keeping people. Uranus is an indication that there will be a lot of sudden comings and goings with employees. Jupiter transiting the Sixth House can mean, if other aspects are positive, that it is time to expand. And of course, look to the Second House to see what your financial situation is and will be in the near future.

Once you are involved in your own business, you should look at the birth of the business and erect a chart. You can use the date and time you incorporated or the date and time the doors opened. In the same way that you can chart the course of a marriage, a business venture's chart will reflect how the planet's transits are affecting your business. Apply all the information you have learned for a personal chart and you will be ahead of the competition because you have astrological knowledge on your side.

ASTROLOGY AND STOCKS

Using astrology to invest in the stock market makes good sense and has been used to good advantage by a number of professional brokers. One individual I know, who is an astrologer as well as a stockbroker, puts out a newsletter relaying his advice for investors according to the motions of the planets. He has been very successful and has attracted a great deal of attention for his work. However, for the average individual, there are a few simple guidelines that will save you a lot of effort and money as far as finances are concerned. The most crucial piece of information is whether or not someone's chart has good potential for investing in the stock market. The Fifth House rules stocks and all speculative investments. If there are hard aspects between the ruler of the Second House and the ruler of the Fifth House, tread carefully and get a lot of good advice before you put your money in the market. If you have malefic planets in the Fifth House, you should also be careful with investments. Also, if Jupiter is located in the Fifth House, you will probably have good luck with investments, but you must watch a tendency to overplay your investments. Lastly, if Neptune is in the

Fifth House in your natal chart, you are not clearheaded in terms of speculation. In this case, it is best to avoid the stock market, or use a very reliable broker or investment advisor.

Once you understand whether or not investing in stocks is beneficial, there are a number of ways to decide whether and when to invest in certain stocks. Please use this information in addition to your own knowledge of the stock markets. Do not buy or sell stocks when the Moon is void. Consider any planets that are transiting your Fifth House, and lastly, look to your Second House to see if you are in a positive financial condition or one that is problematic. If your bank account—as indicated by the Second House—is full, you can afford to speculate. Then, if the Fifth House is unencumbered and not affected by adverse transits, buying stocks will be successful.

ASTROLOGY FOR PLANNING A WEDDING

This is an astrological question that I love to consider, because many times a couple decides to marry after I have counseled them through the ups and downs of dating. I work to find the best possible day and time for a couple to begin their life together. The following rules hold: no v/c Moon, avoid Mercury retrograde, and avoid Venus retrograde. In addition, you want to have the malefics out of the angles, paying particular attention to any malefic planet in the Seventh House. Mars in the Seventh House means there will be fighting and strife. Saturn lends a depressing influence, and Pluto means that there will be a constant power struggle. Uranus, particularly in the Seventh House, can indicate a sudden divorce, and Neptune may reveal some deceit or cloudy issues for a marriage. Find a time when the malefics are safely tucked away in cadent houses and not making hard aspects to the ascendant/descendant axis. Saturn in the First House is never a good time to embark on a marital endeavor.

ASTROLOGY FOR RELOCATION

A frequent question that people may ask you is "Where should I move?" There are a couple of ways to examine this question astrologically. First, look to see if it is a good time to move. For this, you would consider all planets affecting the Fourth House and the ruler of the Fourth House cusp. Once it looks like it is a good time to move, then you can figure out where you should relocate. If you want to move to a foreign country, consider your Ninth House planets and the Ninth House cusp ruler. This will give you information about whether moving abroad would be beneficial for you. To select a location, you could look through *The Book of World Horoscopes* and pick out a country that harmonizes with your chart. Or, you could consider the traditional rulerships of countries and places. These are not based on the incorporation of a location but on signs that have been associated with certain places throughout the history of astrology.

The rulerships of major cities can be taken from Nicholas de Vore's *Encyclopedia of Astrology*. If you travel to any of these places, see if the sign accords with your experience there. Of course, a geographical location has many different factors that create its atmosphere and traditions, but as you travel, see if the place you visit typifies its ruling sign. A client with a Leo Moon and many Leo planets has absolutely no sense of direction, but when he was in Rome, which is ruled by the sign of Leo, he effortlessly found his way through all the twists and turns of the city.

There is also a branch of astrology that was developed by the late astrologer Jim Lewis called Astro*Carto*Graphy. In Astro*Carto*Graphy, a person's chart is translated onto a map of the world to identify powerful positions at the moment of birth. This is a computer-generated chart and is a unique way of studying where in space certain planets dominate. I have not experimented much with this branch of astrology, but if it interests you, get your Astro*Carto*Graphy report and explore.

At a lecture given by Lewis, he mentioned a town in Utah, which he called his "cosmic flat tire zone." Every time he passed through this place (which had been three times at that point), his car would get a flat tire! Interesting, isn't it? Because Astro*Carto*Graphy is relatively new, astrologers are still experimenting with it. See if you can find correspondences between your personal experiences and geographical areas in your life and then experiment with traveling to regions where the planets are positive for you. It could be a fun way to decide where to live.

Lastly, in calculating a move, you want to consider the needs of your entire chart and where you physically feel good. Remember your elements. Fire people need a stimulating environment and lots of space. Earth people need to be able to escape into the country and see fields and hills. Air people usually enjoy the mountains and places where there are air currents from a variety of directions as well as plenty of people to speak with. And, of course, the water signs crave lakes, oceans, and ponds as well as low population density. This is a simplified sketch, but one to keep in mind if you are planning on relocating. There are also books that give charts for many US cities and states. If you want to learn more about relocation charts, consider studying with an experienced Astro*Carto*Grapher.

The most generally benefic stars are listed in the following table. Fortunately, there are more benign fixed stars than malevolent.

TABLE OF BENEVOLENT STARS	
7 Gemini – Aldebaran	8 Libra – Vindemiatrix
14 Gemini – Rigel	19 Libra – Deneb
19 Gemini – Bellatrix	14 Capricorn – Vega
12 Cancer – Sirius	1 Aquarius – Altair
22 Libra – Spica	2 Pisces – Fomalhaut
23 Libra – Arcturus	22 Pisces – Markab

These stars are listed in Ivy Goldstein-Jacobson's text *Foundation of the Astrological Chart* as beneficial fixed stars. There are many opinions about fixed stars, and the best approach is to consider them as you observe them working in a person's chart. This knowledge comes from experience and studying well-known people's charts. The stars' positions were not updated to their current position because unless an individual is going to concentrate on the fixed stars, it is more important for you to know their heritage rather than their current degrees and minutes.

When some fixed stars appear in a chart of a well-known person, oftentimes that person has a special charisma. Vindemiatrix, for instance, is sometimes interpreted as malefic and called the "widow maker" because it was thought to denote the death of a partner. This is not always the case, and Vindemiatrix can indicate special gifts in all areas of Libra's domain. For example, both President Jimmy Carter and Mahatma Gandhi have this fixed star in their charts. Gandhi, born on October 2, 1869, had the Sun at 8♎56 conjunct Vindemiatrix, and Carter, born October 1, 1924, had the Sun at 8♎0 conjunct Vindemiatrix. Rosalynn Carter is alive and well at this time of writing; thus, that interpretation of the fixed star does not apply for Carter's chart. Jimmy Carter has become an active force for diplomacy and peace since he finished his presidency and has arguably better fulfilled his Libra talents as a former president. Gandhi decided for spiritual reasons to abstain from a sexual relationship with his wife, which, in a way, made her a widow of intimacy. He, too, had a special gift for peacemaking. In these two public figures, this particular fixed star exemplifies the positive characteristics of the fixed star's sign; it is as if Carter and Gandhi personify the best aspects of these signs. The meaning in other charts can be true to the original interpretation. For example, in Chart 5, this person had Mercury and the ascendant within 1 degree of orb to Vindemiatrix. She became a widow at age forty-three when her husband died after a short illness. In some of the other charts at the back of this book, there are a few examples of fixed stars. Can you find them? In Chart 2, the Moon in Capricorn located at 14 degrees corresponds to the star Vega. Although I have discussed some of the aspects in this person's chart, which indicate difficulties, this individual is a creative person, and with the Moon in the Fifth House of creativity, she has succeeded in a number of artistic areas.

In Chart 4, Jupiter is located on Rigel at 14 degrees Gemini in the house of partnership. This person married the love of his life, and had a fortunate marriage, which helped him succeed in many of his goals. Lastly, the two charts you learned about in Chapter 6 for Jack and Jane both share the fixed star Sirius, a benefic fixed star, at 12 degrees Cancer. Sirius's position at that time was 13 degrees and therefore conjuncted Jack's Sun as well as Jane's Pluto. This is a powerful connection; Jack was very successful in his career, and Jane urged him on. This is also an indication of past-life connections.

THE ARABIC PARTS

During the late Middle Ages, astrology was not well received by either the Church or the court. At this time the most interesting research and uses of astrology occurred in the Arabic world. Abu Ma'shar and Al-Kindi were two of the most prominent astrologers during these times. Borrowing from Hindu astrology and refining some of their practices, Arabic astrologers used what are now called the Arabic parts. These parts were derived from combining different positions in the chart to yield a point, or part, that furthered interpretation. The most commonly used part, which is calculated on most computer programs, is the part of fortune. The symbol is written like this: ⊗. The part of fortune is a benefic influence and shows where a person derives his or her greatest joy. The house where the part of fortune is located receives a positive influence from this part and will be lucky for a person.

To calculate the various parts, use the system of representing the signs with numbers that you learned in Chapter 5. The following are the formulas for the most commonly used parts:

- Marriage: Ascendant plus Seventh House cusp minus Venus
- Death: Ascendant plus Eighth House cusp minus Moon
- Sickness: Ascendant plus Mars minus Saturn
- Peril: Ascendant plus Eighth House ruler minus Saturn

For the part of death, any prediction must be accompanied by at least three other indicators in the natal and/or progressed chart. And as I mentioned before, it is rare that an astrologer will make a prediction about death. The part of peril warns of major dangers if the part is conjunct the ascendant and square the malefics at birth; otherwise, it is of minor importance.

If you continue your astrological research, you will find that some authors and practitioners use other parts in their readings.

DECANATES

The decanates are further divisions of the sign's influences according to the degrees that a planet is located in. As the name suggests, a decanate is a group of 10 degrees. Each sign has three decanates, because each sign totals 30 degrees. The first decanate is always ruled by the planet ruling the sign itself. For example, 0–10 degrees of Aries is ruled by Mars. In the second decanate, 10–20 degrees of Aries, we look at the next fire sign, which is Leo, ruled by the Sun. The last decanate, 20–30 degrees of Aries, is Sagittarius, ruled by the last fire sign, which is ruled by Jupiter. With each of the signs, note the sign's element and degrees, and locate the sign in the proper decanate. When you consider an interpretation for a planet's sign, the decanate gives you more specific detail. Everyone born under the sign of Libra does not have the same personality. If you were born in the first decanate, the essence of Libra is emphasized because the ruler is Venus. If you were born with Libra at 17 degrees, which is the second decanate, there would be a Uranian influence because that decanate is ruled by Aquarius's planet. Lastly, in the third decanate, there is a Mercury influence because of Mercury's rulership over Gemini. Note that wherever the sign starts, you proceed to the next sign of that element in the natural order.

Usually when the minutes of a sign are more than 30, we round off to the next degree. For example, 24 degrees 32 minutes becomes 25 degrees. In Chart 6, Jupiter is in the second decanate of Libra, because the tenth degree has already been reached. This gives Jupiter an Aquarian as well as a Libran influence. Use the decanates when you are making distinctions between charts that have many similarities. They also can be useful in synastry because they show subtle influences that may help you understand the chemistry or relationship between people. For example, in Chart 7 with all of its Scorpio planets, examining the decanates gives more specific information. The Moon is in the first decanate ruled by Mars or Pluto. Jupiter is placed in the second decanate ruled by Neptune and Venus, and the Sun and Mercury are all in the third decanate ruled by the Moon. When interpreting this chart, we would add a Cancerian influence to this high concentration of Scorpio.

HOUSE SYSTEMS

There are many house systems that astrologers use, and each astrologer has his or her favorites. Usually the house systems are named after their inventor. The two most common are the Placidus and Koch house systems. Other systems are called Campanus and Regiomontanus after their creators. When charts were exclusively hand-calculated, an astrologer used the system that was easiest to calculate. With the computer as your tool, notice on your chart input menu that you can push a button and change the house system you use. Experiment with all the house systems and see which gives you the most accurate results for timing events. As I mentioned earlier, if you do not know someone's birth time, calculate a solar wheel (for noon) on the day, year, and place a person was born. You will not have an accurate ascendant or Moon, but it is a valid chart.

THE ASTEROIDS

Recently astrologers have paid a great deal of attention to asteroids as an additional interpretative tool to add to their skills. These asteroids are a series of small celestial bodies between the orbits of Mars and Jupiter. Some astrologers have hypothesized that they are remnants of a planet that exploded. Usually the asteroids will not be the major factor in an event, but we all puzzle over noticeable traits in a person for which we can find no discernible correlation in the chart. Sometimes a person has a special attraction to someone and there doesn't seem to be any connection until you examine the asteroids between them.

Once you have thoroughly understood the basic symbolism of a chart, look at the asteroids and see what their positions mean to you. The following descriptions discuss the most commonly used asteroids.

CERES

Ceres's symbol is ⚳, and she is the largest of the asteroids. (Even though Ceres is now classified as a dwarf planet in astronomy, for astrological purposes, she's still an asteroid.) Ceres was the goddess of agriculture, harvest, fruits, and abundance. Her Greek name was Demeter, which means "Earth Mother." She refines some of the characteristics of the Moon and represents unconditional and abundant mothering in the chart. A good image for Ceres is of a nurturing mama comforting us. In addition to her psychological attributes, Ceres can also indicate a talent for cultivating plants and gardens.

PALLAS ATHENA

Her symbol is ⚴, and she was the premier warrior goddess of ancient Greece. Her city, Athens, flowered during Greece's golden age, and she was the patron goddess of the magnificent drama, architecture, and sculpture that flourished there. Greek mythology states that Pallas Athena sprang fully formed and armed from Zeus's head. In addition to being a patron of the arts, she also protected soldiers in battle. In a chart, she represents the creative, intelligent woman who can be objective and just. When Pallas Athena is strong in a chart by conjuncting a personal planet, it indicates a person who has tempered sheer intelligence with justice and mercy. There is a strong talent for structure and organization when Pallas Athena is well placed.

VESTA

Vesta's symbol is ⚶. Vesta is the brightest of the asteroids and sometimes can be seen by the naked eye. In Roman mythology, Vesta was the goddess of the hearth and home. Astrologically, she represents the flame that burns away all nonessentials and leaves what is pure and unalloyed. Vesta's interpretation in a chart shows the ability to concentrate on a specific goal to the exclusion of anything extraneous; in effect, that person is at home with whatever mission he or she is carrying out.

JUNO

Juno's symbol is ✴. She was the queen of the gods and known in Greek mythology as Hera. As Zeus's, or Jupiter's, wife she was famous for her forbearance with her husband's many infidelities. She symbolizes relationships and the need for commitment and marriage. The goddess Juno took great care of her beauty and was the patron of marriage, with the viewpoint that only in a committed relationship can beauty and intimacy flourish. She is also the asteroid that indicates the fascinating woman, the kind of woman who makes heads turn when she walks into a room. She represents beautiful and accomplished women throughout history who have fascinated and urged men on to great deeds.

CHIRON ⚷

Chiron is large for an asteroid and small for a planet. Astrologers had predicted that there was an additional planet between Saturn and Uranus, and Chiron was discovered in 1977. We are still learning what Chiron means in individual charts. Chiron in mythology was a centaur and considered a teacher and healer to many gods. The Centaur in astrology is detached from human foibles and sees the world's development in terms of slow healing. In a personal chart, Chiron signifies the wounded healer. Chiron's sign and house position delineates a wound that a person carries within and also suggests the manner of healing for that wound. Stories abound of people having severe problems, and in overcoming such problems, they find their sense of direction and meaning for their lives. This is an appropriate definition for Chiron. When Chiron is in close aspect to any of the personal planets, his effect is magnified.

These are brief descriptions of the asteroids and Chiron. At the end of this book, I have included some books that give more detail on these relative newcomers to astrology. To find out where the asteroids are located in your chart, you can include them in your regular software program's calculation or look at a specialized ephemeris for asteroids. The asteroids are fascinating, and they will add to your astrological toolbox.

THE CUSPS OF A SIGN

Frequently, when people are born at the end of a sign or the very beginning of a sign, they say, "I was born on the cusp." Technically, the cusp of any sign is the position at the end of the sign in 28 or 29 degrees, or at the beginning of a sign at 00 or 1 degree. Astrologers differ as to whether to call such a person, for example, at 29 degrees Cancer, a Cancerian, or a cusp Cancer with Leo influences. The best solution is to remind yourself that this person is on the cusp and to recognize that late and early degrees may have an influence from either the sign that they are leaving or the one they are moving toward. Look at the balance of the chart. If you see that the cusp sign has more evidence from the sign it is leaving, then your interpretation should reflect that. If there is more evidence for the sign it is approaching, then that will color your interpretation. In Chart 7, both the Sun and Mercury are located at 28 degrees. Mercury (at 28 degrees 50 minutes) is only 10 minutes away from 29 degrees of Scorpio; however, with all the Scorpio emphasis, there is very little indication that this person would be influenced by Sagittarius, the next sign, at all. In Chart 5, Mars is located at 1♎25. Should we interpret it with some Virgo? There is no strong Virgo influence in the chart, so the interpretation should emphasize the clear Libra concentration in the chart.

ADDITIONAL BRANCHES OF ASTROLOGY

I want to include some specialized uses for astrology that will help you examine specific questions. Some astrologers specialize in medical, mundane, or feng shui astrology, but as you are studying to be a general practitioner, it is a good idea to become familiar with the following branches of astrology.

MEDICAL ASTROLOGY

As you may remember from when we reviewed the signs and planets at the beginning of the book, each sign is associated with a part of the body. Over the many years that astrology has developed, the correspondence between the signs and the way the body works has yielded a vast wealth of knowledge that can be helpful in healthcare and diagnosis. In ancient times, doctors were frequently astrologers, or they consulted astrologers to help heal their patients. I believe that in the future astrologers and doctors will work together again to help people with their health. There are many books on medical astrology, and it takes good concentration to master the data, but if you find yourself gravitating toward health and healing concerns in your studies, you may want to specialize in this area of astrology.

The area of the body that your Sun sign rules will be the weakest part of your system and where you will have to take care of any matters related to that sign. For example, Capricorn must guard against knee injuries. I always recommend that Capricorns take appropriate precautions when doing high-impact sports. Aries must protect his head from injuries. Sometimes this piece of advice falls on deaf ears, but Aries should always wear a helmet when riding a bicycle or motorcycle. Taurus must protect the throat and wear a scarf during the cold months. Gemini is particularly sensitive to smoke and air pollution and should practice some kind of healthy breathing exercise. Cancer has a sensitive stomach and cannot usually tolerate very spicy food. Leo can have problems with the spine and heart arrhythmia. Yoga or gentle exercise is often a good idea. Virgo's area of weakness is the digestive system and assimilation of food. There can be allergies and bouts with colitis. Many Virgos are health conscious in the extreme. Once they understand that their nerves affect the entire body, they monitor their own health very well. Libra's weak spots are the adrenal glands and the kidneys. It is never advisable for Libra to drink heavily or go for long periods of time without eating.

He must keep his blood sugar level to maintain constant energy. Scorpio must take care that the eliminative systems are working well and be mindful of sexual health. Sagittarius loves exercise but must stretch first or there can be a danger of sciatica or pulling the muscles in the thighs and experiencing difficulties with the hips. Aquarius needs to take care that the nervous system gets rested, that circulation keeps moving, and that ankles are protected. Lastly, Pisces needs comfortable shoes, as there can be foot problems. Pisces also needs to watch for sensitivities to toxins, especially drugs and alcohol.

I have given you a quick look at the major health areas relating to each sign. It is also interesting to consider that each sign's opposite will also give you good diagnostic information. For example, when Taurus has throat problems, a healer versed in astrology would also check the area of the body ruled by Scorpio, the reproductive and eliminative organs, for any imbalances. There is a direct energy connection in the body between each sign and its opposite sign, and a natal astrology chart can be a diagnostic map pointing the way to the trouble spots and also indicating possible therapies and cures.

Consult your chart to help maintain your health. Your chart is a map of the energies that have gone into making you, and disease can be an imbalance or damming up of these energies in one or more areas of the body. If you examine your chart, you can start to see where the blocks have occurred and where they can be healed. This is a rudimentary description of energy medicine. It doesn't work for broken legs, for example, as in those cases you need a doctor to heal correctly, but for many other ailments there is a component of interaction between the body and mind that is amenable to treatment through information in the chart.

SYNASTRY IN MEDICAL ASTROLOGY

In choosing a doctor, surgeon, or healer, it is worth the snooping around it might require to find out his or her birth chart. You may not be able to get the time of birth, but creating a solar wheel for the date (at noon) and place (with the Sun on the ascendant) is good enough.

Most people probably unconsciously respond to doctors who are harmonious with their charts. The primary indications for a compatible doctor-patient relationship are good aspects between the doctor's signs and the patient's Seventh House. The Seventh House is indicated because a doctor and patient are in a partnership to promote wellness. Avoid the doctor's Saturn or Mars in your Seventh House. The other planet to note is Neptune. If there is a close relationship with a healer's Neptune and your Sun or Moon, you could fall prey to a relationship where you cannot clearly evaluate the doctor's advice. The energy between a doctor and patient contributes to the healing process. It is wise to do a chart comparison between your chart and the chart of any doctor, dentist, or healer that you consult.

SURGERY

There are three planets that are essential to examine when scheduling surgery. By surgery, I mean any procedure which requires an anesthetic, including a local anesthetic. The planets are Mars, the Moon, and Neptune. Mars rules the knife and the surgeon. Plan elective surgery when Mars is making harmonious aspects to the Moon, the Sun, and the Eighth House cusp. Do not schedule elective surgery during a retrograde Mars.

When selecting a surgeon, consider a person with many fixed signs indicating steady hands and, as noted, good aspects with your house of health.

Another consideration with surgery is to avoid scheduling any medical procedure when the transiting Moon is in the sign that rules the part of the body needing surgery. For example, I do not schedule dental work when the Moon is in Capricorn. Plastic surgery on the face should not be scheduled when the Moon is in Aries. Exploratory surgery on the throat or esophagus is best done when the Moon is far away from Taurus.

It is also best to schedule elective surgery five days before or after the new moon. Fluids are at low ebb, and there is less chance of swelling. Five days before or after a full moon is inauspicious for surgery because fluids are highest at this point and swelling occurs more easily.

Lastly, examine the aspects between Neptune and all transiting planets. Neptune rules anesthesia, and you want to find time periods where Neptune receives good aspects from all transiting planets so there are no complications with either the anesthesiologist or the drugs themselves.

Even with all these rules in mind, I do suggest that if you need surgery that you consult a professional astrologer; it is difficult to do a comprehensive analysis for yourself when you are facing what is usually a nerve-racking event. Of course, in an emergency situation, don't worry about the astrological aspects. There is always enough time after you have recovered to examine the day's astrological influences.

THE SIXTH AND TWELFTH HOUSES AND HEALTH

Both the Sixth and Twelfth houses hold important clues for health. The Sixth House is known as the house of health, but the Twelfth House rules hospitals and places of confinement. The Twelfth House can give you very good information about a person's mental health and the likelihood of whether the person will need hospitalization. In addition to noting all the parts of the body ruled by the prominent signs of the chart, look at the planets ruling the Sixth and Twelfth houses. This will give you additional information about a person's fortitude and recuperative powers as well as whether or not they generally have good health. When there are malefic planets in the house of health, a person may have psychosomatic illnesses. This means that instead of feeling emotions and creatively dealing with them, someone may experience their feelings manifesting as physical symptoms. I do not mean that a person is necessarily responsible for getting sick; people handle their problems differently. But if a problem does manifest physically, then it is a person's job to do whatever is necessary to heal. The body-mind connection is a sensitive receiving and transmitting system, and whenever something disturbs a person, the body or mind reacts and records the effects. We are all trying to maintain a balance of health in the entire system, and the chart helps to point the way.

For example, in Chart 5, Pisces is in the Sixth House of health. You immediately know that this person is extremely sensitive to toxins, drugs, and alcohol. You also note that Uranus indicates the nervous system and is very close to the Sixth House of health. This person is high-strung, and her nervous system is easily affected by what she eats and drinks. Because of the Neptunian influence (Neptune is Pisces's ruler), there is a strong desire to escape through alcohol or drugs. This person was a heavy drinker and frequently took tranquilizers to calm her nerves. So far, I have not mentioned disease because there is nothing in the chart that directly announces this person would have a disease, but the chart clearly indicates that this client should not drink or take any kind of habit-forming drugs (including smoking).

In Chart 5, this person developed esophageal cancer and died. Heavy smoking and drinking are major risk factors for esophageal cancer. If she had known astrology or had been more aware of her health, she might have stopped these habits long before they inclined her to disease. This example illustrates how a chart can describe a tendency toward an illness, as well as offer information on how to ameliorate a person's destructive tendencies. This person did not, of course, consciously choose illness or begin smoking or drinking to shorten her life. These habits are common, and it takes a lot of self-discipline to give them up. A person also must cope with all the feelings that may have been numbed with nicotine and alcohol. As you saw in Chapter 6, Jane was a very emotional person but could not easily express her feelings. Her nerves were extremely sensitive, and she took a common and seemingly convenient route to deal with life through a haze. If she had channeled her feelings into more self-expression, learned how to communicate better, or used her considerable organizational skills to take care of herself, she may have found a better balance for the stresses in her chart.

In addition to the inclinations outlined, the Twelfth House of Chart 5 shows Mercury in the Twelfth House. Mercury is the natural ruler of Virgo, the sign that rules the digestive system. Jane's Mercury is in Libra, ruler of the kidneys and adrenal glands. There are also many Libran planets in the chart, which indicate a sweet tooth. One piece of advice that an astrologer could give this person is to avoid sweets and sugar because they will take a toll on her kidneys. Alcohol is, of course, a concentrated sugar.

Do you see how you can begin to examine a chart to maximize your health? If a person takes care of the weaker areas of their body and heeds the suggestions for health that the chart suggests, then that person can strengthen their system. For medical astrology, "forewarned is forearmed."

TRANSITS THROUGH THE SIXTH HOUSE

When any of the malefic planets, particularly Saturn, transit the Sixth House, you should be alert to taking care of health matters. Saturn transiting through your Sixth House does not necessarily mean disease, but it does mean that you have to take realistic precautions about your health. Go to the dentist, and attend to any chronic health conditions. Saturn transiting the Twelfth House is also a time to be aware of your body's needs. When any of the outer planets are in the Sixth House, you would be well advised to look at your health habits and readjust any that are not serving you well. When Uranus is in the Sixth House, a person's nervous system is frayed and needs to be replenished. Since Uranus indicates new technologies and healing modalities, this is a very good time to investigate acupuncture or body therapies that can help keep the nerves calm. What do you imagine you should look to when Neptune transits the Sixth House? You should investigate revising the diet, using pure drinking water, and getting second opinions on medical matters, as well as eliminating toxins such as drugs, alcohol, and nicotine. Remember, these planets stay in a house for a long time, so it isn't a matter of going on a diet for one day.

MUNDANE ASTROLOGY

Another very interesting branch of astrology is looking at the charts for different nations. An excellent book called *The Book of World Horoscopes* by Nicholas Campion includes the natal charts of most countries in the world. He has done extensive research concerning when each country was born, meaning when it drafted a constitution or when there was a change in government. In addition to examining world events in terms of astrology, you can study these charts to determine how a country's vibrations harmonize with your chart. This can be useful if you are relocating.

Mundane astrology is also a profound way to follow national events. If you watch the transits to any country's chart, you can tell whether the country is going through a positive or negative phase. Astrologers often make predictions for elections, war, cease-fires, and peace based on these charts.

The key factor in mundane astrology is an accurate chart for a nation or an event. If you time an event yourself or if the time of the event is published in the newspaper, you can erect an accurate chart and see what the event portends. Accurate birth charts for nations are trickier. Although considerable research has been done in this area, nations go through many changes, and determining when a nation began is often not easy. For example, the beginning of the US could be the founding of the Jamestown colony in Virginia, but a more logical date to mark the birth of the US is the approval of the Declaration of Independence on July 4, 1776. This is, in fact, the date most astrologers use. Every once in a while, an astrologer determines that another chart is more accurate, but most major events for the US are reflected in what is known as the Sibly chart. Ebenezer Sibly, an astrologer and Freemason, published his chart for the US in 1787. If you would like to calculate the Sibly chart, the birth information is as follows:

July 4, 1776; 5:10 p.m. in Philadelphia. This chart gives a Cancer Sun, an Aquarius Moon, and a Sagittarius ascendant. This is an interesting combination. The most common Sun signs for a US president has been Aquarius.

If mundane astrology interests you, you can try your prowess with predicting who will win the next election. You can study the US's chart and compare each of the candidates' charts with it. A nation's leader will usually have major connections with his or her nation's chart. If there are no correspondences between a leader and their country, then that nation is in for a difficult time.

FENG SHUI ASTROLOGY

I use this term to combine the Chinese art of feng shui with Western astrology. Feng shui means "water and wind" in Chinese and describes the flow of energy in a physical space. It is a complex and sophisticated art, which is woven into traditional Chinese culture and beliefs. I recommend that students of astrology take a feng shui course, as it will add an interesting dimension to your occult studies. Feng shui astrology means taking the meanings and associations of the astrological signs and applying them to the kinds of colors, designs, spaces, gems, herbs, sounds, tastes, smells, and other factors that each sign enjoys or would find beneficial. If you surround yourself with an atmosphere where you feel comfortable, then life is apt to flow more positively.

To create an astrologically friendly environment, apply what you have learned about all the signs and translate that into how a person will probably feel in his or her physical world. For example, would Sagittarius prefer a small, cozy, dark apartment or a large, bright one? As you know, Sagittarius is ruled by expansive Jupiter, and loves freedom of movement. Sagittarian people are most unhappy when confined to a small space, and you can easily conclude that they would prefer a large, well-lit apartment. If you follow through with each of the signs,

ASTROLOGY FOR COLLEGE
AND UNIVERSITY SELECTION

This question straddles a few areas of the chart, because it involves questions of location, type of school, and available funds. First, look at the Ninth House, which rules higher education. Any planets located in the Ninth House will give you some specific information about what is important to a person in school, whether he or she will finish college, and how difficult it will be to accomplish that. You should also examine the Mercury aspects to see whether a person would benefit from a small intimate school or a large university. People with fire signs on the Ninth House cusp frequently want the prestige of a large, important university. The water signs on the Ninth House cusp prefer a place that is smaller and more close-knit. The air signs usually love any kind of study environment and do well at school. The earth signs will succeed if they feel the goal of their education is practical.

The timing of college is usually right after high school, but sometimes a person's transits are not in tune with studying at that time. A student might benefit from waiting a year or more to begin college. To help someone to decide whether to go to college right after high school or not, you should look at the entire chart and see if there are stressful transits to the Ninth House cusp. Also, if transiting Pluto is adversely aspecting the Sun, Moon, or Mars, a person may be in emotional turmoil and would benefit from waiting to embark on a college education.

ASTROLOGY FOR CAREER CHANGES

There are a few transits and cycles to consider if you want to change your career. First, see if your chart can give you some information on what kind of career you would do well in. Clients who have spent fortunes on personality tests have said that a complete understanding of their astrology chart gave them more information and direction in which to look for a career change. Look at your strengths and see how to translate them into a career where you would feel content. Pay particular attention to the signs on the Second, Sixth, and Tenth house cusps. These three houses show what kinds of occupations you enjoy and the kind of atmosphere where you could work well. If each of these house cusps is in fire, you need a fast-paced, stimulating environment. If the three cusps are in earth, you need a concrete, goal-oriented career. The air signs are communicators and writers, and need a career where they can express their ideas. The water signs tend to be involved with the helping professions and the arts. They need to express their feelings. Of course, you also need to look at a person's Sun, Moon, and Jupiter signs. Your Jupiter sign will often tell you what kind of work is lucky and effortless for you.

Once you have diagnosed the basic aspects of the chart for work and career potential, check if it is a good time to make a change. Pay particular attention to the transpersonal and outer planets crossing the midheaven. According to your knowledge of the signs, you will know if career-related issues or matters regarding worldly success are in a changing, static, fortunate, or unfortunate phase. You can then plan accordingly.

OTHER QUESTIONS

Throughout this book you have learned a variety of ways to consider different questions. All of the techniques you have learned will give you information about certain areas. The more you study astrology, the more you will see that certain practices yield better results for you than others. To review all the tools in your toolbox, remember the following:

- You can look at the transits to the natal chart or the transits to the progressed chart.
- You can draw a solar return for the upcoming year.
- You can look at the aspects to the progressed Moon.
- You can get a general idea of the structure of your life with a Saturn wheel.

Keep practicing these techniques and you will find which ones give you the clearest answers. You may use different techniques according to what you are looking for. Astrologers are constantly researching different ways to interpret the clues of a natal chart and how to apply this knowledge to a person's life. Now, let's look at exactly what to do to analyze a natal chart.

STEP-BY-STEP ANALYSIS OF A NATAL CHART

The following is a list of the basic areas to consider when analyzing a chart. You have learned all these techniques in prior chapters. They are presented here for review and to give you a comprehensive approach.

1. Study the chart and get a general impression of where the planetary concentrations are.
2. Start a worksheet and analyze the elements with the point system. Don't forget to include the ascendant and the midheaven.
3. Analyze the quadruplicities (cardinal, fixed, mutable) with the point system.
4. Note the number of yin and yang signs.
5. Note the two prenatal eclipses.
6. Write down whether any planets fall in critical degrees or fall near fixed stars.
7. Write down whether a planet is in the sign of its ruler, exaltation, fall, or detriment.
8. Note any planets in mutual reception.
9. Note any planets in intercepted houses.
10. Note any retrograde planets, and look in the ephemeris or the progressed chart for the age at which they go direct, as well as planets going retrograde in the future. Note that on your worksheet as well.
11. Draw up your aspectarian.
12. Count the number of different aspects, including the lesser known ones.
13. Note whether there are more separating aspects or applying aspects.
14. Note whether there are any prominent aspect patterns.
15. Take a break, and think about the chart. Write down anything that comes to mind.

16. Take a look at the Moon's nodes and the houses in which they are located.

17. Draw up another worksheet with five headings: Jupiter, Saturn, Uranus, Neptune, and Pluto. Note which house each of these planets is currently transiting. Then list the aspects these planets make to all of the natal placements. Also, write down when any of these planets move across any of the four angles: ascendant, midheaven, descendant, and nadir (the Fourth House cusp).

18. Draw your sheet for the progressed Moon, and record all aspects between the progressed Moon and the natal placements. Then on the second half of the sheet, place the aspects between the current transits and the progressed Moon.

19. Take a look at the eclipses for the coming year and see if any of them exactly aspect a natal planet.

20. Take a deep breath and talk over your findings with your friend, client, or family member.

This is a comprehensive "by the numbers" approach to analyzing any chart. You may find intuitively that you would like to proceed in a different manner. Experiment with a lot of charts and you will find which approach works best for you. The most important astrological skill is synthesizing a wealth of information to extract the salient points. If you follow this list, you will have a method to examine the chart and a way to organize your knowledge.

In addition to this basic analysis, you now know how to look for fine points by examining the asteroids, Chiron and Ceres, the decanates, or Arabic parts. Sometimes you might find a certain astrological technique intriguing and use it for a while. Then the information it reveals doesn't seem to be as important to you and you leave it. Everyone can have his or her astrological moods. But this list will help you approach a chart in basic, solid astrological principles.

When you want to look into the future using a chart, examine the current transits, the cycles of Jupiter and Saturn and the outer planets, the progressed planets and current transits to them, the solar return for the year, the lunar return for a specific month, and the progressed Moon. Any or all of these techniques will give you an understanding of the way a person's life is unfolding. If you want to look at specific questions and themes, you also now know where to look for whatever the question or decision calls for. It takes time to synthesize all of this knowledge. The best way to interpret the plethora of information is to draw up a lot of charts and try out your conclusions on your friends. If you practice and study, you will be amazed at how quickly your intuition and knowledge will grow.

CONCLUSION

Throughout this book, you have studied and learned about the four-thousand-year-old divine subject of astrology. You are now able to understand people and foresee events with greater accuracy than people who do not know astrology. Keeping your astrological knowledge polished will also give you an unparalleled way to understand the infinitely varied and changing world. It can put you within the rhythm of the planets and steady your life when chaos surrounds you, or encourage you to move forward boldly when the time is right.

Your study of astrology is also a spiritual tool to increase your awareness of other people and their paths in life. It is a compassionate art. After practicing astrology for more than twenty-five years, I have learned that as your specific transits and planetary placements manifest themselves, they will help life unfold as it should. An astrology chart can tell you so many things, but the most important message is this: It will be all right.

REFERENCE TABLES AND CHARTS

Name_____ Date _____ Time _____

Place _____ Longitude _____ Latitude _____

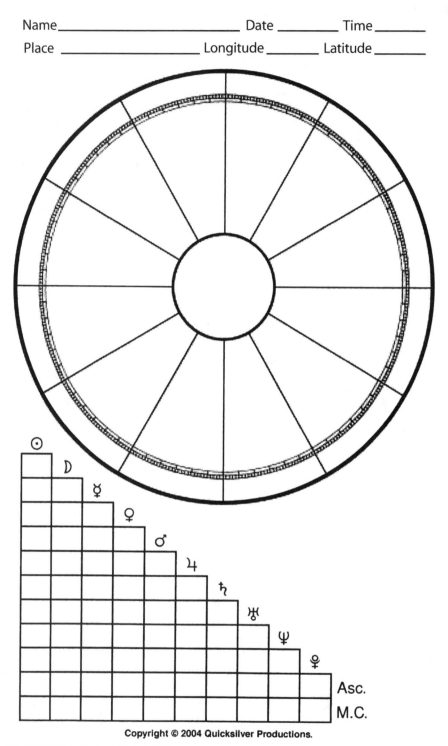

CHART 1

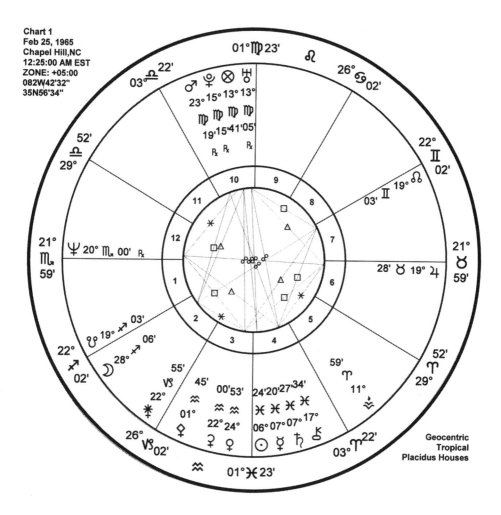

Chart 1
Feb 25, 1965
Chapel Hill,NC
12:25:00 AM EST
ZONE: +05:00
082W42'32"
35N56'34"

Geocentric
Tropical
Placidus Houses

Matrix Software © 2004.

TABLE OF PROGRESSED MOON, RADIX, OR MINOR MOON SYSTEMS FOR CHART I

PROGRESSED ☽	PERSONAL ASPECTS TO ☽										TRANSITS TO ☽									
	☉	☽	☿	♀	♂	♃	♄	♅	♆	♇	☉	☽	☿	♀	♂	♃	♄	♅	♆	♇
January 2019 18♐36	□	☌				□		□		□						☌			□	
February 2019 19♐38	□	☌				□		□		□						☌			□	
March 2019 20♐44	□	☌			⚹	□		□		□						☌			□	
April 2019 21♐50		☌			⚹	□		□		□						☌			□	
May 2019 22♐56		☌			⚹	□E		□		□						☌			□	
June 2019 24♐02		☌			⚹E	□		□		□						☌			□	
July 2019 25♐07		☌			⚹	□										☌			□	
August 2019 26♐13		☌			⚹	□										☌			□	
September 2019 27♐19		☌			⚹	□										⚹			□	
October 2019 28♐25		☌E	⚹		⚹	□										⚹				
November 2019 29♐31		☌	⚹		⚹															
December 2019 00♑37																				

CHART 2

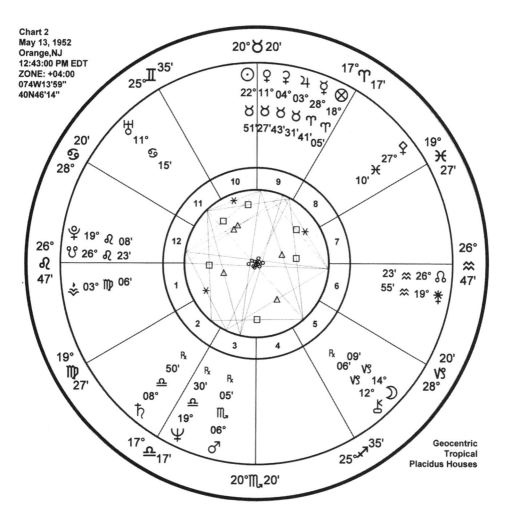

Chart 2
May 13, 1952
Orange,NJ
12:43:00 PM EDT
ZONE: +04:00
074W13'59"
40N46'14"

20° ♉ 20'

25° ♊ 35'

17° ♈ 17'

☉ ♀ ⚷ ♃ ☿ ⊗
22° 11° 04° 03° 28° 18°
♉ ♉ ♉ ♉ ♈ ♈
51' 27' 43' 31' 41' 05'

20'
♋ 28°

♅ 11°
♋ 15'

♀ 27°
♓ 10'

19°
♓ 27°

26°
♌ 47'

♇ 19° ♌ 08'
☊ 26° ♌ 23'
⚷ 03° ♍ 06'

23' ♒ 26° ☋
55' ♒ 19° ♆

26°
♒ 47'

19°
♍ 27'

♄ 08°
♎ 50' Rx

♎ 19° Rx
30'

♏ 06° Rx
05'

Rx 09'
06' ♑
♑ 14'
12°
☋

20'
♑ 28°

17°
♎ 17'

♆ 19°
♎ 06°

♂

25° ♐ 35'

Geocentric
Tropical
Placidus Houses

20° ♏ 20'

Matrix Software © 2004.

CHART 2A

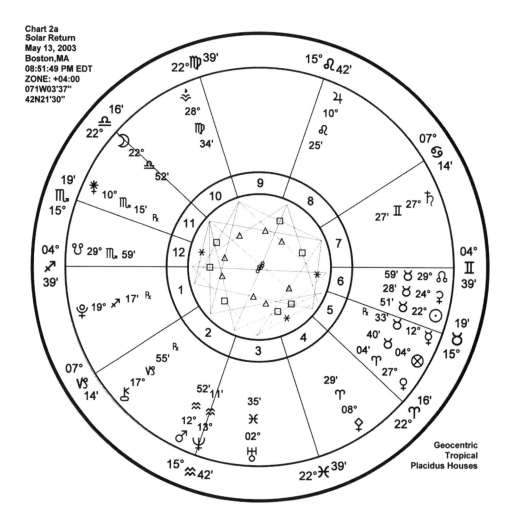

Chart 2a
Solar Return
May 13, 2003
Boston,MA
08:51:49 PM EDT
ZONE: +04:00
071W03'37"
42N21'30"

Geocentric
Tropical
Placidus Houses

Matrix Software © 2004.

CHART 3

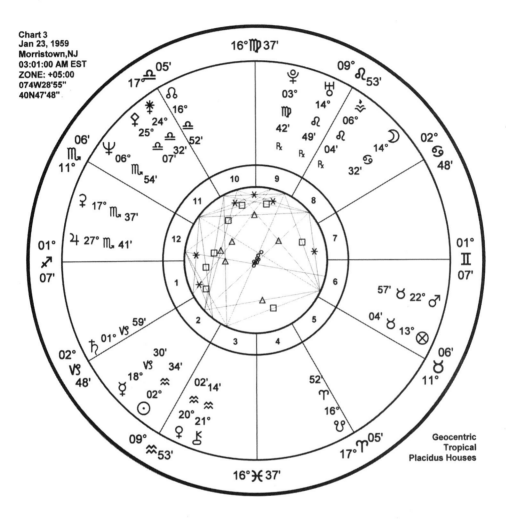

Chart 3
Jan 23, 1959
Morristown, NJ
03:01:00 AM EST
ZONE: +05:00
074W28'55"
40N47'48"

16° ♍ 37'

17° ♎ 05'

09° ♌ 53'

♀ 03° ♍ 42' Rx

⛢ 14° ♌ 49' Rx

♆ 06° ♌ 04' Rx

☽ 14° ♋ 32'

♌ 16°

♎ 24°
♀ 25°
♎ 52'
♎ 32'
07'

02° ♋ 48'

06° ♏ 11'

♆ 06° ♏ 54'

☋ 17° ♏ 37'

♃ 27° ♏ 41'

01° ♐ 07'

01° ♊ 07'

57' ♉ 22° ♂

04' ♉ 13° ⊗

02° ♑ 48'

♄ 01° ♑ 59'

♑ 18° 30'
♀ ♑ 34'
02° ≈

02' ≈ 14'

20° ≈ 21'

52' ♈

16° ♈

06° ♉ 11'

09° ≈ 53'

♀ ☊

17° ♈ 05'

16° ♓ 37'

Geocentric
Tropical
Placidus Houses

TABLE OF TRANSITS TO NATAL AND PROGRESSED PLANETS FOR CHART 3

♃	♄	♅	♆	♀
♃☌Midheaven	♄in Eighth House	♅in Third House	♆in Third House	♀in First House
♃✶♃	♄☌☽	♅☌♆	♆☌☉	♀□Midheaven
♃△☿	♄△♆	♅□♂	♆☍♅	♀□Fourth House Cusp
♃△♂	♄☍♄	♅☍♄	♆□♃	
♃✶☽				
				♀□P☉/☽
P♃☌Ascendant	♄□P☿			♀☍P♂
	♄□P☿			

CHART 4

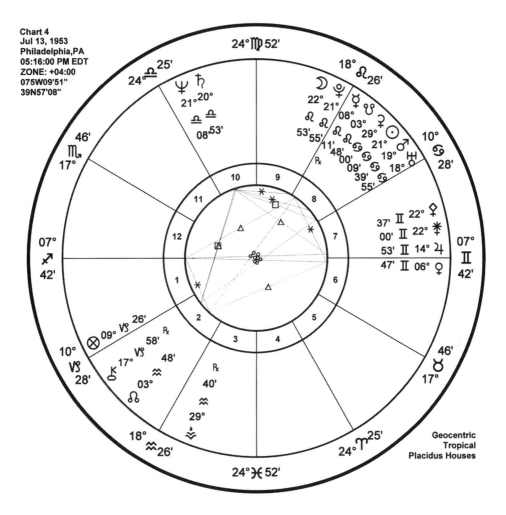

Chart 4
Jul 13, 1953
Philadelphia,PA
05:16:00 PM EDT
ZONE: +04:00
075W09'51"
39N57'08"

24°♍52'

24°♎25'

18°♌26'

♆♄
21°20°

♎ ♎
08°53'

☽ ♇
22° 21°
08°
53' 55' 03° 29° ⊙
11' 48' 21° 19° 10°
00' 09° 18° 28'
39'
55'

46'
♏
17°

07°
♐
42'

♃ ♂ ♅

37' ♊ 22° ♀
00' ♊ 22° ✴
53' ♊ 14° ♃
47' ♊ 06° ♀

07°
♊
42'

⊗ 09° ♑26'
10° ♑
♑58'
♑48'
☊ 17°
03° ♒
☋

♒ 40'

♒
29'

46'
♉
17°

18°
♒26'

24°♈25'

Geocentric
Tropical
Placidus Houses

24°♓52'

Matrix Software © 2004.

CHART 5

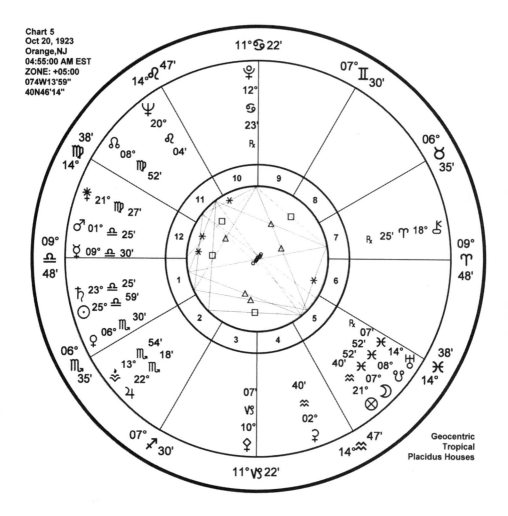

Chart 5
Oct 20, 1923
Orange,NJ
04:55:00 AM EST
ZONE: +05:00
074W13'59"
40N46'14"

11°♋22'

14°♌47'

07°♊30'

♆ 20'

♌ 04'

♇ 12°
♋ 23'
Rx

38'
♍ 14°

☊ 08°

♍ 52'

06°
♉ 35'

⚷ 21° ♍ 27'

♂ 01° ♎ 25'
☿ 09° ♎ 30'

09°
♎ 48'

Rx 25' ♈ 18° ⚷

09°
♈ 48'

♄ 23° ♎ 25'
59'
☉ 25° ♎ 30'

♀ 06° ♏ 30'

06°
♏ 35'

54'
♏ 18'
♒ 13° ♏ 22'
♃

Rx 07'
52' ♓
52' ♓ 14°
40' ♓ 08° ♅
♒ 07' ☋
21° ☽
⊗

38'
♓ 14°

07'
♑ 10°
♀

40'
♒ 02'
♂

14°♒47'

Geocentric
Tropical
Placidus Houses

07°♐30'

11°♑22'

CHART 6

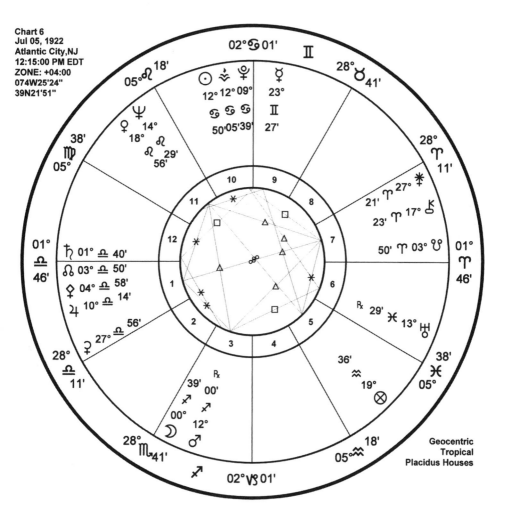

Chart 6
Jul 05, 1922
Atlantic City,NJ
12:15:00 PM EDT
ZONE: +04:00
074W25'24"
39N21'51"

02°♋01'

♊

28°♉41'

05°♌18'

⊙ ⚷ ♇
12° 12°09°
♋ ♋ ♋
50'05'39'

☿
23°
♊
27'

28°
♈
11'

♀ 14°
18° ♌
♌ 29°
56'

�

38'
♍
05°

21' ♈ 27°
23' ♈ 17° ⚷
50' ♈ 03° ☊

28°
♈
11'

01°
♎
46'

♄ 01° ♎ 40'
☋ 03° ♎ 50'
♀ 04° ♎ 58'
♃ 10° ♎ 14'

10   9

11   8

12   7

1   6

2   5

3   4

※

□

△

□

⚹

△
△

☋

△

□

⚹

⚹

01°
♈
46'

Rx 29' ♓ 13° ♅

38'
♓
05°

28°
♎
11'

♊ 27° ♎ 56'

36'
♒
19°

⊗

28°
♏41'

39' Rx
00'
♐ 00'
♐ 12°
☽   ♂

♐

18'
♒
05°

02°♑01'

Geocentric
Tropical
Placidus Houses

Matrix Software © 2004.

CHART 7

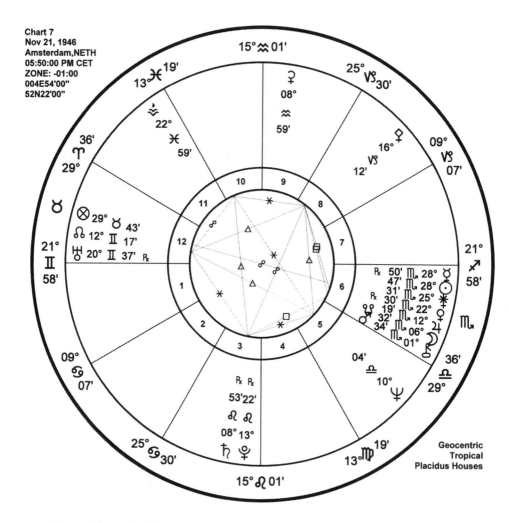

Chart 7
Nov 21, 1946
Amsterdam,NETH
05:50:00 PM CET
ZONE: -01:00
004E54'00"
52N22'00"

15° ≈ 01'

25° ♑ 30'

13° ♓ 19'

♀
08°
≈
59'

♀
16°
♑
12'

09°
♑
07'

♏
22°
♓
59'

36'
♈
29°

10   9

♉
29° ♉ 43'
☊ 12° ♊ 17'
♅ 20° ♊ 37' ℞

11

8

12

7

21°
♊
58'

1

6

21°
♐
58'

2

5

℞ 50' ♏ 28° ☿
47' ♏ 28° ☉
℞ 31' ♏ 25° ♆
30' ♏ 22° ♃
19' ♏ 12° ♀
32' ♏ 06° ☽
34' ♏ 01°

3   4

09°
♋
07'

℞ ℞
53' 22'
♌ ♌
08° 13°
♄ ♇

04'
♎
10°
♆

36'
♎
29°
♏

25° ♋ 30'

13° ♍ 19'

Geocentric
Tropical
Placidus Houses

15° ♌ 01'

Matrix Software © 2004.

CHART 8

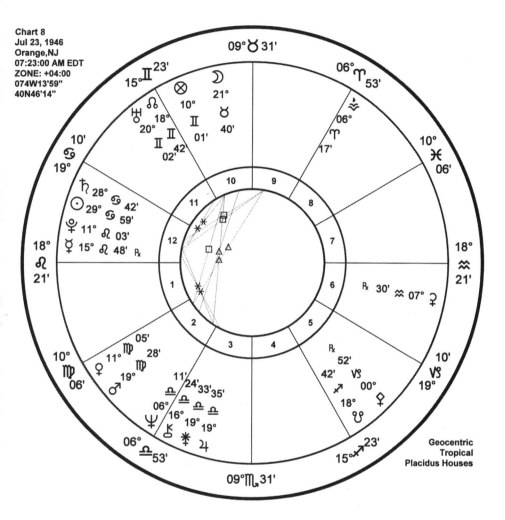

Chart 8
Jul 23, 1946
Orange,NJ
07:23:00 AM EDT
ZONE: +04:00
074W13'59"
40N46'14"

09°♉31'

06°♈53'

15°♊23'

⊗ 10°

☽ 21°

♌ 18°
♅ 20°

♊ ♊ 01'
02' 42'

♉ 40'

06°♈17'

10°♋19'

♄ 28°♋
☉ 29°♋ 42'
♇ 11°♌ 03'
☿ 15°♌ 48' ℞

10
11
12
1
2
3

9
8
7
6
5
4

10°♍06'

♀ 11°♍ 05'
♍ 19° 28'
♂

11'
24'33'35'
♎ 19° ♎ 19'
06° ♎
16°
♆

06°♎53'

09°♏31'

10°♓06'

18°♒21'

℞ 30' ♒ 07' ☊

10°♑19'

℞ 52'
42' ♐ ♑ 00'
18°
☋ ♀

15°♐23'

Geocentric
Tropical
Placidus Houses

Matrix Software © 2004.

RESOURCES

Guides for Chart Calculations

Michelsen, Neil F. *The American Book of Tables*. San Diego: ACS Publications, 1976.

Michelsen, Neil F. *The American Ephemeris for the 20th Century 1900 to 2000 at Midnight*. San Diego: ACS Publications, 2001.

Michelsen, Neil F. *The American Ephemeris for the 21st Century 2000 to 2050 at Midnight*. San Diego: ACS Publications, 1997.

www.alabe.com

www.astro.com

https://lunarium.co

Information for Healers, Rebirthers, and Past-Life Regression Therapists

Brennan, Barbara Ann. *Hands of Light: A Guide to Healing Through the Human Energy Field*. New York: Bantam Books, 1987.

Barbara Brennan School of Healing: https://barbarabrennan.com.

Edgar Cayce's Association for Research and Enlightenment: www.edgarcayce.org.

BIBLIOGRAPHY

Adams, Evangeline. *Astrology: Your Place in the Sun*. New York, NY: Dodd, Mead & Company, 1930.

Adams, Evangeline. *The Bowl of Heaven*. New York, NY: Dodd, Mead & Company, 1926.

Arroyo, Stephen. *Astrology, Karma, and Transformation: The Inner Dimensions of the Birth Chart*. Davis, CA: CRCS Publications, 1978.

Arroyo, Stephen. *Astrology, Psychology, and the Four Elements: An Energy Approach to Astrology & Its Use in the Counseling Arts*. Davis, CA: CRCS Publications, 1975.

Arroyo, Stephen. *Relationships & Life Cycles: Astrological Patterns of Personal Experience*. Davis, CA: CRCS Publications, 1979.

Bills, Rex E. *The Rulership Book*. Tempe, AZ: The American Federation of Astrologers, 1971.

Campion, Nicholas. *The Book of World Horoscopes*. Wellingborough, Northhamptonshire, England: Aquarian Press, 1988.

Clement, Stephanie Jean PhD. *Aspect Patterns: What They Reveal & How They Are Triggered*. Woodbury, MN: Llewellyn Publications, 2007.

de Vore, Nicholas. *Encyclopedia of Astrology*. New York, NY: Philosophical Library, 1947.

Donath, Emma Belle. *Have We Met Before?* Tempe, AZ: The American Federation of Astrologers, 1982.

Forrest, Steven. *The Book of Fire*. Borego Springs, CA: Seven Paws Press, 2019.

Forrest, Steven. *The Book of Neptune*. Borego Springs, CA: Seven Paws Press, 2016.

Goldstein-Jacobson, Ivy M. *Foundation of the Astrological Chart*. Tempe, AZ: The American Federation of Astrologers, 1959.

Goldstein-Jacobson, Ivy M. *The Way of Astrology*. Tempe, AZ: The American Federation of Astrologers, 1967.

Green, Jeffrey Wolf. *Pluto: The Evolutionary Journey of the Soul, Volume I.* St. Paul, MN: Llewellyn Publications, 1985.

Green, Jeffrey Wolf. *Pluto: The Soul's Evolution Through Relationships, Volume II.* St. Paul, MN: Llewellyn Publications, 1997.

Greene, Liz. *The Astrology of Fate.* York Beach, ME: Weiser Books, 1984.

Greene, Liz. *Saturn: A New Look at an Old Devil.* York Beach, ME: Weiser Books, 1976.

Hickey, Isabel M. *Astrology: A Cosmic Science.* Sebastopol, CA: CRCS Publications, 2011.

Loar, Julie. *Goddesses for Every Day.* Novano, CA: New World Library, 2008.

Meridian, Bill. *The Predictive Power of Eclipse Paths.* New York, NY: Cycles Research Publications, 2010.

Oken, Alan. *Soul Centered Astrology.* New York, NY: Bantam Books, 1990.

Reinhart, Melanie. *Chiron and the Healing Journey.* London: Penguin Books, 1989.

Sargent, Lois Haines. *How to Handle Your Human Relations.* Tempe, AZ: The American Federation of Astrologers, 1958.

Stellas, Constance. *The Astrology Gift Guide.* New York, NY: Signet Books, 2002.

Stellas, Constance, Julie Gillentine, and Jonathan Sharp. *The Hidden Power of Everyday Things.* New York, NY: Atria Books, 2000.

Tester, Jim. *A History of Western Astrology.* New York, NY: Ballantine Books, 1987.

Tierney, Bil. *Dynamics of Aspect Analysis.* Reno, NV: CRCS Publications, 1983.

Yott, Donald, H. *Astrology and Reincarnation.* York Beach, ME: Weiser Books, 1989.

INDEX

personal planets and, 35–36

retrograde Mercury, 66–69, 142, 162, 178–79, 219–20, 228–36

transits of, 65–69

Money concerns, 66, 131–34, 216, 220, 237–38

Moon

aspects of, 61–65, 77, 170–71

astrological charts and, 14

astrological signs and, 19, 61–63, 77

chart comparisons, 141

eclipses, 59, 61, 135–36, 215

houses and, 65

karma and, 170–71

lunar cycle, 58, 62–65, 190, 234

lunar return, 134–35

mansions of, 190

Minor Moon, 125–31

motion of, 61–65

nodes of, 165–70, 215, 219–21, 224, 231, 245

personal planets and, 35–36

phases of, 62–65

progressions and, 125–31

Mundane astrology, 207–8

Mutable signs, 20–29, 38, 45, 52–53, 178–82, 190

Mystic rectangle formation, 53

N

Natal chart. See also Astrological charts

access to, 9, 11

analysis of, 34–39, 120, 213–26, 244–46

calculating, 11, 14

explanation of, 9, 14, 58

Natural wheel, 28–29, 222

Neptune

aspects of, 98–103

astrological signs and, 18, 100–101

houses and, 101–3

personal planets and, 35–36

retrograde Neptune, 103, 181

transits of, 102–3

Ninth House, 28, 32

Nodal pairs, 167–70

O

Opposition aspect, 42, 46

P

Parents, 113–14, 147–48

Part of fortune, 38, 195, 215

Past lives

blueprint of, 12

influences on, 12, 88, 159

issues from, 80–81, 162, 170, 177, 182–83, 194, 218

Pisces

characteristics of, 27

decorative styles for, 212

elements and, 20, 21

nodal pairs for, 169

planetary powers and, 36

Planetary cycles, 11–12, 17, 58–77, 80–114

Planetary motions, 12, 57–77, 80–114, 116–20, 132, 136–37

Planetary powers, 36–37

Planets. See also specific planets

aspects between, 41–56, 58–77, 80–114

in astrological charts, 14–19

astrological signs and, 15–19, 67–77, 81–114, 172–80

chart comparisons, 139–59

cycles of, 11–12, 17, 58–77, 80–114

motions of, 12, 57–77, 80–114, 116–20, 132, 136–37

outer planets, 12, 17, 35, 75, 80, 92–119, 123, 140–45, 181, 186, 242

personal planets, 35–36, 41–56, 58–77, 92, 95, 101, 105, 116, 119, 140–47, 177–86, 198–99

powers of, 36–37

progressions and, 119–37

UNIQUE WAYS TO
REFRESH AND RESTORE—
PERSONALIZED FOR YOUR
ZODIAC SIGN!

PICK UP OR DOWNLOAD YOUR COPIES TODAY!